If the
world were a global
village of 100 people, 6 of
them would be Americans. These
6 would have over a third of the
village's income, and the other 94
would subsist on the other two-thirds.
How could the wealthy 6 live "in peace"
with their neighbors? Surely they would
be driven to arm themselves against
the other 94—perhaps even to spend,
as Americans do, about twice as
much per person on military
defense as the total income
of two-thirds of the
villagers.

Yes, but what can I do?

TAKING CHARGE

How you live can make a difference.

TAKING CHARGE

Achieving
Personal and Political Change
Through Simple Living

by
THE SIMPLE LIVING COLLECTIVE
AMERICAN FRIENDS SERVICE COMMITTEE
San Francisco

BANTAM BOOKS
TORONTO · NEW YORK · LONDON
®

RLI: $\dfrac{\text{VLM 9 (VLR 7-11)}}{\text{IL 7+}}$

TAKING CHARGE
A Bantam Book / June 1977

Illustrated by Coburn Everdell.

ISBN 0-553-10511-6

Published simultaneously in the United States and Canada

*Bantam Books are published by Bantam Books, Inc. Its trade-
mark, consisting of the words "Bantam Books" and the portrayal of a bantam, is registered in the United States Patent
Office and in other countries. Marca Registrada. Bantam
Books, Inc., 666 Fifth Avenue, New York, New York 10019.*

PRINTED IN THE UNITED STATES OF AMERICA

Contents

Introduction

Simple living is not a simple issue. At base it is a means of reasserting control over the material objects in our lives and the processes by which they are produced, distributed, and used; in short, it means taking charge of these aspects of our lives.

To us, living simply is one way of consciously returning material things to their proper role, as the means and tools by which human ends may be achieved and human creativity fostered. This is a crucial task in the United States and in other societies that have emulated it, where tremendous efforts are made to turn consumption into an end in itself. In the process, we believe, people tend to become objects of their objects—thinglike beings whose main purpose is to consume whatever is offered them. The human endeavor is thereby cheapened.

Our work and that of many others to be cited later in this book indicate that much of the rest of the world's people are kept poor and hungry in order to maintain high levels of consumption in the United States and other "high-income" countries. American consumers have become unwilling and often unwitting coconspirators in the economic oppression of other human beings and the political oppression that usually accompanies it. Therefore, for us simple living includes, but goes well beyond, regaining control of the materially connected aspects of our personal, family, creative, work, spiritual, and emotional lives. It also includes active engagement in work designed to bring about a fundamental redistribution of political and economic power in this nation and the world. Meeting the basic material and political needs of the hungry and powerless is as much a task of the simple living movement as reclaiming control over our own lives.

Reorienting production so that its first priority is meeting basic human needs such as health care, adequate nutrition, housing, education, and clothing is a closely related task. The United States and other industrialized nations are among the world's most productive—using resources and often labor provided by the Third World. We believe that much of our production—weapons, advertising, fast food, private automobiles, and many other items—contributes to the deterioration of our quality of life as well as that in poorer countries.

We think that these problems of overconsumption, maldistribution, and production for profit rather than use are closely linked. Simplifying our own lives, creating alternative economic institutions, and bringing about a redistribution of corporate political and economic power are ways by which we can begin to solve them.

Using This Book

The queries, analyses, and projects included in these chapters are meant as suggestions rather than prescriptions. Everyone's personal and social situations are a little different, and what is simple living for us, a group of essentially young white veterans of middle-class upbringing and countercultural expectations, may not fit the situations of others. At its best, this book will provide an introduction to simple living rather than a complete guidebook on the subject. We hope it will inspire readers to go beyond our recommendations and come up with new ones of their own. This is a part of the ongoing process of taking charge.

Only you can determine the ways in which this book can best be of service to you. These may become clearer if you glance through the various chapters before reading any part thoroughly. Skimming will also help individual readers locate those problem areas that concern them most. Most chapters include lists of resources for further work and exploration, as well as projects and alternatives that may be developed by individuals or groups.

This book can also be used as a basis for seminars,

workshops, and other group activities. There are a number of ways it can do this, depending on the time available, the number of participants, and their specific interests and levels of commitment. Here are a few:

1. The book could be used as a general introduction to simple living. A study group could spend several weeks considering the issues and questions raised in this introduction and the first two chapters. Then it could take a week or two to discuss other chapters of interest. This study could be enriched if members of the group each read a different supplementary source (these are listed at the end of each chapter) and reported briefly on them to the group as a whole. Following group study and discussion, the group might want to carry out one or more of the projects that are suggested.

2. The book could be the basis for exploring individual topics in depth by groups, subgroups, or individuals with special interests. Each chapter beyond this introduction and the two that follow it can be a means of finding out what inner resources, skills, and talents we have that can be applied to developing less complex and consumption-oriented lifestyles.

3. The implications of simple living could be explored for issues that our group did not investigate in depth. These include, among others, birth, death, shelter and land, decision-making and value-clarifying techniques, and law and security.

4. Some of the projects suggested in this book could be used to begin outreach and consciousness-raising work with others. New projects in related areas might also be developed.

How This Book Came to Be

This book originated from two more or less simultaneous, but unrelated events. In the spring of 1974, a macroanalysis seminar in Palo Alto, California, finished its work. (For a description of the seminar, see chapter 14.) Meanwhile, a Simple Living program was just getting under way in the Northern California regional office of the American Friends Service Committee in San Francisco. Several of the authors had been involved in both projects.

As the seminar participants considered what to do with the experience, knowledge, and close personal ties they had gained, someone suggested that they prepare a small packet of materials for people interested in simple living but unfamiliar with the subject. This seemed like a good idea, and we went to work on it, expecting to be finished in time for the annual gathering of the Pacific Yearly Meeting of the Society of Friends in August 1974. There it would serve as a focus for discussion and a means of introducing the Simple Living program to a wider audience.

After typing and mimeographing far into the night, we produced five hundred copies of our initial packet. These vanished almost at once at Yearly Meeting. Additional orders came in so fast that the San Francisco AFSC staff could not keep up with the demand. We soon became aware of a number of errors, inaccuracies, and stylistic problems in our initial packet. Faced with the choice of either laying the project down or expanding it, we chose the latter. The result was a privately printed book which has now gone through three printings.

This edition of *Taking Charge* has been revised and enlarged yet again. Going from the original packet to the present book has not been easy. It has often been difficult to keep a group of authors who vary widely in perspective, experience, and principal concerns between the same pair of covers, and in fact we have not always succeeded. Decisions made at one group meeting have been overturned at the next, and feelings have sometimes gotten in the way of clear thinking. We all learned how much we had to learn, often about our subjects as well as those of our coauthors.

Not all of our differences concerning the meaning of simple living or the emphasis that ought to be put on its various aspects have been resolved. Nor are they likely to be. But we have learned from each other.

Some of us have a clearer idea of the importance of the political and institutional aspects of simple living than we did in the beginning. Others are more sensitive to the very real personal pleasures of a simpler way of life.

One thing is certain: this book would have been much easier to write if our various lives had been simpler. The incredible demands made on everyone's time by life in the 1970s has taken its toll. Less than three years has seen a group originally centered in Palo Alto, California, move to several parts of the United States, Canada, and as far away as Norway. As these changes occurred, it became more and more difficult to continue working collectively as we did in the beginning. So in many ways our individual realities have challenged our collective ideas and have shown us how far we have to go to make true simplicity a reality in our own lives as well as in the society we live in.

Acknowledgments

Over the three years of this project, many people have been involved in it to whom the authors of this edition of *Taking Charge* owe a great debt of gratitude. The staff members of the Simple Living Program of the Northern California regional office of the American Friends Service Committee, in addition to participating in writing the book, have provided a great deal of time, energy, and organizational support in keeping the project going. Lillian Pohlman of the Northern California office did the lion's share of the work in distributing earlier versions of the book. Marge Bacon of the National AFSC office, who read and commented on the manuscript several times, also has our special thanks. The Palo Alto Monthly Meeting of the Religious Society of Friends provided many kinds of assistance in the early stages of the project.

Several people who helped write earlier versions of the book are not among the present authors. Without their valuable contributions, this book would not be what it is. They include Bob Burnett, Barbara Fuller, Bill and Sherry Gross, Dan Gurney, Eric Sabelman, and Kelly Seifert. Dorie Wilsnack did the graphics for an earlier version of *Taking Charge,* and Michael Larsen, originally put the collective in touch with Bantam Books.

Others who have contributed valuable ideas, advice, and energy to the project include Susan Gowan, Al Krebs, Carol Marsh, Joan Montesano, Bill Moyer, David Pingitore, Bill Leland, and Lee Swenson. Jack Stuart, one of the authors, edited an earlier version, and Chuck Fager lent his editorial expertise to the final version of the book. Peggy Oakley did the critically important work of typing the manuscript with unfailing skill.

Special thanks go to our editor at Bantam, Toni Burbank. We also appreciate the many helpful suggestions and criticisms we received from readers of earlier versions of the book. In addition, as the various chapters indicate, we have benefited from many other sources on questions related to simple living. However, the final responsibility for each chapter rests with its author or authors, and for the book as a whole with all of us.

Lucy Anderson	Alice Newton
Nancy Burnett	John Shippee
Beth Collison	Marie Simirenko
David Hartsough	Alan Strain
Jan Hartsough	Jack Stuart
Susan Lee	Coby Everdell (Graphics)

1

Simple Living:
Personal and Political Change

BY JOHN SHIPPEE

Toward a Definition of Simple Living

When we started working on this book, in early 1974, relatively few people in America seemed concerned with simple living. Since then, the simple living movement has "come out of the commune"—and with a vengeance. The governor of California abjures limousines and refuses to live in his mansion. His administration now includes an (appropriately small) Office of Appropriate Technology. Laurance Rockefeller in *Reader's Digest* in February 1976 extolled the virtues of the simple life. E. F. Schumacher's path-breaking book *Small Is Beautiful* is now found on the office shelves of business executives, architects, and planners of the future, and Frances Moore Lappe's *Diet for a Small Planet* is in their kitchens! Simple living has not only achieved middle-class respectability, but some elements of it are even being assimilated into the American way of life.

We do not view this as a totally positive phenomenon, although it is one that might well have been predicted by intelligent observers of most social and cultural innovations of the last decade or so. Just as rock music and Peter Max cartoons are used to sell 7-Up to the Pepsi generation, so "simpler living" can be used to sell granola—along with reductions in social services, public education, and other such resources. The "domestication" of simple living in this fashion— so that it serves the long-range interests of private enterprise and profit making at the expense of poor working people—is not what we had in mind.

We understand simple living to be an active involvement in maximizing human well-being, autonomy, and creative involvement with the world while minimizing waste of natural resources and human capabilities. For us, simple living includes:

—An emphasis on replacing wasteful consumption with creativity and usefulness wherever possible.

—The use of energy, natural resources, and technology as means for facilitating human growth, self-reliance, mastery of skills, and sharing, rather than as ends in themselves.

—The redistribution of resources and restructuring of institutions so that everyone's basic needs are met before luxury items are produced which benefit only the few.

—Working to end production that threatens human life or makes it less enjoyable. This includes noninformative advertising, arms production, and planned obsolescence.

—Recognition that material goods are the basis for human existence, not the source of abundance. Real abundance is found in human creativity, individual and shared self-reliance, and richness in personal relationships, culture, and the human spirit.

Where We Are Coming From

We originally became interested in simple living for several reasons. It seemed like a saner way to exist in an economic system where things often appear more important than relationships with others. We also saw it (perhaps naively) as a way of lowering resource consumption and divorcing ourselves from exploitation of Third World nations and natural resources. Simplicity is also an important part of the Quaker religious tradition that many of us share.

A concern for simplifying our ways of living is not new in the United States. Quakers and other Anabaptist religious groups (such as the Mennonites and the Amish) were among the first immigrants to articulate and attempt to live out such concepts here beginning in the seventeenth century. The religious origins of the concept, however, important as they have been historically, are not the only sources from which we have drawn.

We have also learned from the work of authors like Ernest Callenbach, Ralph Nader, and E. F. Schumacher, who have pointed out the connections between American-style consumption and pollution, depletion of resources, and health risks. They also show how the cumulative impact of these connections reduced the human endeavor to consumption for its own sake. One task of the simple living movement, as we see it, is to help create alternatives to these dangers.

Our understanding has also been strongly influenced by the insights of scholars and researchers like Richard Barnet, Ronald Muller, John Woodmansee, and Jim Hightower, who have identified links between corporate domination on a national and international scale and the spread of American-style consumption patterns and aspirations throughout the world.[1] Their work has helped make us aware of the common corporate sources of both overconsumption in the United States and continued poverty, underdevelopment, and oppression in Asia, Africa, Latin America, and poor areas of the industrialized parts of the world.

Johan Galtung, Ivan Illich, the authors of *Moving Toward a New Society,* and others who have examined the matrix of overdevelopment and underdevelopment have also made important contributions to our thinking.[2] They have analyzed such matters as the relationships between economic growth, capitalist relations of production and distribution, complex organizational structures, the imperatives of industrial technology, and the dependency and helplessness most people feel in consumerized mass societies as well as poor countries. They helped move our thinking about simple living beyond issues of personal change, growth, and the development of small alternative institutions.

We have also been influenced by the many authors who argue that simplicity can improve our personal lives by helping us to become more self-reliant, better able to relate to one another, and freer to use our skills for purposes other than amassing wealth. Ralph Borsodi, Stephen Gaskin, Helen and Scott Nearing,

Aldous Huxley, the Vocations for Social Change people, and the group who produce the *Whole Earth Catalog* are among them.

Simple living has been and remains primarily a middle-class concern. The backgrounds and outlooks of the group who wrote this book reflect this fact. We are principally university-educated people who have had considerably more training in working with our heads than with our hands. We realize, that as Adam Finnerty, a simple living organizer in Philadelphia, has put it:

> We must work to link our concerns and energies with those of the poor and oppressed here in this country. Many of the minorities struggling for justice in the United States have based their hopes in the continued growth of the U.S. economy and thus cast a decidedly wary eye at a movement that talks about "living on less." They fear that their legitimate aspirations for a decent life may be ignored in the clamor over "dedevelopment of the rich countries." The simple-living/global justice movement is challenged to develop a specific vision of a re-developed United States in which the needs of the poor are met.[3]

Failure to do so would merely perpetuate the conflict of interests that transnational capitalism has created between working people in the United States and poor people abroad. Inexpensive CB radios, calculators, stereo equipment, clothing, and many other goods are available in the United States largely because of cheap and docile labor in countries such as South Korea, Taiwan, the Philippines, and (until recently) Mexico. Such goods make it possible for working people to maintain a moderately comfortable standard of living in spite of rapid inflation. Nonetheless, the international division of labor that produces them lowers employment here while keeping wage levels abroad at a minimum. Successfully ending this situation under present circumstances would only move the burden created by the "profit imperative" from workers in the Third World to lower-income people here.

Tony Mullaney, a Catholic activist engaged in working-class organizing, and others have made criticisms of the simple living movement on similar grounds, which must be taken seriously. Mullaney, writing in *Peacework,* suggests that simple living is one more capitalist strategy for preventing serious declines in the rate of capitalist profits in the face of major increases in the prices of raw materials and labor.[4]

Approaches to simple living that are limited to personal change and alternative institution building cannot answer this criticism. Both such activities in and of themselves are perfectly consistent with increased prices and profits. They make it easier for people to reconcile themselves to live lower on the economic scale. As long as this is not accompanied by an overall redistribution of economic and political resources and power in favor of poor and working people, we do not believe that it constitutes simple living. Instead, it is a manifestation of the kind of economic oppression that must be stopped.

Developing an economic system that facilitates simple and nonoppressive living conditions for all people will not be an easy task. Many of us will have to pay serious attention to basic questions that we may never have given much thought to before. One of these is the question that underlies most of the debate about simple living: How much is enough?

Of what?

—Sugar-coated breakfast cereals and deodorants for every part of the body?

—Freeways, smog, traffic jams, and auto accidents?

—Redwood trees?

—Unemployment, unused skills, and creativity?

—Intimacy and deep friendship?

—Direct and effective participation in important political and economic decisions?

And for what purposes?

—So that we can have more things while enjoying them less?

—To increase the profits and power of a small group

of corporate and financial institutions, executives, and power-brokers?
—To help us become healthier, more aware, and more loving people?
—To increase the opportunities for sharing, co-operation, and self-reliance in our society?

Our answers to these questions have a lot to do with our ability to build ways of life, communities, and eventually societies based on living simply and taking charge. These questions are hard to answer, however, because most of us have been effectively taught not to question underlying values like:

—Bigger is better.
—Newest is best.
—Experts and elected officials are the best decision makers; the rest of us do not (and can not) know enough to question what they do.
—Science and technology will solve all of the really serious problems.
—Anyway, there is no such thing as enough; everyone will become more prosperous if we learn to produce more.

We recognize that a concept like Simple Living implies at least a middle-class existence, one having some possessions and resources to simplify, as well as the leisure to consider and try out options. It is easy these days to make many middle-class people feel guilty about their life-styles. That is not the purpose of this book. If efforts at simple living involve us in guilt-laden austerity competitions (I bake my own bread, yours comes from the community store, they eat Wonder Bread), a little consciousness raising is in order. This is not a society in which it is easy to live simply.

The idea that simple living means voluntary poverty is one we have often run into, but it is erroneous. Poverty (whether of goods or of the spirit) is often accompanied by such an emphasis on material goods and their accumulation that other sources of human enrichment go unperceived. By contrast, living simply involves explicitly analyzing the role of material goods in our lives. When are they enriching or degrading? How do they help us to accomplish our goals more easily and how do they get in the way of living more fully? People who feel owned by the surfeit of things in their lives and the obligations incurred to obtain them are not living simply. Neither are people whose lives are dominated by the lack of such material necessities as adequate nutrition, health care, fulfilling work, or housing. This double-edged character of the concept is important, because to us simple living demands a collective response to the maldistribution of resources here and throughout the world, which results in overconsumption and personal alienation in some places and grinding poverty elsewhere. It also involves an attempt to create and institutionalize alternatives to an economic system that lays waste the material world (and most of the people who live in it) in the name of profits and economic growth.

The simple living process is therefore one of change on many levels. And it is not something which, like arithmetic or how to bake a cake, can be learned in ten easy lessons. Instead, it develops out of a constantly unfolding interaction and integration of many activities, including:

—Personal change and growth
—Empowerment and the reinvention of a politics of participation and action
—Building economic alternatives

These can complement and reinforce each other as we work together to take charge of our lives. However, there are no guarantees that simply because such a process is possible, it will automatically occur. Hard work and well-thought-out strategies are required to overcome the obstacles that confront us in all of these areas.

Political Action and Personal Change

We think combining political action with personal change is important, because, in our experience, it does little good to create institutions and structures which help us to live together more openly, caringly, and creatively, unless at the same time *we* are becoming more open, caring, and creative people. Providing opportunities for participatory decision making is of little use unless people have reason to feel that their insights and inputs make a real difference. That's why we have included chapters on personal growth, creative simplicity, and community in this book.

Alternative institution building is another important part of living simply together. Cooperative grocery stores, worker-owned businesses, food conspiracies, co-op auto and appliance repair shops, alternative schools, free clinics, and farming collectives are all laboratories for a simpler future. Many areas now have whole networks of alternative businesses and cooperative enterprises. Examples of alternative institutions are described in most chapters of this book.

Alternative institutions can help take many specific aspects of our lives at least partially out of the hands of the dominant economic system. They help us to "bring the future into the present" by providing opportunities to transform limited parts of our reality.

On the other hand, it is very unlikely that such institutions alone can bring into being an economic order based on simplicity and participation.

At present, alternatives are too small and scattered to provide their mainstream rivals with any serious competition. People's food networks are not a major economic threat to Safeway, Del Monte, or Continental Bakeries (the branch of IT&T that brings us Wonder Bread, Twinkies, and similar goodies).

Along with changes in our own life-styles and the development of alternative institutions, simple living challenges us to reinvent a politics based on public participation in consciousness raising, discussion, and action. Its object is to regain control of the decisions that affect our relationship to resources and consumption at all levels.

Thus our approach to simple living includes, but goes beyond, personal choice and change. It involves empowerment and shared self-reliance. When people learn through experience and practice that they not only have the ability to understand and control skills, abilities, processes, decisions, tools, and institutions, but that they also have the right to do it, they have become empowered. When Brazilian workers and Chilean peasants learned to read by using, recognizing, and recombining words that meant something in their daily existence (*slum, worker, landlord,* etc.), they were empowering themselves on a number of levels at once.[5] They were mastering a skill that most had thought beyond their capacities. Even more significantly, they were learning that they had a right to analyze and discuss things of importance to them and to act on their conclusions.

The struggle of the United Farm Workers for the right to organize, to earn living wages, and to live in decent conditions has produced many instances of empowerment. One middle-aged farm worker learned English in three weeks when he started working for the UFW and then became one of the union's main fund raisers. Members of the UFW operate their own gas stations and medical services, and some are planning cooperative farming ventures. Such activities empower people by increasing self-reliance and cooperation. They also require shared decision making from people who have always been taught to submit to the decisions of others.

Even though most of us may not be desperately poor, we can all think of many situations in which our lives are controlled by people and conditions about which we believe we can do nothing. For many years there has been a steadily increasing tendency in most industrialized nations (led by our own) to substitute increases in consumer goods and creature comforts (at least for middle-class and steadily employed working people) for reductions in self-reliance and autonomy.

Most of us, for instance, have no choice over what happens to our children in a monopolistic public school system, which is effectively controlled from above (especially in larger cities). To know what helplessness feels like, it is only necessary to be admitted to a hospital—an institution for the repair of physical damage and the prolongation of terminal illness.

Ivan Illich has labeled the institutions and systems

that foster such conditions of choicelessness and de-pendence "radical monopolies." [6] It is an appropriate term for services that offer no alternatives to increased dependence and their own growth.

Like the huge multinational corporations that domi-nate the economy, we see these radical monopolies in fields such as education, medicine, decision making, communications, and transportation as antithetical to simple living.

Reinventing Politics

In its finest sense, politics consists of discussion and action by equals on issues of public concern. Politics thrives in an environment that allows all problems to be presented and all relevant alternatives to be argued and considered before decisions are made.

This kind of politics is almost extinct in America today. And whenever a particular issue is stamped "private," "secret," or "for consideration by experts, elected officials, and other authorized persons only," real politics dies a little more. The rebirth of politics depends on active public insistence on meaningful and effective participation in decisions of every kind.

We believe this process is an integral part of simple living. One-way media, the two-party system, and concentration of decision-making power in the hands of national economic, bureaucratic, and political elites have turned too many of us into passive con-sumers of packaged candidates, predigested issues, and predetermined decisions. Most of us have very little to say about the conditions that govern our relationships to:

—Foreign policy

—The price of meat

—The kinds of food provided in supermarkets

—Our children's education

—The conditions under which we work (if at all) and what our work produces

—And a host of other concerns.

All of these items are directly related to our ability to live simply and securely without exploiting others. Taking charge involves lifting these issues out of the realm of passive consumption and returning them to the arena of active and participatory politics.

The economic and political interests opposed to this kind of politics have a great deal of power but very little legitimacy. A nationwide poll conducted in 1975 by Hart Research Associates on behalf of the People's Bicentennial Commission is one case in point. It stated that most Americans (57%) think that both major parties favor big business over workers in their policies and actions. Fifty-eight percent believe that corporations dominate the actions of federal government officials. More people (49%) think that business causes most of our problems than disagree with this conclusion. Forty-nine percent also think that political challenge to the power of big business would be a good idea, while only 39 percent disagree. Majorities also favor such measures as employee ownership and control of economic enterprises and consumer representation on corporate boards of directors.[7] Other polls have reported similar results.

Yet there is little serious public discussion of these problems and alternatives by political figures or in the establishment media. Nor can we expect this to occur unless we actively take a hand in the process.

One starting point is to stop treating the irritations and oppressions we all feel as members of a consumption-oriented society as either private matters or issues over which we can have no control. Job insecurity and unemployment, unrepairable appliances, poisonous food additives, and such things as oppression by class, sex, race, or age are not basically individual problems. They are public social issues. Making this connection can initiate a political process in which we assert the power to define problems and initiate programs of our own rather than accept solutions carefully tailored to advance political careers or private interests.

Reinventing a politics that is relevant to simple living and economic justice also means reeducating ourselves. Alternative newspapers, listener-supported and community radio stations (the best known of which are the Pacifica stations in various parts of the country), and many of the consumers and progressive research groups around the country are potential allies in this effort.[8] Other possible sources of empowerment in relation to various simple living issues include:

—Formation of neighborhood councils which work to make political issues out of problems that affect local residents.

—The politicization of alternative institutions. Food co-ops, which provide educational material on agribusiness and help organize consumer actions related to the food system, are one example.

—Churches, relief organizations, and civic groups which take their international activities beyond charity. Such groups could sponsor study groups on conditions in specific Third World countries and their links to the American economic system. Such groups could then help publicize situations of special concern (torture, political arrests, increased economic oppression) that go unreported in the establishment media.

—Consumer organizations can sponsor public campaigns for strong representation on corporate boards and for consumer review of corporate policies and products.

—Consumer organizations could also organize task forces to dig out and disseminate information on conditions in nations where the raw materials for our consumer goods originate.

—Union members and other workers could form study groups around issues such as production to fill human needs rather than stockholder pockets, and worker control of industry. Other study groups might be concerned with humanizing working conditions and replacing jobs devoted to wasteful or antihuman production.

Basic social change will not come all at once, but as people move from education to action, our work will begin to have impact. We will then need to be able to distinguish between reforms (called "revolutionary reforms" by Andre Gorz, who developed this concept) which actually begin to redistribute power and resources while dealing with specific problems, and token changes which dissipate and co-opt the struggle for change.[9] To help make these distinctions, three questions can be asked about any specific proposed reform:

1. Does it begin to redistribute the power of dominant political and economic institutions, especially by creating or expanding the opportunity for popular participation in decision making?
2. Does it help make visible the links between the immediate situation and the larger causes and consequences?
3. Does it promote participatory politics by raising the public's level of critical awareness and involvement with the issues it concerns?

Thus, for instance, a campaign to change the distribution of power on corporate boards of directors by adding worker and consumer representation would constitute a "revolutionary" reform. By contrast, attempts to pressure existing boards to change particular exploitative policies (e.g., mining activities in South Africa) would not.

Ordinary political activity can also often be helpful. It is important to write letters and take part in specific campaigns to bring about simple-living-related legislative reforms (such as an end to the construction of nuclear power plants) and to support officeholders whose policies and actions further goals that are consistent with simple living.

Reinvention of politics based on popular discussion and action is the first step in redistributing power. Education and confrontations which expose institutions and practices that are obstacles to simple living are additional steps, as in planning alternatives which reduce consumption, waste, and dependence while raising the general quality of life. Work on all these tasks is under way in many communities in the United States. It remains for us to make them powerful and widely recognized forces which can claim the legitimacy our existing institutions have lost.

Is Small Beautiful?

Size can be a tough problem for people and organizations interested in various aspects of simple living. Organizations have a tendency to grow in size, particularly if they are successful and popular. Moreover, the problems we are addressing are so thoroughly interwoven with the dynamics of American society that only a widespread and broadly based movement is likely to overcome them. Yet large-scale organizations are, in our judgment, generally inconsistent with simplicity, self-reliance, and nonhierarchical cooperation.

Thus, as interest in simple living increases, we think that organizational strategy should be based on proliferation of small decentralized and autonomous groups and organizations rather than a few large ones. To a considerable extent this exists today. Alternative economic institutions, consumer action groups, public interest research groups, communities with simple lifestyles, people's health collectives, and other such organizations have popped up all over the country. This is a good beginning. Further progress will make it important to learn to communicate and coordinate actions without building massive, self-perpetuating bureaucracies or "alternate empires." How this can be done is by no means as clear to us yet as are some of the advantages we hope to gain from doing it.

Smallness can help protect against co-optation and repression by the powerful institutions we oppose. Growth in itself renders co-optation easier as organizations find themselves forced to employ increasingly standardized and bureaucratized methods of work in order to survive. Participation of membership in decision making can also become a matter of form rather than substance as the same people get elected to boards of directors year after year, and membership meetings become more and more infrequent. Highly centralized mass organizations run from the top down are easy to co-opt by buying off or pressuring the top leadership. A network of small autonomous organizations which are responsible to their members is much less vulnerable in this respect.

Smallness can also help to protect us from some of the other pitfalls of growth and success. Inevitably some people will try to turn simple living into a source of profits and power. Just as the counterculture generated a pack of hippie-millionaires, so the simple living movement may produce its own entrepreneurs. Indeed, this is already happening: *The Whole Earth Catalogs* have generated several millions of dollars, many of which have been distributed to groups involved with simple-living-related concerns. This cannot be said of another successful "alternative" product, granola cereal; most of it is now sold by the same food manufacturers that make the other worthless sugar-coated cereals. Keeping simple-living-related enterprises small and accessible to their clientele can help to keep profits (where they exist) both reasonable and circulating within the community. Better and less-expensive products and services can also result.

Small organizations are also more likely to have happier participants, workers, and clients than large ones. More personal interaction, flexibility, and participation are possible when people have a chance to work closely with one another—not that smallness alone, however, guarantees these advantages!

Small working groups and collectives can also have greater scope for flexibility and experimentation than large ones. Psychological and objective stakes in status quo preservation are usually less powerful. Risks and obstacles to change are also lessened. Participation in decision making can be facilitated by limiting the size of an organization. People have more opportunities to keep up with what is going on and to take leadership roles in a movement composed of many small organizations than in one that consists of a few large ones. Leaders are also more accessible to members for both criticism and appreciation.

Proliferation of small, but interacting, groups and organizations can also provide us with the experience and examples of an alternative to hierarchical, centralized, and impersonal forms of human organization. We think these are absolutely necessary if simple living is ever to become more than an adjunct and safety valve for our overdeveloped society.

We do not pretend that smallness will easily or rapidly replace many of the huge capital investments (factories, office buildings, medical centers, universities) and systems (telephone, highway) that we all now depend on for survival. Nor does anyone yet know how to operate such systems in a participatory and antibureaucratic, yet still effective, way. We hope that people who have experience with them but who are interested in building a simpler, more just society will begin to do concrete planning and educational work along these lines—both in their work places and with the general public.

Where to Begin

Knowing where to start is something difficult, and no one should feel bad about spending time exploring issues and groups, and then beginning slowly with a project or activity that is challenging but not overwhelming.

One way to start could be to find out where the present system hurts you most and to join with others (who may already be working on the problem) to bring about some changes. Another could be to focus on an issue or issues related to the ways in which our patterns of consumption contribute to the oppression of others. Either way, as our work and understanding progress, we are likely to find that the two kinds of oppression are related.

The list of questions below was put together to help in this process. They cover a variety of simple-living-related issues. You can quickly scan them to see which most clearly speak to your condition. The questions and projects listed elsewhere in the book can also be consulted.

You might try taking those questions that are most meaningful to you and discussing them with your family or other people who have concerns in the area of simple living. This is one way of focusing energy for further study and action. Another would be to discuss with others the kind of future you would like to see and begin to make specific plans (however preliminary) for bringing it about. It may be helpful to make these plans at the three levels that have been discussed in this chapter: personal growth and change, alternative-institution building, and redistribution of political and economic power. Following this, you and others may want to set concrete goals for yourselves in one or more of these areas. Such goals should be achievable, and it is a good idea to be time-specific (i.e., in one week, six months, one year, five years, etc.). Goals can be helpful as guidelines and a good source of self-affirmation when they are accomplished. In group goal-setting, the goals can be written down on large pieces of newsprint or recycled printout and kept for further reference by the group.

Questions

A. Simple Living

1. If we could be doing any work we wanted to, would we continue in our present jobs? What kind of work would we prefer? Why?

2. From what sources do we derive our ideas of "the good life"? To what extent do these ideas differ from the way we are now living?

3. To what extent is our recreation either heavily commercialized or basically passive, rather than active?

4. Do we think the "American Way of Life" can be maintained at its present level of resource consumption indefinitely? Who would benefit? Who would suffer? What would be the costs? What can we do about it?

B. Personal Growth

1. What do we know about how the food we eat and the activities we engage in every day affect our health? How do our patterns of consumption and living arrangements affect the health of people in other parts of the world?
2. How many things do we own which cost over $150 (the approximate annual income of the poorest third of the world's population)? What possibilities exist for sharing such resources with others?
3. What are the influences that determine our eating habits and those of our children?
4. How much meat do we eat? Can the amount be reduced? Should it be?
5. Outside school, what three activities involve most of our children's time and energy? Are they passive or active? Are they dependent on things or on other people in order to take place? To what extent do they consume nonreplaceable resources and energy?
6. How could we become more self-reliant this week?
7. What can we do to increase facilities in our neighborhoods for nonconsumerist and cooperative play? Can children be involved in designing and building their own parks and play equipment in our area? In inventing their own games? What could we do to help facilitate this?

C. Alternative Institutions

1. What kinds of human-scale cooperative institutions can we develop to provide products and services for which we now depend on multinational corporations? How can such institutions be structured to encourage community participation and thus help bring people together? Can they be designed to encourage other community-controlled enterprises to develop out of them?
2. How difficult is it to find and purchase unprocessed and organically grown foods in our area, as opposed to processed and perhaps poisoned ones? Are individual or community gardens a viable

alternative for us? How about food co-ops or conspiracies?

3. How would we like to see our savings invested? Do banks, insurance companies, pension funds, and the like pursue similar objectives? Do we have any control over these institutions? What alternatives either exist or can be developed?

D. Redistributing Power

1. Do we know which goods and services we use every day would not be available in the absence of cheap labor and raw materials from poor countries? Can we do without or find substitutes for such things? What political and economic measures can we promote to bring about equitable compensation for such resources and the labor involved in their production?

2. What changes are needed in our government policies, business practices, and personal consumption patterns in order for us to consume less energy? How do these changes relate to each other? Is the individual consumer responsible for the bulk of energy consumption in the United States? If not, who is?

NOTES

1. See the notes and bibliographies for this section and for "Consuming Ourselves," "Consuming the World," and "Food" for information about works by the authors listed and related works.

2. In addition to the bibliographies mentioned above, Johan Galtung's major writing in this area is an article, "A Structural Theory of Imperialism," in *The Journal of Peace Research,* 1971, No. 2, pp. 81–100.

3. "What's Happening in the Simple Living Movement," in *WIN* Magazine, April 1976, p. 8.

4. "Small Is Not Beautiful," in *Peacework,* available from the American Friends Service Committee, 2161 Mass. Ave., Cambridge, MA 02140.

5. Cf. "Small Is Not Beautiful," above, and Paolo Freire, *Pedagogy of the Oppressed* (New York: Seabury, 1971), p. 62.

6. Ivan Illich, *Tools for Conviviality* (New York: Harper and Row, 1973), passim.
7. Jeremy Rifkin, "The People Are Passing Us By," *The Progressive,* October 1975, pp. 13–14.
8. Many of the underground papers that have survived the 1970s are valuable sources of information on community happenings and political rip-offs at the local level. The news services to which many of them subscribe, Pacific News Service and Internews, provide information on international happenings that is rarely available elsewhere.

   Pacifica stations are located in Berkeley, California (KPFA and KPFB); Los Angeles, California (KPFK); Fresno, California; New York City (WBAI); and Houston, Texas. They will soon be broadcasting in Washington, D.C., as well. They provide programs on a wide variety of subjects of interest to simple living adherents, from vegetarian cooking to alternative childcare, local and international political happenings, and cross-cultural entertainment. Their regular evening news and special reports are unrivaled anywhere in the conventional electronic media and rarely in the press. If you are in a Pacifica area, listen and subscribe (their entire income comes from listener subscriptions and donations).

   As to research outfits, see listings at the end of the next two chapters.
9. This summary is based on the discussion of revolutionary reform found in Susan Gowan, et al., *Moving Toward a New Society* (Philadelphia, Pa.: New Society Press, 1976), pp. 271–275. Parts 3 and 4 of this book helped clarify and reinforce much of the thinking that has gone into this chapter.

SOURCES OF FURTHER INFORMATION

Borsodi, Ralph. *Flight from the City.* New York: Harper and Row, 1933, 1972.

Domhoff, G. William. *The Higher Circles.* New York: Vintage, 1970.

Eller, Vernard. *The Simple Life.* Grand Rapids, Mich.: Eerdmans, 1973.

Fellowship Magazine, Nyack, N.Y., April 1974. Issue on Simple Living.

Friends General Conference. *The Simple Life*. Available for $1.50 from FGC, 1520 Race St., Philadelphia, PA 19102.

Gandhi, M. K. *All Men Are Brothers*. Chicago: World without War Publications, 1972.

Illich, Ivan. *Tools for Creativity*. New York: Harper and Row, 1973.

Lakey, George. *Strategy for a Living Revolution*. San Francisco: Freeman, 1973.

Movement for a New Society. *New Society Packet*. Available for 35¢ from MNS, 4722 Baltimore Avenue, Philadelphia, PA 19143.

Moyer, William. *De-Developing the U.S. through Non-Violence*. Available for 25¢ from Philadelphia Macro-analysis Collective, 4722 Baltimore Avenue, Philadelphia, PA 19143.

Nearing, Helen, and Nearing, Scott. *Living the Good Life*. New York: Schocken Books, 1954.

Shepard, Odell. *The Heart of Thoreau's Journal*. New York: Dover, 1927.

2
Consuming Ourselves
BY JOHN SHIPPEE

Queries

1. How often do I buy things because my needs for love, friendship, celebration, job satisfaction, personal recognition, or cultural identity are not being met? How often have I bought someone something instead of showing my friendship or love more directly? Are "gifts" in my family or group things that we do, things that we are, things that we make, or things that we buy?

2. Of the things that I own, which help me or my family or group to be more active, self-reliant, and involved with each other and others?

3. Are my freedom of choice and my political and social values restricted by businesses and other institutions whose survival is dependent on high and growing levels of consumption? How?

4. To what extent are possessions and social status an important part of my self-image and that of my family? Are our feelings of self-worth based on the things we have and the "quality" of the neighborhood we live in or on who we are as human beings? What educational, media, and social messages do we get which reinforce tendencies to evaluate ourselves and others in terms of possessions rather than of personal qualities? How could we change these messages?

5. Which of my children's demands and expectations are shaped by advertising?

6. How much of what I spend on consumer goods goes for nonfunctional packaging, needless repairs, needless decoration, advertising, corporate lobbying, market research? Do these contribute anything to quality or use value?

7. Is my present job dependent on continued growth of a high-consumption economy? Was I thrown out

of work by reduced consumption during the economic slump that began in 1973? If not, do I know people who were?
8. What alternatives to employment based on high and growing consumption do I have? What alternatives should I have? What can I do to help make these alternatives real?

Introduction

What does it mean to live in the overdeveloped sector of a maldeveloped world, as the authors and most of the likely readers of this book do? To us it means we are surrounded by a gigantic machinery of production and consumption which is set up to keep going and growing at all costs. It means that we are caught up in this machinery in a multitude of ways, more than we even realize. It means that we are the objects of continued and many-leveled pressures aimed at keeping us plugged into this machinery as workers and consumers. Among these pressures are advertising, the credit system, and the transformation of gift-giving into "gifting." Let's look more closely at these pressures and the people who benefit from them.

Buying Instead of Being

Women and children are two key targets of consumerist advertising in American society. Their cooperation is needed if our male-dominated, profit-oriented society is to keep running smoothly.

The images used in these efforts are illustrated by the following Mattel Toy Company advertisement:

> Because girls dream about being a ballerina Mattel makes Dancerina. . . . A pink confection in a silken blouse and ruffled tutu. . . . Wishing you were older is a part of growing up. . . .

Barbie, a young fashion model, and her friends do the "in" things girls should do—talk about new places to visit, new clothes to wear, and new friends to meet.

By contrast, according to Mattel,

Because boys were born to build and learn, Mattel makes Tog'l [a set of building blocks for creative play].[1]

This may have changed somewhat as a result of increased feminist consciousness ("You've come a long way, baby!"), but not much.

Little if any of this is left to chance. Advertising firms put tremendous amounts of creative energy into developing associations between their products and desirable characteristics which, it is implied, we lack. Paradoxically, "newness" is one of the oldest of these. You can never get enough newness. Hence, the addition of color and smell to detergents ("New Blue Cheer," "Lemon-fresh Joy"), annual changes in automobiles and major appliances, and the development of standardized, stackable potato chips (Pringles). Winning ("Wheaties, the Breakfast of Champions"), enjoyment ("Grab all the gusto you can"—Schlitz), cleanliness—and soft-core racism ("Whiter than white"), pollution-free country environments ("It's springtime" —Salem cigarettes), and of course, sexiness ("just flick your Bic")—all these are among the traits used to sell products.

The Malnourishment Industry

A substantial part of the annual advertising budget is spent getting kids to malnourish themselves. Coca-Cola spends $89 million a year on advertising (enough to buy over 21.7 million bushels of wheat for hungry people); General Foods spends $170 million (enough for over 30 million tons of soybeans to supplement protein-poor diets). One result is that

Californians (alone) spend $3 billion dollars annually (which would pay for nearly 20 million tons of wheat or 14.6 million tons of soybeans; 1 ton equals 36.7 bushels) on unnecessary medical and dental bills because of health problems related to poor nutrition and, in particular, to increased sugar intakes.[2]

How is this advertising money used? In January 1972, Joan Gussow, a professor of nutrition education, along with her colleague Ruth Eshleman and eight graduate students, studied the ads that appeared in 29 hours of children's TV in order to find out. Of 388 commercials (one every 3½ minutes), 319 were for food. They were distributed as follows:

Breakfast cereals	38.5%
Cookies, candy, gum, popcorn, snacks	17.0
Vitamins	15.0
Canned desserts, frozen dinners, drive-ins, peanut butter, oranges	9.0
Beverages and beverage mixes	8.0
Frozen waffles and poptarts	7.5
Canned pasta	5.0

Professor Gussow and her students found the accumulated impact of these ads "blatantly antinutrition." After watching 33 of them, one student had to be relieved for something akin to battle fatigue. The report concludes, "watching children's television if one likes and respects food—and children—is sickening." [3]

During a February 1, 1975, monitoring of 3 hours of children's programming in California, the youthful audience saw 66 commercials—one every 2.7 minutes. The researchers found that 48 percent of the commercials advertised sugared cereals, drinks, candy, gum, and cookies; 20 percent more suggested drinks to go with the featured product. Ten of the cereals advertised contained an average of 48 percent sugar. A study by the Berkeley Consumers Co-operative criticized all ten for their sugar content and/or lack of nutritional value.[4]

Imagine how different our diets, food options, and media fare would be if those in favor of good nutrition "for children and other human beings" had even 10 percent of the funding now commanded by food processors and their allies in advertising!

Credit: I Owe My Soul to the Company Store

Things control us through the commitments we make to get them. There was well over $170 billion in consumer credit outstanding in the United States during 1975.[5] This is over $770 per person—more than eight times the per capita annual income of the 900 million inhabitants of the world's poorest countries (under $95 per year by this writer's calculation).

BankAmericard, Mastercharge, and other revolving credit systems, the main sources of consumer credit, are little more than modern, internationalized versions of the old-fashioned company store. Such charge systems, with their plastic-coated keys to the consumer goody box, have several features in common with their nineteenth-century predecessors. They make it easy to achieve instant gratification by spending beyond our incomes. The resulting chronic indebtedness helps tie us to our jobs and aspirations. Moreover, all of us pay to keep these systems operating, whether we use them or not.

Credit card holders pay very high interest rates for their credit: 18 percent on unpaid balances is not uncommon. Four percent more is extracted for the use of "instant cash" or check guarantee features. We all pay for the 3-percent commission on credit sales which the credit companies charge merchants using their services. Very few merchants take advantage of laws allowing them to charge 3 percent less to their cash customers.

Nonparticipants are also penalized. Cashing a check where you are not well known, renting a car, or, in some places, even opening a bank account can be difficult if you are not a member of the plastic generation.

The consumer credit system is also a threat to privacy. Your credit rating and all of the personal and financial information and misinformation that go with it are available to any bank, merchant, employer, police agency, or private investigator who can give the rating company a plausible reason for wishing to see them. Until recently, however, we ourselves had no right to access to such records in order to correct any misinformation that might appear in them.

We Are What We Buy—Aren't We?

The advertising industry widely promotes product identification as a solution to alienation. We are told that loneliness and lack of contact with others may be remedied by joining the Pepsi Generation or the Dodge Rebellion. Trademarks also show up on clothing—by their brand of beer shall ye know them—to the delight of the manufacturers of Budweiser and Coors, which are far ahead on the T-shirt front.

The media also participate in a more subtle version of the product-identification mania. By reinforcing the desirability of wealth and high consumption in costuming, setting, and background, TV shows underline the messages of the advertisers who underwrite them. Kojak, America's sexiest cop, lives in an endless series of expensive, hand-tailored suits. Cannon, the barrel-shaped private eye, is almost never without his telephone-equipped Lincoln Continental. The detectives in *Ironside* are always going out to dinner when they are not busy lowering the crime rate in San Francisco.

Family shows go further. Product identification is less evident than "life-style" identification. To be sure, shows like *All in the Family, Maude, Lotsa Luck,* and their ethnic spin-offs—*Chico and the Man* and *Sanford and Son*—are considerable improvements over their predecessors (*The Honeymooners, I Love Lucy,*

Father Knows Best). They continue to present working-class people, however, as objects of ridicule, unless they talk and act as if they have college educations. We think television will have achieved something when workers (other than cops and the occasional truck driver) are considered worthy of respect.

Nostalgia shows are just as unrealistic. Wouldn't it be nice to live as cozily and simply as the Waltons? It would certainly be easier if each of us were issued our own private family mountain to do it on.

Even *Sesame Street* makes a subtle contribution to consumptionism. It sells the art of selling. The program unabashedly uses Madison Avenue techniques to give numbers, letters, and learning skills a positive image. In addition to teaching the subject matter, this process also teaches kids to be positively oriented toward advertising techniques and images. It also teaches them to expect and respond to short-term, easily accessible stimulation, rather than more demanding and substantial fare. We think *Sesame Street* would be considerably improved if it taught children how to analyze the open and hidden messages in the advertising to which they are constantly exposed.

These are relatively minor problems compared to the blatant consumptionism of the giveaway shows. Women and a few token men shrieking and yelling on cue as the plastic-faced emcee produces a new consumer goody are, in our opinion, a national media disgrace.

One effect of this barrage of not-so-subtle media commentary is to reinforce feelings that many people have about their lives and jobs—often dull, monotonous, exhausting, and devoid of real personal satisfactions. They are clearly not the heroes of all of the glamour and adventure shows or even the self-confident, upwardly mobile (if struggling) Waltons. With the addition of advertising there is little wonder that increasing consumption of increasingly worthless consumer goods is the result. Many people have few other sources of satisfaction and pleasure in their lives.

"Gifting," a Perversion of Giving

In few areas is the antihuman impact of advertising and the compulsive consumption it promotes more evident than in the transformation of giving, expressed through gifts, into "gifting."

Gifting activity peaks during Christmas/Chanukah/winter solstice (hereafter referred to as Xmas) in America. Many of us run around for a month or so worrying and feeling guilty if we cannot find exactly the right things to buy for one another. Often we measure our worth by the extent of our involvement in Xmas gifting. Is it only a coincidence that December is a peak month for suicides?

The main economic reason for Xmas is profit. Many department stores and other retail outlets, as well as toy manufacturers and other industries, can afford to break even during the rest of the year if they come out far enough ahead in December. Their message to us is that the best way to show our love and appreciation for one another is to buy something.

Giving has been an important part of almost all human cultures. Giving and sharing have been the basis of the economic system in some traditional societies. In others, festivals in which gifts were given or goods were distributed were a means of insuring the survival of the community as a whole and compensating for inequalities in strength and skill. Among the Sioux Indians, high status was partly based on the ability and desire to provide for the old and helpless. During a hunt,

... the council sent for certain young men who were being noticed by the people, and to these the chief said: "Good young men, my relatives, your work I know is good. What you do is good always. So today you will feed the helpless and the old and feeble. Maybe there is an old woman or an old man who has no son. Or there may be a woman who has little children but no man. You will know these and hunt only for them. Today you belong to the needy!" This made the young men very proud, for it was a great honor.[6]

Contrast a typical gift-giving in consumerist America:

The company gave me a fine Christmas bonus for staying with them another year, and together with our credit cards we really felt flush. We bought a lot of stuff. On Christmas Eve there were well chosen gifts for everyone, a roaring fire, eggnog, carols, family, and our tree centered on a pile of presents.

January twenty-eighth we got a bill from Master Charge and the next day from the Emporium, and Penney's, and Wards. Even Mobil got into the act. "Please remit the amount shown in the box above. Your minimum payment is $10." The Christmas spirit was gone and the bills were there to pay and I was wondering what was happening to us that we had to buy Christmas.[7]

Gifting has other unhealthy side effects. Fashionable weddings and those attending them are gauged by the values of the gifts given. Kids rate themselves against each other on the number of presents they receive for Xmas, Bar or Bas Mitzvahs, or their birthdays. Many people fear being unable to meet the gift expectations of others when they have financial problems or lose their jobs.

One excellent source for taking giving back from the corporate "Grinches who stole Christmas" is the *Alternative Celebrations Catalog*. It contains many suggestions for nonconsumptive gifts for the new ways of celebrating various holidays and special events.

We can create alternatives by our own efforts. Other alternatives, such as increased autonomy and satisfaction on the job and respect for people who do hard but necessary work, can come only with the changes we make in our society and the cultural messages and standards that we are willing to accept.

Meanwhile, we are paying for this sort of consumption with much more than money.

Corporations and Consumerism

A small number of individuals, families, and institutions reap most of the financial benefits of American consumer habits and determine most of what will be offered the American consumer. For example, it should be obvious that our transportation choices are largely determined by what is offered by the major manufacturers—not by what is ecologically sound, economic for us, or consistent with worldwide economic justice.

It is no coincidence that Charles E. ("What's good for General Motors is what's good for the country") Wilson, former chairman of GM, was secretary of defense in 1956, when the decision was made to spend $33 billion of gasoline tax money on a nationwide freeway network. The result is the present freeway system, which Congress funded as a contribution to the national defense system. Meanwhile the nation's railways have been allowed to deteriorate, and public transportation in many cities is a bad joke. Consumers had very little to say in all of this.

Corporate irresponsibility and exploitation are even clearer in the saga of smog control. After much corporate resistance, the major car manufacturers decided to go along with government-imposed emission-control standards (considerably modified from original mandates). The control device chosen was the catalytic converter, despite a study by the National Academy of Sciences indicating that such a choice would be far less satisfactory than a complete change to stratified charge engines, such as those employed in Honda cars.[8]

As an "add-on" the converter was much less expensive for the manufacturers than a change in the basic engine design (the rights to which had been sold to Honda by a U.S. firm in the first place and would have to have been bought back—a matter of considerable expense and potential corporate embarrassment).

Catalytic converters use platinum and palladium to

reduce emissions of carbon monoxide and hydrocarbons in engine exhaust. National Institute of Health studies have shown that it replaces them with sulphates and "sulphuric acid mist." [9] These, when inhaled by an unsuspecting public, injure the lungs—particularly those of people already suffering from breathing problems of various types. Further, General Motors obtains its platinum through the Charles E. Englehardt Company, which gets it from a new mine in South Africa.

Catalytic converters are thus the products of exploitation. They are also exploitative. These devices have to be maintained every 30 to 50 thousand miles at a cost of $75 to $250 per car. They also lower gas mileage.

In sum, catalytic converters replace one kind of pollution with another, which may be worse; and exploit poor people in the Third World and consumers in the United States on the basis of the same corporate decision.

The decision to control pollution by this means would in all probability not have been made had those affected by it had any real power in corporate policy making.

Our economic powerlessness is also evident with respect to the food industry. A few national food-processing companies and regional supermarket chains determine what foods will be offered and how they will be displayed.

Fifteen per cent of all food stores control 75 per cent of the market; Campbell's makes 90 per cent of the soup sold in the U.S. and other giants (Del Monte, Stokely-Van Camp, Libby and a few others) grow or contract for processing and/or sale 80 per cent of all vegetables produced in the U.S.[10]

The results? Supermarkets now carry over 10,000 different items, compared with about 900 in 1928.[11] There has also been a tremendous increase in frozen instant everything——from pizzas to TV dinners.

In other industries control is even more concentrated. Four companies control 80 percent or more of car sales, interstate bus transportation and the production of cigarettes, locomotives, steam engines and turbines, telephone equipment, and over 70 percent of typewriter, tire, laundry equipment, and metal can production.[12]

Such enterprises, often abetted by government regulations, are also the main consumers of energy in American society. Disneyland, electric advertising, high-energy manufacturing processes, and the air-conditioning, heating, and lighting of huge office buildings and factory complexes all contribute to this.

The corporate interests that dominate consumption also control most of the jobs in the United States. If consumption falls off, workers are laid off in large numbers. (The reduced demand for large American cars in 1973 and 1974 cost over 100,000 workers in the automobile industry their jobs.) Others cannot find jobs that they might otherwise have expected to get.

The pressures that can be brought to bear on people who need their jobs to maintain a high-consumption standard of living are illustrated by the case of Kermit Vandiver. In 1967, the B. F. Goodrich Company was asked to design a brake for the A7D jet fighter. For various reasons, the resulting brake failed most of its qualification tests. Kermit Vandiver, a technical writer for the company, was told to falsify the results in the test report. He writes:

Before coming to Goodrich in 1963, I had held a variety of jobs, each a little more pleasant, a little more rewarding than the last. At forty-two, with seven children, I had decided that the Goodrich Company would probably be my "home" for the rest of my working life. The job paid well, it was pleasant and challenging, and the future looked reasonably bright. My wife and I had bought a home and we were ready to settle down into a comfortable, middle-age, middle-class rut. If I refused to take part in the A7D fraud, I would have to either resign or be fired. The report would be written by someone anyway, but I would have the satisfaction of knowing I had had no part in the matter. But bills aren't paid with personal satisfaction, nor housepayments with ethical principles. I made my decision. The next morning, I telephoned Lawson and told him I was ready to begin on the qualification report.[13]

Recently, however, even unquestioned loyalty has been no guarantee of job security for American workers. Nor does increased consumption any longer automatically increase employment.

In the last few years, many American corporations have been moving their manufacturing operations overseas to take advantage of reduced labor costs and high labor discipline. According to the AFL-CIO, 900,000 jobs were lost in the United States between 1966 and 1971, before the recent economic decline.[14] Once again victimization of American workers goes hand in hand with the exploitation of cheap labor abroad.

Corporations are also replacing human labor with automation and machines wherever possible. Machines and computers do not go on strike, demand higher wages, or require fringe benefits. Soon even supermarkets may be computerized, which would eliminate thousands of checkstand jobs and the necessity for pricing each item. The resulting unemployment burden falls most heavily on the young, the poor, the nonwhite, and the old (women often continue to be employed because their labor is less expensive).

Our present economic structure is geared to constantly increasing consumption and steadily declining employment.

A Few Modest Proposals

The challenge facing us goes far beyond simply consuming less. If we all were to do this, basic changes in the American and international economic systems would still be necessary to prevent widespread unemployment and economic chaos.

Our larger task is to take charge of our consumption patterns and begin to develop forums for collectively deciding what should be produced, consumed, and used. One way to begin might be to start a network of Consumers Anonymous groups. Such groups could offer mutual assistance to members in curbing their "thing addiction"—the tendency to buy things or to "gift" people in order to compensate for unmet human needs. We hope these Consumers Anonymous groups would not confine themselves to placing responsibility for overconsumption entirely on individuals, but would also confront the industrial sources of consumptionism and "thing addiction."

It is not now possible to exercise public control over corporations, the advertising industry, and the other promoters of high consumption in industrialized societies. But we can begin to create working models which challenge the legitimacy of the existing system. Among these models could be the following:

1. Self-selected boards of consumers to point out products that are either unnecessary or overproduced (breakfast cereals, deodorants and beauty products of various kinds, snack foods, and camper trucks might be a few examples), and suggest where the resources involved could be better used.

2. Citizen groups engaged in analysis of corporate structures and decision making. These could study and recommend alternatives to the present semimonopolistic corporate structure that dominates business and most government in the United States and most of the rest of the capitalist world.

3. Citizens' industry study groups to study and begin to design more human and ecological uses for the resources currently exploited by the advertising, armaments, automobile, and junk food industries.

4. Anticorporations or boards made up of consumers, corporate employees, and other citizens to propose alternatives to corporate decisions concerning resource use, product mix, corporate size and structure, executive salaries, and other privileges. Proposals would be based on nonexploitation of the Third World, development of human capabilities, product durability, customer service, and resource conservation.

These "counterinstitutions" could perform important services by educating their members and the public to the existence of real alternatives to present ways of doing things, which too often are seen as unchangeable. They would give people a chance to analyze critically the conditions of their lives and could provide useful, interesting activities for elderly, unemployed, and other people with considerable free time. They could also create the skeletons of alternative institutions and thus "bring the future into the present."

Bringing the future into the present is also an important reason for changing our consumption patterns as individuals and groups. The great mass of unconvinced people are not going to buy the principle of "less and better rather than more and worse" unless they see it working for others. Thus deconsumerization which is carried out by degrees may be as important as rapid and radical change. Unconvinced, but possession-ridden, people may feel encouraged to simplify their own lives if they see people much like themselves doing so. Those who are willing to go further have their own importance as experimenters, leaders, and pioneers in new approaches to having, being, and doing.

Goals for Change

Some of the structural changes we believe are needed to build an economic system that meets actual human needs are the following:

1. The detaching of income level from jobs and job status, accompanied by heavy taxation of unearned income (such as profits, dividends, and inheritances). In short, guaranteed minimum and enforced maximum income levels for all—with comparatively little differentiation based on type of employment or lack of it.

   This would require partial or total subsidization of those whose jobs either provide benefits not easily measured in dollars (teachers, artists, grandparents —real and substitute, and others filling presently unmet social and community needs) or for whom there is no employment available.

2. A concerted effort to create new jobs based on community needs and enhancement goods (music, art, celebration, individual and group creativity). Employment based on fulfillment of human needs would make liberation of the energy and creativity of workers a higher priority than increasing the use of impersonal, energy-intensive machinery.

What community does not need more day-care centers, teachers, health people, local repair shops, and other services? These could conceivably be made available in an economy based on service and full employment rather than on profit and accumulation.

What You Can Do

1. List the goods and services on which your current way of life depends. Of these, which were not in general use 75 years ago? What advantages do they provide? What added costs?

2. Which of the goods and services on which you rely for comfort and survival depend on centralized sources of fuel, energy, water, transportation, or supply which are beyond your direct control? Could you in fact survive if these sources suddenly failed? What changes would you have to make? What alternatives are available? What alternatives ought to be available? Does our dependence on such sources help limit our freedom in relation to major political, social, and economic institutions?

3. For a period of two weeks pay close attention to the advertising to which you are exposed. What is it telling you about what you are as a human being? How does it seek to influence your goals and desires? Those of your children? What kinds of threats and promises does advertising use? Do these reflect reality or not? Record and discuss some ads that are especially striking for one reason or another. Analyze the in-

fluences and messages associated with our patterns of consumption and those of other segments of our society.

4. Find some popular magazines from Third World countries and discuss the extent to which American consumption patterns are put forth as something to be aspired to in poor parts of the world.

5. List all your possessions which you would have to own in order to live without great discomfort and inconvenience. What proportion are they of your total possessions? How do you define "great discomfort and inconvenience"? Try living without some of the non-essentials for a period and sharing some of the others with neighbors and friends. You may discover that most of your real needs can be met at relatively little cost.

6. Try saying no the next few times you are asked to solve any kind of a problem by making a purchase of goods that do not seem absolutely essential to you. What are the alternatives?

7. List the things you own which help you be more active, self-reliant, creative, and convivial. List those which promote passivity, dependence, and alienation, or have a strong tendency in that direction. Which depend on how they are used? What are the differences between them? How do you use things in the second category? What might be some alternative ways of using them or sharing their use?

8. Get together with others and try to find out the investment and loan policy of a bank, pension fund, or insurance company of which you are a client. To what extent is it loaning your money to military contractors, exploitative multinational corporations, or companies operating in countries with racist or oppressive military regimes (South Africa, the Philippines, Spain, Nicaragua, Brazil)? See sources of Further Information below that could help with such projects.

9. Discuss (with your family, living group, friends, or simple living seminar) how you might go about deconsumerizing your own life. List three suggestions for simplifying your life and try them out for a month.

Afterward, evaluate the experience and, if appropriate, add a few more suggestions to your list.

NOTES

1. Advertisement in *Life* magazine, December 1969, quoted in "The Image of Women in Advertising," in Gornick and Moran, eds., *Woman in Sexist Society* (New York: Signet, 1972), p. 305.
2. Hearings of the California State Senate Subcommittee on Nutrition and Human Needs, Feb. 7, 1975; Senator George Moscone's opening remarks, pp. 5–6. Wheat and soybean costs are based on prices at the beginning of September 1975.
3. Joan D. Gussow, testimony before the Senate Commerce Committee, March 2, 1972, reprinted in *Journal of Nutrition Education,* Spring 1972, p. 49.
4. Testimony of Sally Williams, California State Senate Select Committee on Nutrition and Human Needs, Feb. 7, 1975.
5. *New York Times,* Feb. 17, 1975, p. 1.
6. John G. Neihardt, *When the Tree Flowered* (New York: Pocket Books, 1951, 1973), p. 33. Neihardt's fictionalized account, based on extensive interviews with Black Elk and other Oglala Sioux who remembered the prereservation period, is reinforced in Jeannette Mirsky, "The Dakota," in *Cooperation and Competition among Primitive Peoples,* ed. by Margaret Mead (New York: McGraw-Hill, 1937), pp. 383–384.
7. Gary Sweatt in *Working Loose,* AFSC New Vocations Project (New York: Random House, 1971), p. 4.
8. *New York Times,* October 15, 1973, p. 40.
9. Ibid.
10. Margaret Lobenstein and John Schommer, *Food Price Blackmail* (San Francisco: United Front Press, 1973), pp. 8–10.
11. Gussow, op. cit., p. 48.
12. Steve Babson and Nancy Brigham, "Why Do We Spend So Much Money?" (Somerville, Mass.: The Popular Economics Press, 1973.)
13. Kermit Vandiver, "Why Should My Conscience

Bother Me?" in *Sin in the Name of Profits,* ed. by D. Obst (New York: Doubleday, 1972), p. 24.

14. Richard J. Barnet and Ronald E. Muller, *Global Reach* (New York: Simon and Schuster, 1974), pp. 304–305.

SOURCES OF FURTHER INFORMATION

(See also: Food, Health Care, Consuming the World, Personal Growth, Economics)

Books

Alternatives. *Alternative Celebrations Catalog.* Greensboro, N.C.: Alternatives Press, 1975.

Many concrete suggestions on how to decommercialize Christmas. Order from Alternatives, 1924 E. Third St., Bloomington, Ind., 47401.

Brand, Stuart. *The Whole Earth Epilog.* New York: Penguin, 1974.

———. *The Updated Last Whole Earth Catalog.* New York: Random House, 1974.

Both of these books are very thorough guides and reviews of hundreds of books, tools, resources, and sources of ideas for simplifying our lives.

Callenbach, Ernest. *Living Poor with Style.* New York: Bantam, 1972.

A well-written, entertaining, and very practical guide to living well on very little money. The book is intended as a guide to living outside the consumerist economy.

Diamond, Stephen. *What the Trees Said.* New York: Dell, 1972.

This book relates the experiences of a communal farm in Massachusetts which came into existence when a group of Liberation News Service collective members moved onto the land. The book is a journal of simple living on a day-to-day basis as a group of very different people become a family.

Ehrlich, Paul, and Harriman, Richard. *How to Be a Survivor.* New York: Ballantine, 1969.

An introduction to the world population problems and the American overconsumption problem. This book gives a number of concrete suggestions for changes in the American economic system, to take pressure off world resources.

Ehrlich, Paul, and Pirages, Dennis. *Ark II.* San Francisco: Freeman, 1974.

This book examines the interrelationships among resource use, economic structures, and the political system in the United States, and the pressures placed on world resources by American consumption. The linkages between political and economic power are examined and analyzed. The authors also discuss alternatives to existing economic arrangements, such as guaranteed incomes and restrictions on consumption.

Fritsch, Albert, et. al. *99 Ways to a Simpler Lifestyle.* Washington: *Center for Science in the Public Interest,* 1976.

Gish, Arthur. *Beyond the Rat Race.* Scottsdale, Pa.: Herald Press, 1973.

How to escape from "the poverty of affluence." Many concrete suggestions.

Goodman, Paul. *Growing Up Absurd.* New York: Random House, 1960.

A classic reflection on the irrationality of childhood in modern middle-class America.

Gorney, Roderic, *The Human Agenda.* New York: Bantam, 1973.

A large and major study of human nature. The author refutes the argument that humans are essentially violent and conflictful. One section of the book compares simple and complex societies in terms of the human relationships they foster and their propensity to violence. The author also discusses the various alternative futures that American society faces.

Gornick, Vivian, and Moran, Barbara K. *Woman in Sexist Society.* New York: New American Library, 1972.

A collection of articles on the role of women in American society.

Hunnius, Gary, et al. (eds.). *Workers' Control: A Reader on Labor and Social Change.* New York: Random House, 1973.

A collection of articles on workers' control of business enterprises, including a number of case studies.

Huxley, Aldous. *Island.* New York: Harper and Row, 1972.

A utopian novel which describes Huxley's vision of a sensible society in which human growth and creativity

are emphasized. The role of high material consumption
in obstructing social and personal development is explored.

Furgenson, Barbara. *How to Live Better on Less. A Guide
for Waste Watchers.* Minneapolis: Augsburg.

The author recommends five Rs for moving toward new
life-styles—repair it, reuse it, reclaim it, restore it, reac-
tivate it. The book contains many examples and pro-
poses a concept of abundance that does not depend on
high consumption.

Kemp, Judy Lynn. *The Supermarket Survival Manual.*
Chatsworth, Calif.: Books for Better Living, 1973.

How to buy and keep food more intelligently. Talks
about living with supermarkets rather than changing
them.

Lakey, George. *Strategy for a Living Revolution.* San
Francisco: Freeman, 1973.

Outlines and discusses a five-stage strategy for nonviolent political, economic, and social revolution in the
United States.

Lakey, George, et al. *Moving toward a New Society* (title
of early editions: *Revolution: A Quaker Prescription
for a Sick Society*). Philadelphia: New Society Press,
1976.

The authors analyze the reasons why a revolution is
needed in order to change the U.S. economic and political system. Power relations in the United States,
the domestic U.S. economy, American economic imperialism, and the effect of our economic practices on
the environment are among the topics discussed. The
book presents a large amount of data to back up its
arguments.

Lappe, Frances Moore. *Diet for a Small Planet* (revised
edition). New York: Ballantine, 1975.

Emphasizes better distribution of world protein resources through drastically lowering the meat content
of diets in the United States and other industrialized
countries. The first half of the book deals with protein-
calorie requirements for good nutrition. The rest is
devoted to meatless recipes which emphasize vegetable
protein.

Morgan, Robin. *Sisterhood Is Powerful: An Anthology of*

Writings from the Women's Liberation Movement. New York: Random House, 1970.
Articles, poems, and other materials from the Women's Liberation struggle.

Nearing, Helen, and Nearing, Scott. *Living the Good Life* and *The Maple Sugar Book.* New York: Schocken, 1970.
These two books chronicle the Nearings' experiences moving from New York City to a run-down farm in Vermont, where they earned enough money through "bread labor" to support intellectual and political work. Many practical suggestions for building and surviving in the country taken from the authors' experience and that of rural people over the last 400 years.

Neihardt, John G. *Black Elk Speaks.* New York: Pocket Books, 1970.
A classic, first-person description of life among the Sioux during the period of their destruction as a nation by the U.S. military. Contains valuable information on living in harmony with nature, sharing, and celebration in this traditional society. It also provides a history of the U.S. invasion of the northern plains for economic reasons from the Sioux Indian point of view.

————. *When the Tree Flowered.* New York: Pocket Books, 1973.
Novel, also based on factual material from Neihardt's conversations with Black Elk and other Sioux who grew up in the 1860s and 1870s.

Obst, David (ed.). *Sin in the Name of Profit.* New York: Doubleday, 1972.
Six articles chronicling various kinds of double-dealing, misrepresentation, and mistreatment of customers by large corporations. Suggests the difficulty of making these institutions carry out internal reforms. The book takes specific cases from the automotive, drugs, and military contracting industries.

Pendick, Jeanne, and Pendick, Robert. *The Consumer's Catalog of Economy and Ecology.* New York: McGraw-Hill, 1974.
Helps consumers evaluate purchases from the point of view of self-cost and earth-cost. The food and home-furnishing sections are especially good.

Schumacher, Ernest. *Small Is Beautiful*. New York: Harper and Row, 1973.
A thorough analysis of the implications of a Buddhist approach to economics for modern industrial society.

Shell, Adeline Garner. *Supermarket Counter Power*. New York: Warner Paperback Library, 1973.
Comprehensive, calls attention to some hidden costs of food. The book discusses iron, calcium, and other nutritional values in food. It also deals with the protein situation. There is detailed information on breakfast cereals and junk and fake foods.

Shortney, Jane Ransom. *How to Live on Nothing*. New York: Pocket Books, 1973.
Advice on how to live well on a small or limited income. Discusses food, clothing, furniture, health, housing, and vacations.

Wright, Austin T. *Islandia*. New York: Arno, 1971.
A monumental utopian novel which concentrates on the decision being made by an isolated agricultural nation on whether to accept industrialization. Placed at the beginning of the twentieth century, the book deals with many of the values sacrificed to material prosperity by industrial society.

Periodicals and Newspapers

Alternatives. (1924 E. Third St., Bloomington, Ind., 47401.) Newsletter of the group that publishes the *Alternative Celebrations Catalogue*. Carries on discussion of simple living related topics described in catalogue.

CA News. (San Francisco Consumer Action, 26 Seventh St., San Francisco CA 94103).
Newsletter of San Francisco Consumer Action. Contains valuable information on consumer legislation in California, consumer rip-offs, and major issues which tie consumer problems to other activities of multinational corporations including food imperialism and raw materials exploitation.

Co-Evolution. (P.O. Box 428, Sausalito CA 94965).
A quarterly journal published by the *Point Foundation* which distributes the profits earned by the *Whole Earth Catalog*. Articles on activities and groups in which the

foundation is interested, including survival, alternative games, and the Black Panthers.

Creative Simplicity (Shakertown Pledge Group, W. 44th and York Ave. S., Minneapolis MN 55410).

Simple living topics are explored and many resources gathered together. Especially good for organizers working with religious groups.

Dandelion (occasional; Movement for a New Society, 4722 Baltimore Ave., Philadelphia PA 19143).

Deals with issues of interest to the the MNS, including simple living, nonviolent revolution, political organizing, and sex-role liberation.

Dollars and Sense (Union of Radical Political Economists, 41 Union Square West, New York NY 10003).

Articles on the current economic situation and its relationship to the distribution of political and economic power in the United States.

Mother Earth News (P.O. Box 70, Hendersonville NC 28739).

Articles on issues of interest to people involved in communal farming, organic food, simple living in rural areas, etc.

The Progressive (408 W. Gorham St., Madison WS 53703).

This is a left liberal monthly which is getting increasingly concerned with the effects of monopolistic corporate activities in the United States.

Simple Living Newsletter (514 Bryant, Palo Alto CA 94302).

Provides a philosophical grounding to simple living concerns and practical accounts of actual situations and experiments.

Pamphlets, Articles, Monographs, Manuals

Babson, Steve, and Brigham, Nancy. *Why Do We Spend So Much Money?* Somerville, Massachusetts: Popular Economics Press, 1973.

Entertaining and informative description of the relationship of corporate economic and political power to high prices.

California State Senate Select Committee on Nutrition and Human Needs. Hearing February 7, 1975. Testimony and Appendices.

Much useful information on junk food advertising aimed at children.

Cathey-Calvert, Carolyn. "Sexism on Sesame Street." Pittsburgh, Pa.: KNOW, Inc., no date.
A study of *Sesame Street* showing the sexism involved in distribution of roles, dialogue, and portrayal of the sexes. Several years old, the program is now much better.

Corporate Action Project. *Corporate Action Guide.* Washington D.C., 1974.
A manual for community action in organizing against multinational corporate power.

Council on Economic Priorities. *Guide to Corporations: A Social Perspective.* Washington D.C., 1974.
A study of 43 of the most powerful U.S. corporations and their social impact. Includes data difficult to obtain from the companies themselves.

Gussow, Joan G. "Testimony before the Senate Commerce Committee, March 2, 1972," in *Journal of Nutrition Education*, Spring 1972, pp. 48–53.
An interesting, humorous, and solidly backed analysis of antinutrition in the United States and the forces spreading it. Focuses particularly on food advertising aimed at young children.

Komisar, Lucy. "The Image of Women in Advertising." In Gornick and Moran, *Woman in Sexist Society.* New York: New American Library, 1972.
Discusses the sexism implicit in advertising aimed at women.

Lobenstein, Margaret, and Schommer, John. "Food Price Blackmail." San Francisco: United Front Press, 1973.
Suggests by a combination of cartoons and hard data how workers, consumers, and small farmers are all being victimized by agribusiness.

"No More Miss America." In Morgan, R. (ed.), *Sisterhood Is Powerful.* New York: Random House, 1970.
A comprehensive critical analysis and indictment of the Miss America pageant and beauty contests in general.

Philadelphia Macro-Analysis Collective. "Organizing Macro-Analysis Seminars." Philadelphia: Movement for a New Society, 1975.
A guide to organizing and conducting such seminars, which emphasize democratic teaching-learning processes,

the connections among political, economic, social, and international problems, and the necessity for action.

Sivard, Ruth Leger. "World Military and Social Expenditures, 1974." New York: Institute for World Order, 1975.

A digest of the comparative costs of armaments and social services to the nations of the world in 1972 (latest available data).

Woodmansee, John, et al. *The World of a Giant Corporation.* Seattle Wash.: North Country Press, 1975.

This report, compiled by the GE Project is a comprehensive critical report on the activities, power, and influence of GE in the United States and internationally. GE is presented as a specimen of the giant multinational—not as a special case that is in any way exceptional. Available for $1.95 from P.O. Box 12223, Seattle WA 98112.

Organizations

American Friends Service Committee, 1501 Cherry St., Philadelphia PA 19102.

The corporate religious service body associated with American Quakerism. The AFSC maintains 10 regional offices, which feature programs in peace action, women's issues, prison reform, community relations, etc.

Agribusiness Accountability Project, c/o San Francisco Study Center, P.O. Box 5646, San Francisco CA 94101.

Black Bart, P.O. Box 48, Canyon CA

An organization interested in turning people on to alternative life-styles and in creating alternative institutions and ways of living.

General Electric Project/New England Action-Research, New England AFSC, 48 Inman St., Cambridge MA 02139.

Research on the various involvements of multinational corporate enterprise, using GE as a primary example. They may be able to be of considerable help to others interested in carrying out similar or related work.

Movement for New Society, 4722 Baltimore Avenue, Philadelphia PA 19143.

National organization interested in developing and organizing nonviolent revolutionary change in the United States and elsewhere. MNS people have a multidimensional and community-based approach to this problem. They work on the basis that personal growth, community living, simple living, and radical political and social change are all involved in the process of building meaningful revolutionary alternatives to what we have now.

Point Foundation, 330 Ellis St., San Francisco CA 94102
Publishers of the *Whole Earth Catalog, Whole Earth Epilog,* and *Co-Evolution*. When they have the money, they also fund research and action on a whole range of alternatives to the consumerist, sexist, industrialized social order in which we find ourselves.

Shakertown Pledge Group, c/o Minneapolis Friends Meeting, W. 44th and York Ave. South, Minneapolis MN 55410.
These people developed and distribute the Shakertown pledge, reproduced at the end of this book. They also produce the newsletter *Creative Simplicity,* (see Resources in "The Shakertown Pledge" for more information.) available for $5 a year.

Simple Living Program of the Northern California Region, American Friends Service Committee, 2160 Lake Street, San Francisco CA 94121.
Helped produce this book, distributes simple living information, facilitates workshops that connect politics and lifestyle, and is working to build a national network of groups addressing simple living issues. It is also participating in the development of programs to stop nuclear power plants in California. Publishes newsletter called *Simple Living,* available for $3 contribution a year.

Union of Radical Political Economists, 41 Union Square West, New York NY 10003.
Professional organization of radical economists. They publish *Dollars and Sense,* a journal for general readers on current economic problems as well as background materials on the energy and food situations which are available as packets.

3
Consuming the World
BY JOHN SHIPPEE

In a world economic context, simple living is one part of an approach to curing a worldwide combination of overdevelopment and underdevelopment which we will call "maldevelopment." [1] The maldevelopmental symptoms of overdevelopment—dependence on technologies and institutions we don't understand or control, self-destructive overconsumption, industrial pollution, and interpersonal alienation—are most apparent in countries like our own. The outward signs of underdevelopment are most apparent in poor countries. However, both aspects of maldevelopment can be found in most nations of the world. For instance, Mexico City is often smoggier than Los Angeles; Americans can travel to many poor nations in the Third World and never leave the same hotel, courtesy of Hilton, Sheraton, and Holiday Inn; Third World elites often consume at levels far beyond their American counterparts. Underdevelopment is also found in the United States.

As long as maldevelopment continues, only a small number of the world's people can ever hope to have the health, education, and nourishment that the average middle-class American takes for granted. Those who enjoy these benefits can do so precisely because exploitative, oppressive, and degrading conditions exist in much of the rest of the world. This conclusion is based on evidence that is both convincing and compelling. [2] In a world economy characterized by maldevelopment, it can be no other way.

A Few Facts

A few examples will suffice to illustrate this situation. In order to support the way of life to which we have become accustomed, Americans, who comprise 6 percent of the world population:

- Consume 61 percent of the world's total annual production of natural gas and slightly more than one-third of most energy and mineral resource production (1968).[3]
- Import a great part of the mineral resources our economy depends on, principally aluminum (87 percent), chromium (85 percent), tin (90 percent), iron ore (24 percent), manganese (90 percent), asbestos (85 percent), and steadily increasing amounts of petroleum and natural gas.[4]
- Consume over 5.7 times the average world energy consumption per person. This is over 29 times the annual per capita energy consumption of the people of the Middle East, Latin America, Asia (except Soviet Asia and Japan), and Africa.[5]
- Eat 212 pounds of meat and poultry per person per year. The animals involved consume over 20 million tons of vegetable protein annually of which only around 10 percent is converted to animal protein. The 18 million tons of protein thus wasted is almost enough to end hunger in the world.[6]
- Take billions more in profits and other returns on investment out of Third World countries than foreign aid and direct private investment puts into them. In 1970 this surplus amounted to $4.9 billion. In that year, 13 percent of total U.S. corporate profits (figured as a percentage of sales) was derived from Third World countries.[7]

Many western development strategists have argued that economic growth on the American or Japanese model, an increase in food production, and controlling population are the keys to ending underdevelopment. Their arguments pass over, or do not take seriously, the need for prior international and domestic redistribution of political and economic power as prerequisites of real development.[8]

None of these solutions seems adequate to us. High growth combined with limited redistribution such as that produced by the Marshall Plan and the GI Bill tends to benefit powerful economic interests as much or more than the supposed beneficiaries, and is one source of the destructive overconsumption which now prevails in much of the United States and other "developed" countries.

Third World development strategies based on this model have occasionally resulted in startling economic growth, but rarely in major benefits to the poor. Brazil, for example, has achieved an economic growth rate of 10 percent or more annually over the last decade; yet the real wage of the average Brazilian worker during this time has fallen. Foreign investment on very attractive terms has driven out and replaced local ownership in many sectors of the economy. Huge areas of the country are being auctioned off to foreign firms for mineral exploration and exploitation, while the Indians native to these areas are subjected to various genocidal practices. Political dissent and labor organizing are regularly punished with torture.[9] Is this development or maldevelopment?

The so-called "Green Revolution" in Third World agriculture is another case in point. Sponsored by the U.S. Agency for International Development and the Rockefeller Foundation, the Green Revolution was intended to build up food supplies through the introduction of high-yielding varieties of wheat and rice. The catch is that cultivation of such crops requires large doses of Western technology in the form of tractors, artificial fertilizers, and highly disciplined farming operations. Plots of land much larger than the average in India and Pakistan (where the Green Revolution approach was pushed very hard) are required for successful cultivation. More rice and wheat were in fact produced. But the results have also included:

- Increased rural and urban unemployment due to farm mechanization.
- Increased migration from rural areas to already overcrowded cities.
- Higher profits (and greater incentives to adopt Western consumption patterns) for the comparatively few able to take advantage of Green Revolution agricultural technology.
- Severe dislocations when oil prices quadrupled,

affecting in turn the prices of lubricants, fuel, and fertilizer, needed for this approach.

Much of the additional yield ended up in the stomachs of beef cattle, whose owners could pay more for it than displaced peasants. More grain was also exported from the countryside to urban centers and the tables of those fortunate enough to be able to pay the cost. The net result, before petroleum price increases, was more food for fewer people at higher costs accompanied by lessened self-reliance.

Clearly, another approach is necessary.

We believe it is similarly misguided to select population, rather than the grossly unequal distribution of economic power and resources, as the root of underdevelopment. Famines, for instance, occur in underpopulated areas, like African Sahel, as well as in overpopulated areas of the Third World. And China, the world's most populous country, has not had a famine since the establishment of the People's Republic in 1949. Moreover, world food production grew fast enough over the last generation so that, were it distributed evenly, everyone would have had 10 percent more to eat in 1973 than in 1954.[10] Distribution, not population, is our problem. The increase in food was largely consumed in the rich areas of the world.

High birth rates are the result of poverty and maldistribution, not their cause. Third World parents will keep having large families as long as infant mortality is high and as long as children are their only social security.

"This has proven true," write Susanne Gowan and her colleagues, "not only in China and Cuba, but also in Western Europe and the United States. Few people know that for the 130 years preceding 1930 there was a major population explosion among the world's white people. In that time the white population grew from 22 per cent of the world's total to 35 percent. Even the advent of effective birth control devices did little to slow the growth rate until relative affluence and security were attained."[11]

Development—Whose Problem?

Much recent developmental thought supports a simple living perspective.[12] New definitions and guidelines are being discussed in many parts of the world and are gradually beginning to be implemented. A conference of development experts (largely from economically disadvantaged countries) held in Algeria in 1975 emphasized the following points: [13]

- Development is a human-centered process. Technology and organization must serve the concrete needs of people rather than vice versa.
- Participation in making and carrying out decisions is not simply a means to development; it is in itself development.
- Self-reliance and cooperation rather than rigid division of labor and dependence are the basis of true development.
- To succeed, development strategies must give highest priority to meeting the basic needs of the poor rather than providing more luxuries for the rich and comfortably off.
- High levels of consumption are inconsistent with development because they are unattainable by the vast majority of the population. They breed passivity among the consumers, or are otherwise undesirable in themselves.
- All countries need development, rich as well as poor.

By these standards, the United States is in many ways not a developed country. It is overdeveloped in some ways, with technologies and institutions which defy understanding and control by average human beings. It is underdeveloped in many others, including the self-reliance of its citizens, their level of personal and economic autonomy, and their knowledge and use of emotional, spiritual, creative, and cooperative abilities.

These manifestations of overdevelopment and underdevelopment reinforce each other in many ways. The impersonality and competitiveness of many American work, school, and family situations weaken creativity and spontaneity and encourage individuals to take refuge in passive consumption. This leaves people open to exploitation (though to a lesser degree) by the same institutions that profit from exploitative activities in the Third World.

Simple Living and Development

It is our belief that to overcome world poverty and the exploitation that perpetuates it, development strategies must replace the objective of unlimited material growth and consumption with the benefits associated with taking charge of our lives and futures. The United States and other wealthy nations have an especially urgent responsibility in this regard. This should not be threatening to us; we believe our lives can be richer in many ways without being destructive to the planet or to other human beings. Many examples are given in the chapters on community, child rearing, personal growth, creativity, and alternative economic institutions.

We have the task of creating a society based on thoroughgoing redistribution of wealth, power, and consumption. We also need to find ways of eliminating our dependence on the exploitative use of resources elsewhere in the world. Instead of encouraging material consumption by artificially limiting nonmaterial (and potentially abundant) satisfactions like participation, mutual support, feelings of competence, self-respect and self-worth, creativity, trust, and love, a developing American society would encourage growth in these areas. Limitations on material consumption and redistribution of material goods and services on the basis of human needs are unlikely to be accomplished on any other basis.

To suggest that it can be accomplished at all may seen incredibly idealistic. Even for our comparatively privileged selves, however, the alternatives are rather bleak. Without a redistribution of wealth and power in our society and others like it, the consequences of economic and social change will fall heaviest on the poor and middle classes. Increased raw materials prices, for example, could well result in still shoddier and more expensive goods than we have now, higher prices for them, and further increases in unemployment. The effects of increased world petroleum and wheat prices in the early 1970s were a mild example of what could occur. Dependence on employers, increased competition for available jobs, and increases in other social costs would also be likely.

Yet higher prices for raw materials here and smaller markets for the products of present American-style technology abroad are both necessary if the spread of maldevelopment is to be reversed at all. Domestic redistribution under such constraints, without widespread and enthusiastic acceptance of the necessity for self-reliant development and material simplicity, is a political impossibility. Even a revolutionary government would very likely have to impose unacceptable levels of authoritarian constraints if the ground were not very well prepared for such measures. Easy ways out of this dilemma are unlikely. We certainly do not pretend to know the answers. But we do know that up until now very few people have even been willing to face up to the questions.

Taking Charge of Our World

From our simple living perspective, studying, understanding, and confronting the exploitative institutions that dominate the American and world economic systems are the first steps toward redistributing their economic and political power. If we are to undertake these tasks, we need to understand our own relationship to the maldevelopmental machinery of our society. Are we all unreconstructable exploiters of ourselves and each other? Is it necessary or even particularly helpful to think of ourselves in this way as we go about the task of simplifying our lives?

Victims or Executioners?

We approach this question by considering our relationship to the consumption process and the amount of power we exercise over this relationship. From the perspective of consumption, most of the world's population can be divided into four major groups. A relatively small group of individuals, families, corporate enterprises, and financial institutions own a vastly disproportionate share of economic resources and control a vastly disproportionate share of political power in the United States and through the world. Members of this group and the senior officers of the economic enterprises and institutions that belong to it have almost complete control over how much they personally choose to consume and the sources from which it comes. One-tenth of one percent of the United States population (222,000) are millionaires, and two-thirds of these made it in the last ten years. Individually and collectively, they exercise tremendous power over the consumption patterns and distribution of resources among all the rest of us. For instance, the 200 largest corporations control fully two-thirds of all manufacturing assets.[14]

Who controls the corporations? Sixty-one percent of all individually owned corporate stock is owned by 1 percent of the population. Ninety-six percent of it is owned by 20 percent.[15]

In spite of the recent growth in millionairedom, economic setbacks have served to concentrate economic power even further. Over the last five years, the number of American stockholders shrank by over 5½ million. Those who dropped out were both younger and less affluent than their fellow capitalists.[16]

Those of us who do not own stock usually put our reserves into banks, insurance companies, and investment funds. These institutions use our money to con-

How would our lives change if we were suddenly transformed into members of the victim group in the Third World?

First, take out the furniture; leave just a few old blankets, a kitchen table, one wooden chair (the car went long ago—remember?).

Second, throw out the clothes. Each one may keep the oldest suit or dress, a shirt or blouse. The head of the family has the only pair of shoes.

Third, all kitchen appliances have already gone. Keep a box of matches, a small bag of flour, some sugar and salt, a handful of onions, a dish of dried beans. Rescue those moldy potatoes from the garbage can: those are tonight's meal.

Fourth, dismantle the bathroom, shut off the running water, take out the wiring and the lights and everything that runs by electricity.

Fifth, take away the house and move the family into the toolshed.

Sixth, by now all the other houses in the neighborhood have gone; instead there are shanties —for the fortunate ones.

Seventh, cancel all the newspapers and magazines. Throw out the books. You won't miss them—you are now illiterate. One radio is now left for the whole shantytown.

centrate economic control even more. Some of them control tens of billions of dollars of other people's assets. They use these to purchase stock in and make loans to economic enterprises.

The second category of resource users is a much larger group, which enjoys access to both necessities and varying degrees of luxury as long as the economy is in reasonably good shape. This is the "middle class," the broad category of powerless possessors and users. These people have access to goods and services undreamed of a century ago—as long as they remain use-

Eighth, no more postman, fireman, government services. The two-classroom school is 3 miles away, but only half the children go, anyway.

Ninth, no hospital, no doctor. The nearest clinic is now 10 miles away with a midwife in charge. Get there by bus or by bicycle, if you're lucky enough to have one.

Tenth, throw out your bankbooks, stock certificates, pension plans, insurance policies, social security records. You have left a cash hoard of $5.

Eleventh, get out and start cultivating your three acres. Try hard to raise $300 in cash crops because your landlord wants 1/3 and your local moneylender 10 per cent.

Twelfth, find some way for your children to bring in a little extra money so you have something to eat most days. But it won't be enough to keep bodies healthy, so lop off 25 to 30 years of life expectancy.

(Adapted from the FAO magazine *Freedom from Hunger,* based on excerpts from *The Great Ascent* by Robert L. Heilbroner (New York: Harper and Row, 1963).

ful to those who purchase their time and services.

However, their positions are by no means assured. When unemployment goes up and sales go down, many of these people can find themselves suddenly both poor and powerless. A professional, managerial, or otherwise skilled job today is no guarantee of comfort and security tomorrow. It may guarantee just the opposite if this comfort and security have been purchased on the installment plan. Those who have been fired or laid off in the current recession are well aware of this.

If this sounds a bit feudal, it's not. It's worse. Under most feudal arrangements, retainers, serfs, and other subordinates were assured of lifelong tenure and protection in exchange for their services.

The middle classes are dependent on those who rule for economic security and access to consumer goods. Most of us who wrote this book, and most of those likely to read it, belong to this category. We are in an anomalous position where we could be described as being both victims and unwilling executioners. We do not determine the consumption and resource use patterns of our part of the world. These patterns have instead taken charge of us and have made us considerably less self-reliant and able to participate in many decisions concerning our lives than most of our grandparents were. They have also made us, perhaps unwillingly but nonetheless actually, complicit in the existing unjust patterns of resource distribution and use.

Among the clear victims of American-style consumption patterns and the economic structures that support them are people for whom poverty, rather than comfort, is both a way of life and the most likely future. They make up the third category of resource users. There are over one billion of them—*over 40 million of whom live in the United States.* For most of these people, the only hope of escape lies in the transformation of economic structures now based on competition and unlimited private accumulation of wealth.

The fourth group grows whenever the fragile conditions for the survival of the third group are upset or disturbed. It consists of those people who are condemned to death by the present international economic system.

Recently this has included large parts of the population of the African Sahel region on the edge of the Sahara desert, the Indians in Brazil and elsewhere in Latin America, and the poor peasants in Ethiopia, India, and Bangladesh. People who have no protection against predictable and regular crises such as famines, epidemics, and lack of work form a part of this group. Such situations (in the absence of effective emergency assistance) mean their deaths. People whose life spans are shortened and who are weakened both mentally and physically as a result of chronic malnutrition and the diseases associated with it are also included. Almost inevitably, children (girls before boys) are the chief victims. Women follow. The men continue to eat the longest in most famine-prone societies because they are believed to be the cornerstones upon which new families may be built.

Getting Started

Once we understand where we fit into the world picture, we can start working for change.

Much work is already underway in such places as worker-managed and collective enterprises, people's health clinics, and other small-scale alternative institutions which are described elsewhere in this book. Groups like the New Alchemists (energy systems), National Land for People (land redistribution), the Agribusiness Accountability Project (agribusiness), Briarpatch (small and cooperative economic enterprises)—are all actively accumulating experience that will be useful when self-reliant development takes hold in this country. Other people still working in conventional institutions also have interests, knowledge, discontents, and skills which can contribute to this process.

Taking charge of and simplifying our own lives is a second important part of self-reliant development. People who are already limiting their consumption will find the transition to a materially more frugal society easier than those who continue to consume as if there were no tomorrow. Such people also create a market for tools that can help us become more self-reliant. Their lives, homes, and communities are living models of the ways in which self-reliant development takes place.

Self-reliant development, however, also means confronting and changing the maldevelopmental institutions and practices that presently dominate overdeveloped societies like our own. Growing our own vegetables, by itself, is not going to get Safeway out of American stomachs or Del Monte off Mexican or Namibian backs. Nor can small alternative economic and service enterprises do much to change the rigidly hierarchical, highly competitive, and overspecialized employment structure that prevails. Such phenomena, as well as the underlying organizational principles, legal protections, and economic incentives that fuel and support profits and growth-oriented maldevelopment, have to be challenged directly. Such efforts have been gaining strength and legitimacy for the last fifteen years, as public interest research and action groups have challenged the private transportation industry, agribusiness, nuclear power plant programs, and the military-industrial complex. Much still needs to be done, however, and of a fundamental nature, to bring about self-reliant development at home and end resource misuse and systematic exploitation abroad. Some specific changes that would help achieve these goals include:

- Legal limits in the size and foreign operations of corporate enterprises and other economic ventures.
- Changes in the organization and distribution of work to provide truly full employment and the opportunity to develop both mental and manual skills and creativity to every worker. In China, for instance, workers and peasants have been actively involved in management, decision making, scientific research, and technological innovation.
- Measures to facilitate simple and self-reliant living on an individual and community basis. These include job sharing, tax benefits to communal living arrangements other than nuclear families, and redistribution of agricultural land presently controlled by highly industrialized absentee agribusinesses—often in violation of federal laws. National Land for People, a land-reform group in California, is presently campaigning vigorously for the redistribution of over 500,000 illegally concentrated, federally irrigated acres in the San

Joaquin Valley of California. Most of this land is presently owned and/or operated by such giants as Southern Pacific (106,000 acres), Bangor Punta (over 10,000 acres), Getty Oil, Standard Oil, and a variety of other absentee landlords.[17]

- Worker and consumer participation in management and direction of economic enterprises.
- Bringing an end to open and covert government support for multinational corporate dominance in Third World countries. In the past this has led to CIA-directed overthrows of governments in Guatemala and Iran and U.S.-sponsored invasions of Cuba and the Dominican Republic; it also played a role in the U.S. involvements in Indochina and Angola.
- The conversion of resources presently employed to maintain such maldevelopmental institutions as huge armed forces and expensive spy organizations to uses that are consistent with a process of self-reliant development.

The human and material resources now employed for such maldevelopmental purposes are urgently needed elsewhere. Many parts of New York City look as if they had been firebombed. Schools in many urban and rural areas in the United States are notorious for their inability to provide people with useful educations. Adequate health care is unavailable to many Americans; what is available is too often narrowly focused on the physical aspects of disease and injury, with no concern for prevention or the emotional and psychological effects. All of these development problems require the application of currently used or misused resources and human capabilities if they are ever to be dealt with adequately.

Development also implies recognition that non-material poverty is a public problem. Much energy and ingenuity could usefully be devoted to neighborhood and community arts and creativity programs for all age groups. Similarly, we have a long way to go in learning to trust, respect, and love people who are not from our families, neighborhoods, and communities, to say nothing of overcoming the widespread feelings that we ourselves are not worthy of love and respect. Much effect is also needed to overcome the deeply ingrained effects of racism, sexism, classism, and even national chauvinism, which most of us, however unconsciously, continue to carry around with us. All of these development needs are at the same time potential jobs, which many people are ready to do. In a developing society, such jobs would be publicly funded and under community control.

The Third World

Not much has been said here about development in the countries we usually think of as underdeveloped. We feel that, beyond seeing to it that they have a much larger share of the world's resources and greatly increased access to markets in technologically advanced countries and development capital, this is not our problem. They must and will find their own ways out of poverty. Some nations are already doing this. In China, for instance, the GNP per capita is under $200. Most middle-class Americans spend more than that annually on clothes. But from all reports, hunger, illiteracy, dependence, slaverylike conditions, lack of basic health care, unemployment, and most of the other symptoms of poverty have been eliminated there. The survival and development needs of the Chinese people are being met without foreign aid.

Since 1961, Chinese development has proceeded increasingly on the basis of self-reliance, popular participation in decision making and overcoming obstacles, and reliance on human energy and creativity rather than on outside expertise.

The Chinese model of development may not be entirely applicable elsewhere. The underlying principles, however, are much the same as those on which the approach to simple living outlined in this book is based. As a strategy, it has proven much more successful than anything sponsored by the industrialized countries for the elimination of poverty and overconsumption.

China's development, however, was not possible until political, economic, and military power were taken from those who held it by people in the third and fourth categories of resource users. With very few exceptions (such as in Tanzania and, for a period, Chile), this has been accomplished only in the wake of long, violent, and extremely destructive liberation struggles. Not even revolution, however, is an ironclad guarantee of development. Victory in an armed (or, we hope, nonviolent) struggle is only the beginning of a process which may or may not end in the kind of development of which we are speaking.

Conclusion

American, European, and Japanese capitalists, experts, and scholars have spent over thirty years systematically underdeveloping the Third World and overdeveloping their own societies, and it is time this process stopped. Any technological assistance that is really necessary will undoubtedly be asked for and can undoubtedly be given on terms designed to benefit the receiver rather than simply to guarantee continued profits to the donor. Meanwhile, our principal development problem is overcoming maldevelopment at home and creating an economic system that is no longer dependent on consuming the world.

NOTES

1. Denis Goulet, *The Cruel Choice* (maldevelopment). Johan Galtung (rapporteur), *Resolution*, Commission A of the First Conference of the U.N. International Development Center, Algiers, 1975. The Dag Hammarskjöld Trust, *What Now*, Special edition of *Development Dialogue*, spring 1975.
2. Johan Galtung, "A Structural Theory of Imperialism," *Journal of Peace Research*, 1971, No. 2, pp. 81–100. Andre Gunder Frank, *The Development of*

Underdevelopment; Pierre Jalee, *The Pillage of the Third World;* Harry Magdoff, *The Age of Imperialism;* Lenin, V.I., *Imperialism, The Highest Stage of Capitalism.*

3. Dennis Pirages and Paul Ehrlich, *Ark II* (San Francisco: W. H. Freeman, 1974), p. 230.

4. Ibid.

5. Calculations based on figures from Joshua Goldstein, "World Energy Dynamics: 1969–1989," *Alternatives,* Vol. 1, No. 1: March 1975, tables, pp. 105–106.

6. Based on data in Frances Moore Lappe, *Diet for a Small Planet,* New York: Ballantine, 1971, pp. 8–9; and Georg Borgstrom, *This Hungry Planet,* rev. ed. (New York: Collier, 1967), pp. 8, 45.

7. Carroll, Lakey, et al., *Revolution: A Quaker Prescription for a Sick Society,* Philadelphia: Movement for a New Society, 1972, pp. VI-12, VI-24.

8. See, e.g., Walt W. Rostow, *The Stages of Economic Growth.*

9. A. Fishlow, "Some Reflections on post-1964 Brazilian Economic Policy," working paper No. 19, Department of Economics, University of California, 1971; "Brazilian Size Distribution of Income," *American Economic Review,* 62 (May 1972), pp. 391–402; Teresa Hayter, *Aid as Imperialism* (New York: Penguin Books, 1971), pp. 135–143; Walter L. Ness, Jr., "Financial Market Innovations as a Development Strategy: Initial Results from the Brazilian Experience," *Economic Development and Cultural Change,* Vol. XXII, No. 3, April 1974, pp. 469–472.

10. Lakey, et al., *Moving Toward a New Society,* Philadelphia: New Society Press, 1976, pp. 45–48, 61.

11. Ibid.

12. See note 1 above.

13. See Galtung, in note 1 above.

14. Millionaire data from "An Inside Look at America Today," *San Francisco Chronicle,* Dec. 25, 1975, p. 1. The U.S. Bureau of Census estimates there are 24.3 million poor people in the United States; the Catholic Church puts the number at 40 million.

Robert McNamara, president of the World Bank, estimates that over 900 million people in the world have incomes of less than $75 annually: cited in an editorial in the *San Francisco Chronicle*, Sept. 8, 1975.

15. 1962 data from Proctor and Weiss, *Survey of Financial Characteristics of Consumers*, pp. 110–114, and Friend, Crockett, and Blume, *Mutual Funds and Other Institutional Portfolios: A New Perspective*, p. 113.

16. "How the Small Investor Has Dropped Out," *San Francisco Chronicle*, Dec. 10, 1975, p. 29. "Changing Profile of the Capitalist," Sylvia Porter column, *San Francisco Chronicle*, Dec. 10, 1975, p. 29.

17. For information, write to: National Land for People, 1759 Fulton, Room 7, Fresno CA 93721. Monthly newsletter, $10 a year.

SOURCES OF FURTHER INFORMATION

(See also: Consuming Ourselves, Food)

Books

Borgstrom, Georg. *The Hungry Planet*. New York: Collier-Macmillan, 1967.
A study of protein shortages and their relation to the consumption of vegetable protein in the production of meat.

Domhoff, G. William. *Who Rules America?* Englewood Cliffs, N.J.: Prentice Hall, 1967.
A comprehensive study of the relations between power, wealth, and social status in the United States.

Goulet, Denis. *The Cruel Choice: A New Concept in the Theory of Development*. New York: Atheneum, 1971.
One of the first and only books to discuss development in an ethical context. Discusses the need for a new approach to development in industrialized as well as nonindustrialized countries. Excellent throughout, but slightly marred by use of academic language.

Heilbroner, Robert. *The Great Ascent*. New York: Harper and Row, 1963.

———. *The Human Prospect*. New York: Harper and Row, 1974.

A projection of the future of the United States in a profoundly pessimistic vein. The author suggests that if we do not learn to live simply very rapidly, changes in the U.S. economy will force the country into a very oppressive kind of authoritarianism.

————. *The Limits of American Capitalism.* New York: Harper and Row, 1966.
A critical study of the American economic system.

Jalee, Pierre. *Imperialism in the Seventies.* New York: Third Press, 1973.
An analysis of the effect of pre-energy-crisis imperialism on relations between wealthy countries. Presents quite a bit of information on the relationship between industrialized and Third World countries and the exploitation and dependency resulting therefrom.

————. *The Pillage of the Third World.* New York: Monthly Review, 1967.
An earlier work, which analyzes and exposes the dependence of rich nations on raw materials derived from the Third World.

Lakey, George, et al. *Moving toward a New Society.* Philadelphia: New Society Press, 1976.
Described in Chapter 2.

Lappe, Frances Moore. *Diet for a Small Planet.* New York: Ballantine, 1975 (revised edition).
Described in Chapter 2.

Magdoff, Harry. *The Age of Imperialism.* New York: Monthly Review, 1969.
A slightly dated, but nonetheless important, discussion of the role of U.S. imperialism in the world economy.

Meadows, Donella, et al. *The Limits to Growth.* New York: Universe, 1972.
A computer analysis of the rates of population increase, resource depletion, environmental pollution, energy use, and other factors that threaten continued life on this planet. The value assumptions and conclusions of this book are highly controversial, but indicative of the consequences of resource use in industrialized countries.

Oxford Economic Atlas of the World (4th edition). Oxford: Oxford University Press, 1972.
Somewhat dated, but still useful, geographic mapping of resource production, trade, and use in the world.

Proctor and Weiss. *Survey of Financial Characteristics of Consumers.* Washington D.C.: Federal Reserve System.

Periodicals

Alternatives (Institute for World Order, 1140 Avenue of the Americas, New York NY 10027).
Concentrates on problems of development and alternative world futures.

The Corporate Examiner (Interfaith Center on Corporate Responsibility, 475 Riverside Drive, New York NY 10027).
Monthly newsletter critically analyzing domestic and international activities of U.S. corporations.

Development Dialogue (The Dag Hammarskjöld Memorial Foundation, Ovre Slottsgatan 2, Uppsala, Sweden).
Quarterly journal devoted to discussion of issues in development. The editors see lack of development as a problem in rich as well as poor countries.

The Guardian (New York).
Radical weekly newspaper. Thorough reporting on U.S. imperialism and exploitation and movements that oppose this.

NACLA's Latin America and Empire Report (North American Committee on Latin America, P.O. Box 226, Berkeley CA 94701, or P.O. Box 57, Cathedral Station, New York NY 10025).
Current research on economic, political, social, and military aspects of U. S. imperialism in Latin America.

Pacific Research and World Empire Telegram (Pacific Studies Center, 1953 University Ave., East Palo Alto, CA).
Current research on economic, political, social, and military aspects of U. S. imperialism in Asia.

Pamphlets, Articles, Monographs, Reports

Berry, Philip, et al. *Guide to Global Giving: A Critical Introduction to Voluntary International Aid Agencies in the United States.* Philadelphia: Movement for a New Society, 1976.

Dag Hammarskjöld Memorial Foundation. "What Now?" *Development Dialogue,* 1975, No. 1/2.
This special issue discusses some of the requirements

for self-reliant development and restructuring of the world economy to allow equitable distribution of world resources.

Galtung, Johan (rapporteur). "Resolution: Commission A, 1st Conference of the International Development Center, Algiers, June 24–27. 1975."

This is a comprehensive resolution calling for a total reassessment of the meaning of development for industrialized and nonindustrialized countries alike.

Goldstein, Joshua. "World Energy Dynamics: 1969–1989." *Alternatives,* Vol. 1, No. 1, Spring 1975, pp. 101–132.

A projection of world and national energy use and its environmental consequences in the period named.

Hueem, Helge. "The Political Economy of Raw Materials and the Conditions for Their 'Opecization.'" PRIO, Oslo, mimeographed, 1975.

An analysis of the economic and political consequences of the development of OPEC-like organizations among raw-materials-producing countries. Also analyzes conditions favorable and unfavorable to the development of such organizations. Considerable data on raw materials production and trade is also presented.

Moyer, William, and Haines, Pamela. "How We Cause World Hunger." *WIN* Magazine, January 30, 1975, pp. 10–16.

Shows the relationship between American eating habits and starvation in other parts of the world.

Povey, George. "Hunger, Disease, War and the Class Struggle." Speech given at the 1975 Annual Meeting of the American Friends Service Committee, Northern California Regional Office, San Francisco, February 8, 1975.

Povey ably argues for the view that development requires a victorious struggle by the oppressed against the owning classes in the world. He also analyzes the negative consequences of employing violence in this struggle.

Organizations

Institute for Policy Studies, 1901 Q St. N.W., Washington, DC.

This is a research institute which focuses on alternatives to present American government policies and transnational corporate involvements. IPS researchers have done important work in exposing the U.S. role in the Indo-China war, the actions of multinational agribusiness, the multinational energy industry, and other aspects of multinational corporate enterprise. An ongoing project is the development and publication of a "Peoples Encyclopedia," which will contain extensive descriptions of alternatives to present American institutions and involvements, and tools for implementing such alternatives.

Institute for World Order. 1140 Avenue of the Americas, New York NY 10036.

Principally concerned with transforming the international system and the societies that compose it into one where values such as peace, social justice, and environmental improvement can be realized. Deeply involved in peace education and peace studies at all levels in the United States and, to some degree, elsewhere.

Interfaith Center on Corporate Responsibility. 475 Riverside Drive, New York NY 10027.

Principally interested in researching and exposing the investments and involvements of U.S.-based multinational corporations in southern Africa and other areas with oppressive and exploitative regimes and/or economic policies. Especially interested in corporations that are partially church-owned.

National Land for People. 1759 Fulton, Room 7, Fresno, CA 93721.

Land redistribution in the United States.

North American Committee for Latin America, P.O. Box 57, Cathedral Station, New York NY 10025, and P.O. Box 226, Berkeley CA 94701.

NACLA puts most of its energy into research on the role of U.S. imperialism in Latin America and exposing U.S. government and corporate actions and policies in that region.

Pacific Studies Center, 1953 University Avenue, East Palo Alto CA.

Similar to NACLA except that its geographic focus is on Asia and other areas of the Pacific rim. They have an extensive library and clipping file, which can b` used by people in the area interested in carrying out research on the activities and multinational involvement of industrial and financial enterprises in the Bay Area which have investments in Asia.

4

Personal Growth

BY LUCY ANDERSON

Queries

1. How would I describe myself to someone else? What do I really like about myself?
2. Whom do I feel closest to? Why?
3. How much do I live in the present, past, or future? Why?
4. Do I take time to know myself better and those with whom I live and work?
5. Do I treat persons of other sex, race, or age differently? How? Why?
6. How do I handle conflict or disagreement in my home or work place?
7. What does the spiritual mean to me? Do I set aside a time for quiet or meditation each day?
8. What does my body tell me about myself? Do I listen to what it says? Am I at home with my body?
9. Can I see or feel the signs of strain or tension in my body? How do I respond to it?
10. What beliefs or visions govern my political and personal actions?
11. If I had very little time to live, what would I want to do with it?
12. What types of life experiences do I value most?
13. How do I feel today?

What is personal growth? Why do we now talk about growth? Isn't growth cancerous, a waste of resources, energy consuming, and contrary to simple living?

No. Growth does not have to mean opulence or waste. We have read earlier in this book that by living simply we can find time to work to correct injustices. We can understand and begin to overcome the effects of consumerism and the influence of advertising. And by living simply, we also have the chance to improve our personal and spiritual lives. We see that consumerism cannot bring us inner peace; we have to find that in the nurturance and love we give one another. Personal growth is the process of learning to tap these inner resources or reservoirs of strength as we do the hard work of bringing about social changes.

As we explore simple living and personal growth, we discover that there is both a replenishing growth and a growth that takes us to new places. Replenishing growth can be compared to the organic material composting in a garden. It takes several months for all the matter to be fully broken down and composted into rich soil which can be returned to the garden beds and used as mulch. A rich new crop of healthy vegetables will then be able to grow in soil that had been worn and drained of important nutrients by last year's garden. This is growth that is not exploiting or disproportionately large, but rather a recycled, conserving type of growth.

Likewise there are parts of our daily experience that we need to work well into the soil of our being, that we need to fully digest in order to foster new growth and nourishment for ourselves. It sometimes takes a long while to really confront our experiences, our struggles, or our decisions. If we can resolve our conflicts and come to terms with our experiences, we feel replenished and able to support new growth. Then when new seeds of experience are sown, we are able to let them grow and come to fruition.

So for those of us who want to live in a simple way, one of the key objectives of personal growth is the integration of our personal lives and our political actions, the acceptance of our unity and our uniqueness. If we can respect both the personal and the political in their own right, then their inseparable nature will become clear. Problems in the world lead us to respond to cries for justice in personal ways. We refuse to eat lettuce or grapes that are not grown under contract with the United Farm Workers, we decline to buy nonunion-label clothes, and we think seriously about trying to curb our meat consumption.

We realize that our personal actions are political statements.

Elsewhere in this book there is much to read on the purely political implications of simple living. Here I will try to separate out and discuss three of the personal aspects: (1) the right type of environment for growth, (2) the quality of relationships, and (3) simple living and spiritual concerns.

1. Environment and Growth

Creating the right type of environment for growth can be compared to preparing soil for germinating plants in the early spring by turning the earth and spreading mulch over the beds. Similarly, people need a good environment for growth: a supportive setting where we can feel good with our bodies, our spirits, our emotions, and our intellect, yet always be challenged to a greater awareness of these parts of our being. We need a community, a collective (e.g., a wòmen's/men's group), or family to grow with and move with toward simple living, personally and politically. Without this supportive atmosphere we are likely to feel inwardly hungry—and to fall into a pattern of ceaseless, unsatisfying consumption. With this support, however, we can better take what is really nutritious for us—the acceptance, the understanding, the love.

Learning to challenge each other in ways that foster growth can be a difficult process. Often we pussyfoot around and avoid directly speaking our differences; or we are judgmental and try to shove people into seeing things as we do; or perhaps we are self-righteous about our way of life. None of these attitudes creates a supportive, nurturing environment for growth. Ideally we stimulate growth in one another by expressing our care and our support and by straightforwardly stating our differences, decisions, and points of view. Then we can make changes in our way of life not because we feel deprived or pressured, but rather because we experience rebirth and renewal of our creative energy as we explore alternatives, and because our lives are enriched by deeper, more meaningful relationships.

One family I know, in the course of simplifying their lives, went through a long and struggling time of shifting priorities, evaluating their actions, and trying to create a better environment for growth. Nancy had played the role of housewife for about ten years. She spent most of her time doing the cleaning, the laundry, the cooking, and the dishes and keeping the house perfectly neat and spotless. There was little room for anyone's personal expression in the house except Nancy's own. Meanwhile, her husband, Bob, played the breadwinner role and came home from work with little energy for the family and with requests and expectations. The submerged tensions between them finally became intolerable and burst into the open. Neither really felt satisfied with the roles they had locked themselves into. Both felt stifled and bored. Neither could grow or support the other in growing or expanding her or his self-awareness.

After some real struggle, Nancy and Bob decided to separate for a time. During this period, Nancy became able to let go of her feelings of needing to maintain the perfect house and put her energy into new things. She told me that the feminist books she read and her women's group were fundamentally important to her as she endeavored to explore her own identity apart from Bob. Nancy got her first job (a part-time job so that she would still have time for her children), went back to school part-time, and really began to take responsibility for her own life. Bob also did a great deal of growing. On weekends, when their three children came to stay with him, he was confronted with having to cook and care for them—something he had never taken responsibility for before that time.

Nancy and Bob live together again now—but a lot has changed. They have been able to come back together because both have been willing to live more simply and to shed old roles. As Nancy says, "If my needs are simpler I can meet them." The house is no longer Nancy's picture of perfection, but it expresses the various interests and personalities of each member of the family. Nancy admits, "Now it is *our* home." Not only Bob but the children as well share in the cleaning, cooking, and gardening, and because their home is simpler and easier to care for, Nancy is freed to put time into her job and school. Bob found a job closer to home and is better able to share in household responsibilities. Nancy points out that they are still learning and there are often hard times, but she has seen a great deal of growth. Today their home provides a supportive atmosphere for growth and change. The different emphasis on the material, and the warmth it creates in the physical, environment reflects the warmth and love they have for one another.

2. Quality of Relationships

Personal growth can expand and enrich the quality of our relationships with others. In fact, it is in relationships with others, our community, and the world that we grow. The things that probably most hinder that growth are our self-images, our possessions, and our lack of time. In order to grapple with these obstacles, we first need to be honest with ourselves—really recognize our physical, psychological, and spiritual needs. It is so easy to evade being honest with ourselves by putting material things around us, by working ceaselessly to earn prestige or money and leaving ourselves no quiet time, or by getting behind some world-saving cause which we feel is so critical that taking time for personal growth seems frivolous, luxurious, or worse.

Once we begin struggling with restrictive roles, self-images, and monetary needs, it will become apparent that it will take time to make changes. It is hard to move from taking very little time for our personal growth to make it a priority. At first we may have to be very intent and strong-willed about it, determining that a certain number of hours a day will be devoted to personal growth activities such as spending time with our family, taking time for meditation, writing in a journal, or even going for a walk. This does not mean becoming consumed by every minute detail of our actions, but rather searching for a balance between action and reflection. It is not easy getting to know ourselves or others well. As we do so, the resulting changes and new understandings may threaten existing relationships and shake up old patterns and responses. The conflict can be hard and unpleasant for us, but it can also be creative. The breaking up of old patterns can be our first step toward a more fulfilling life and a more open, honest attitude toward ourselves and others.

My friends David and Penny, after considerable effort, have achieved a graceful motion to their relationship. They devote time to personal growth both because it enriches their relationship and because they see it as a prerequisite to the social work they do. But this was an issue they struggled with. Four years ago, when Penny and David took a job-sharing position as campus ministers at a nearby university, David was bothered by the fact that the quantity of his production, in terms of programs, was not as great as the church where he had previously worked. He had, he thought, wanted to be a successful activist minister. But as he stretched to live up to this image, in a part-time job, he had less and less time for Penny, for himself, and for his son, Joshua. Joshua, their first child, had been born shortly before David and Penny became campus ministers. David was fascinated with Joshua and with becoming a father. His full participation in parenting helped him let go of his concern to "make it" in the work world and instead really take time during outside work for his own growth and his relationship with Penny. There were hard times trying to sort out priorities and letting go of old images of who they were going to be. They started a parents' liberation group, which helped create more time to be thoughtful and honest with themselves and each other in their changes. Today, neither of them could imagine not taking time for personal growth. They feel it has enriched both their family and their work lives.

3. Simple Living and Spirituality

For me, the spiritual is that which fuses all of life and makes the whole world *sacred,* that is, entitled to reverence and respect. It is in the world, in relationship to other things and people that the spiritual, the holy, manifests itself and is discovered. For many others too (including Christians, Jews, Buddhists, and people of no particular denomination) the motivation to live simply comes from the fact that it is consistent with our spiritual beliefs. From our perspective, this section should have introduced not only this chapter but the entire book.

We see all life as sacred, or, as the Quakers would say, there is that of God in each of us. There is a universal bond that connects us all, through which we can truly see our commonality. Sometimes I like to attach imagery to this concept; I think of it as a light within each of us, a light which shines through us individually and yet emanates from a common source. This source I choose to call God; and he/she is a living presence. Each person's light shines out and connects with the light of other people. Sometimes these touchings are scarcely noticed; other times they are extremely profound.

It seems that today there is violence everywhere—wars, political oppression, racial and sexual discrimination, starvation, loneliness, and sorrow. The violence seems so overwhelming that some of us try to shut it out. We become blind or insensitive to the pain we hear and read of through the media. We ask, "How can I make a difference?" As we look for answers, God is not a distant abstraction for us, but a personal presence who shares our condition and our experiences. Our joys are God's joys; our suffering is God's suffering. Thus our responses to suffering are religious acts as well as humanitarian and political efforts.

Of the people I know who share a similar religious approach to simple living, some choose to respond to God's suffering voice by becoming political activists. They are on the picket line with the Farmworkers, demonstrating at GE stockholders' meetings, or sitting in at Lockheed and encouraging dialogue about the need for and cost of the Trident missile. Others respond by creating alternatives; they develop uses for wind and solar energy or establish low-income housing, free medical clinics, or cooperative markets. For still others, the most meaningful response is to raise their children with this respect and reverence for all life. In all cases our work in the world is a reflection of our spiritual beliefs. At the same time, the hard social and political realities challenge and force us to be honest about our perception of the spiritual. I do not feel God is a source of magic powers who will reverse or excuse human irresponsibility, oppression, or violence. I agree with the German theologian Dietrich Bonhoeffer, who was executed by the Nazis for working in the Resistance against Hitler, that there is no such thing as "cheap grace." Religion is not a way to avoid the struggle to bring about a world where each person's basic needs are met, a world of peace.

I believe that some sort of spiritual exercise, be it contemplation, meditation, or worship, is important to our lives whatever kind of work we do in the world, but especially so if we want to work effectively to bring about a more just world. Even if we are not formally religious, we need time for renewal and strengthening of our physical and spiritual energy. For some, periods of contemplation are times of insight and understanding, when they can find solution and make weighty decisions. Periods of quiet can be times for putting events into a clearer, more realistic perspective. Gathering for worship can also provide for rejuvenation and celebration. It is an opportunity for friends to gather and express not only their faith but also their love and support for one another in their common struggle. For me, setting aside places and times as sacred spaces reminds me that all the world is sacred.

Recently I heard Elie Wiesel, renowned poet, writer, and Jewish theologian, give the Kent State Memorial Lecture at Stanford University. He concluded the lecture with a Hasidic story, one of his favorite modes of presentation, about a man whose wife and two of three sons die of starvation. Although his grief and despair increase with each death, each time the man recites the Kaddish, the Jewish prayer of mourning and praise of God. Finally, with his one remaining son, the man says to God, "No, I won't stop reciting the Kaddish—I will believe in you in spite of you." Wiesel drew from the story a parallel affirmation about humanity—that we must believe in one another in spite of ourselves. This attitude, it seems to me, is an example of the basic spiritual hope that makes it possible for us to pray for and practice peace in the midst of war, to cry out for and affirm meaning in a time of meaninglessness, to celebrate and build community in a world where there is so much isolation.

Thus a sense of the spiritual not only enables me to see the need of working and praying for peace, but also enables me to hold on to the signs of meaning and joy in life. Paradoxically enough, it seems as if it is easier for many of us to tap our inner resources, touch the spiritual, and experience the depth of our being in the face of suffering. On the other hand, it is harder for us to reach these depths simply by letting the hushed whisper of beauty penetrate our bodies, or experiencing the depth of laughter and the spiritual dance and celebration of life. It is almost as if we were fearful of awakening that part of our being, fearful of the encounter with the spiritual we might have through the craziness of laughter or the profundity of happiness.

As I struggle to grow toward being a more mature, honest, open, and loving person, I see more clearly what it means to be human both through developing my personal relations and through deepening my political action. Simple living and the living presence of the spiritual invite us to be together, to dance together, to rejoice together.

What You Can Do

In our search for personal growth, we have found the following activities helpful:

1. Keep a time log for several days accounting for all your time (include sleep) in one-hour intervals. After you've recorded a representative sample of your days, ask:
   —What five activities took the most time?
   —What activity did I most enjoy?
   —What activity would I like to be doing more?
   —What was left undone?
   —How much time did I give myself for personal growth or meditation?
   —How much am I controlled by events or others?
   This exercise is helpful in getting a realistic picture of our time and in measuring our priorities (which may need reordering).

2. Balloon game. Make a circle (balloon) in the center of a piece of paper and put your name in it. Around this balloon, make a balloon for each of the activities that occupies your time each day, such as work, family, sharing with others, spiritual life, and so on. The size of each balloon should represent the amount of time you give to that

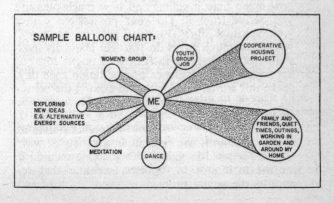

SAMPLE BALLOON CHART:

WOMEN'S GROUP

YOUTH GROUP JOB

COOPERATIVE HOUSING PROJECT

EXPLORING NEW IDEAS E.G. ALTERNATIVE ENERGY SOURCES

ME

MEDITATION

DANCE

FAMILY AND FRIENDS, QUIET TIMES, OUTINGS, WORKING IN GARDEN AND AROUND MY HOME activity. Next draw a line from your balloon to each activity balloon, with the thickness of the line representing the strength of your commitment to that activity and the pleasure you receive from it. If you are doing this in a group, discuss with one another what your charts tell you about your own lives. For example, do you have a big balloon for work with only a thin line to it, and thick lines to family, sharing with friends, and spiritual life, but with small balloons for each of them? WHY? What are your priorities? Have people allowed time each day for their own nourishment? How does your balloon chart compare with what you would like it to look like? Play the game again in a couple of months and see what changes take place.

3. A healthy spirit wants a healthy body. Make a chart with five columns, headed Nutrition, Exercise, Sleep, Posture, and Hygiene. Each day, become aware of what you have done for yourself in these areas and make a short note of them at the end of the day. Try to improve as you go along until you attend to these concerns as daily habit.

4. As your body is the physical extension of your spirit, your possessions are a physical extension of your body. List all your personal possessions that cost more than $50. Assess each one in terms of how much time it claims and how much pleasure you derive from it. Do your possessions clutter your spiritual life? Do your possessions "own" you? How much stress do you feel about the possibility of breakage or theft of your possessions?

5. Set aside a time of silence or meditation each day. Make this a time to explore and expand the peaceful and harmonious parts of life. How do you emerge feeling?

6. Role Playing. One useful tool for conflict situations is role playing. It can be done in a variety of ways and can be used in many contexts. One method is for the facilitator to design a scenario that resembles the actual problem at hand. Each person

plays a role different from his own position. After this is done, a situation more similar to the real conflict could be role-played. Another method is to have other persons playing the alter egos of the participants. Each of these should stand behind a role player and blurt out comments he believes the participant is really intending to make. There should be one or two observers who look for times when the players are being unfair or holding back. Following the role playing, allow time for careful sharing of what has occurred.

7. Counseling Groups. Experiences in counseling groups can have deep and lasting impact. They can help us get to the roots of our feelings with other group members who are struggling. Hospitals, women's groups, and university and adult education programs frequently offer a variety of counseling groups, often at reasonable rates. The Co-Counseling Movement, for example, has an effective and almost free self-help counseling approach in which participants are both counselor and client. Write the National Headquarters at 719 Second St., N, Seattle, Washington 98109, to find out what's available in your area.

8. Dialogues or Creative Listening. Dialogues are structured group interaction, particularly suited to people who may be leery of professional counseling approaches. They are organized and conducted entirely by group members. At each session a question, such as What is the greatest source of problems in your close relationship? or What gives you the most joy? is asked. Group members meditate on the question. Each person has an opportunity to respond orally once, at a time of the person's choice. The process emphasizes supportive listening, equal opportunity for both the timid and the long-winded, and gut feelings instead of analysis. Discussion among members is prohibited while the dialogue is in progress.

9. Organize a simple living workshop for a group of which you are a part. Focus on where all participants feel they are now and let the content of the

workshop develop from participants' specific concerns. The following issues you might consider discussing during the first day of your workshop:

- Why simple living? What experiences have challenged you to live more simply? To think about your way of life? What personal oppressions related to your way of life at present do you feel?
- What are the societal causes of oppressions you feel? What kind of society would you like to live in? What style of life do you want for yourself—both from a personal and societal view?
- How do we get from here to there? What specific actions can we take, as individuals or as groups? How shall we change our lives? Our institutions?

Further topics for discussion could include specific queries or chapters in this book.

In creating and having your workshop, try to be aware of:

- Personal relationships and interactions. Even preparing for the workshop could be a time of growth.
- Process; means are as important as ends.
- Sex roles; divide tasks and leadership roles equally between men and women.
- Individuality; realize that people will have differences about the ideas discussed.

10. Decision making is often a period of internal confusion, uncertainty, and growth. It is particularly difficult when alternatives seem nearly equally desirable or undesirable. When I am making a decision, do I listen to what my body tells me and to my gut reactions? Do I consult with others who might have relevant input? Am I able to make a firm choice and live with it, or change it if it proves to be wrong for me?

   The following decision-making tool has been helpful in making decisions where the alternatives seem approximately equally desirable. List factors that you consider important criteria for assessing the alternatives in one column. The example shows just a few. Rank each alternative on the basis of each criterion, on a scale of 1 to 10 with 10 indicating that the alternative completely satisfies that criterion. (Note that for any criterion, each alternative may rank 10.) When finished, total the numbers and try to assess what they indicate about your preferences.

Important Factors in My Decision	Alternative A	Alternative B
1. Matches my long-term goals		
2. Meets the needs of my spouse and family		
3. Location		
4. Time required		
5. Feel good about it		
6. Matches my experience and interests		
7. Unknowns		
TOTAL		

SOURCES OF FURTHER INFORMATION

(See also: Community, Clothing, Children)

Berrigan, Daniel, and Thich Nhat Hanh. *The Raft Is Not the Shore.* Nyack, NY: Fellowship Books, 1976.

Douglass, James. *Resistance and Contemplation.* New York: Delta Books, 1971.

James, Muriel, and Jongward, Dorothy. *Born to Win: Transactional Analysis with Gestalt Experiments.* Reading, Mass.: Addison-Wesley, 1971.

Merton, Thomas. *Contemplation in a World of Action.* New York: Doubleday, 1970.

Neal, Robert E. *The Art of Dying.* New York: Harper and Row, 1973.

O'Neill, Nena, and O'Neill, George. *Shifting Gears: Finding Security in a Changing World.* New York: Avon, 1975.

Reps, Paul. *Zen Flesh, Zen Bones.* New York: Doubleday/Anchor, 1976.

Schutz, William. *Joy.* New York: Ballantine, 1973.

Suzuki, Shunryu. *Zen Mind, Beginner's Mind.* New York: Walker/Weatherhill, 1971.

Thich Nhat Hahn. *The Miracle of Being Awake.* Nyack, NY: Fellowship Books, 1973.

Trungpa, Chogyam. *Cutting Through Spiritual Material-ism*. Berkeley, Calif.: Shambala Publications, 1973.
————. *Meditation in Action*. Berkeley, Calif.: Shambala Publications, 1970.

5

Community

BY DAVID HARTSOUGH

Wendell

Queries

1. Do we seek closer, more meaningful relationships with others?
2. Do we need a support group larger than our immediate family for our personal growth?
3. Could a living community help us cut our financial needs and free us to do what we want with our lives?
4. Are society's values alien to us? Do we wish that we and our children could interact more with people whose values are similar to ours?
5. Do we seek security not found in material possessions or a big bank account? Could we find needed support and security from living or associating closely with a group of people who care deeply for each other?
6. Do we often feel powerless against advertising, large corporations, and big government?
7. Could a community help us take charge of our lives and live in greater harmony with our beliefs and values?

If we answer yes to any of the above questions, we are probably interested in, or perhaps already trying to build, some form of community. In this chapter we will share ideas about three kinds of communities: communities whose members share one household and interact in many aspects of their daily lives; communities whose members choose to reside in a limited geographical area or "neighborhood" to make "sharing and caring" easier; and communities of spirit or concern, which can develop even though considerable geographical distance may separate their members.

Community and Simple Living

Living contentedly without great material consumption goes against the grain of our culture. But it is possible in the context of community. Incomes can be reduced if washing machines, tools, automobiles, and houses are shared. Material overconsumption can be considered an addiction similar to alcoholism, a hard habit to kick. It helps to have a supportive community of people struggling to kick the same habit.

For people who find their present occupations incompatible with their ideals, a community can be a source of support as they make radical changes, in employment, particularly if the changes involve leaving the full-time, career-oriented work world to live on earnings from part-time jobs.

Living a simpler material existence has helped many community members shift from "having" to "being." For instance, when Paul and Selma Thompson were married back in 1958, they wanted lots of kids, lots of money, and a well-ordered life. The things they considered absolutely necessary in those days—new home, second car, big savings account, steak, fancy clothes—they now consider nonessential luxuries. They decided that the pleasures of accumulation were not worth the price of the rat race. Paul "retired" early, at the age of 39. The Thompsons, their four children, and three other families with children formed the Open House Community, a religious living community in Lake Charles, Louisiana. They like their new life. According to Paul, "the greatest factor contributing to our satisfaction with our present lifestyle is the strong support, physical, emotional, and spiritual, that we received as a family and as individuals from the other community members. We understand how hard it is for an individual, or an individual family, alone in society, to live a life different from that which is considered normal. This new life," he says, "is fundamentally satisfying because we support one another in an almost daily decision to share and grow. People are so infinitely more than what they own that there is no limit on the amount of themselves that they can give."

Why Community?

What kinds of people are attracted by the idea of community? While researching this chapter, we came across all kinds. Let's look at a few examples Ken and Nancy, a married couple in Palo Alto, California; Kathleen and Robert in Philadelphia; and Virgil and his family who live in Chicago. All these people at one time led comfortably conventional lives, with houses, cars, TV sets, lots of appliances and clothes, and money in the bank. The men worked hard to support their way of life: Ken as a teacher, Robert in social work, and Virgil as a minister. But they came to be dissatisfied with the way they lived. Ken felt he had no close friends. Robert was so consumed by his job that Kathleen and their two children rarely saw him. Virgil found his personal values increasingly out of step with mainstream life.

Joining with others in community was their response to these dissatisfactions. Ken and Nancy joined a group of people in Palo Alto who share cooking, child care, tools, and skills while continuing to live in their own homes. Kathleen and Robert moved into the Philadelphia Life Center of the Movement for a New Society. They shared their new house with another family and adults. Virgil joined the Reba Place Fellowship in Evanston, Illinois, a religious community.

All these people feel that their new living arrangements have simplified and enriched their lives. Ken has made a number of close friends, and he enjoys the group's gatherings for work and fun. Nancy has had some of the load of child care and housekeeping taken off her shoulders. Robert and Kathleen found at the Life Center that they no longer needed an income of $20,000 a year; they could now live better on $5,000 a year. So Robert quit his job and got involved with the United Farmworkers Union and nonviolent resistance to the Vietnam War, two concerns he had had for a long time. He also found he now has more time to spend with Kathleen and their children, while Kathleen, a trained nurse, has been able to return to work part-time at a job she enjoys. Virgil's family found that the extended-family life of the Reba Place Fellowship gave their religious expressions a deeper meaning than they had found in ordinary churches. The more than 130 members of the Reba Place live in houses and apartments within a three-block area; they share money and possessions and believe serving one another gives them a chance to practice Christian love.

Virgil summed up the benefits all these three families have found in community in an interview with *Fellowship* magazine. "We have come to realize," he says, "that there is no way you can really live a set of values different from those of the rest of society unless you have a community, a social network, that will be strong enough to compete. Mainstream social values and the American lifestyle are perpetuated by such powerful institutions as General Motors, the Pentagon, universities, and so on. These corporate institutions keep getting more powerful and more sophisticated. They swallow up the individual. . . . Reba Place Fellowship is by far the most powerful influence on the lives of members of this community and what we are doing. That kind of a shift in power is what has to take place, and that is what community is all about." [1]

Once begun, a community of concern or spirit must be consciously developed and nurtured. People can work together or interact without any real sense of community or meaningful sharing as, for example, when people work in the same office or factory, and hardly know each other. But most people discover that a sense of having something in common brings much more joy and fulfillment to their lives.

Here are some ideas for starting communities which we have used successfully or learned about from others.

1. If you belong to an existing group or club, express

your need for community. You may be surprised to find others who feel the same way. If so, get together and talk about your needs; share your ideas about the community you envision and how together you can begin to make that vision a reality.

2. Plan a series of potluck dinners with people who share your values and want to live in a more closely knit community. At these gatherings discuss what you hope to gain from your envisioned community, what kind of community would best meet your needs, and how you can begin building that community.

3. In your neighborhood, find out from people who live nearby what common interests and needs they have. One woman who lives near us in San Francisco decided to try to do this on her block. She circulated a flier to everyone on her street which said:

Is It Time to Revive the Downey Street Association?
Possible reasons:

1. block party
2. car pools
3. children's activities
4. praises
5. complaints
6. petitioning city hall
7. buying clubs
8. politics
9. cleaning up
10. a newsletter
11. block garage sale
12. directory of skills, services, talents, advice, available on street, in neighborhood
13. city programs
14. neighborhood programs
15. petitioning landlords to fix up
16. groups for music, study, crafts, etc.
17. keeping sidewalks clear for pedestrians
18. drafting suggestions or requests to government agencies or companies or ???
19. trading
20. ? ? ? ? ?

If these ideas or others that might benefit our lives on Downey Street interest you, or if you want to run a meeting or have one at your house, please contact. . . .

Her name, address, and phone number were listed at the bottom of the flier. The response she received has been exciting. She says people are beginning to feel related and involved and needed, and also that they are having their needs met in their neighborhood.

4. Begin projects that will help a group grow together. Start a food cooperative. Organize a child care facility. Start a macroanalysis seminar (see "Another View of Economics," chapter 14; write Macro Collective, 4722 Baltimore Avenue, Philadelphia, PA 19143, for more information).

5. Start a resource and skills exchange. Get a group of friends or neighbors together and ask them to list on a card what resources and skills they are willing to share with others. On another card have them write the resources and skills they need. Then have people read their cards aloud or post them on a wall for others to read and see how many needs can be met within the group.

How a Community Gets Started

To see how a community can actually get started, let's look at one that originated in Palo Alto, California, in November 1974. For many years Dorothy Fadiman, a housewife and mother of two, had had a vision of a community where she and her friends could be more responsible for themselves and less dependent on large impersonal corporations. She shared this vision with her friends and found that many felt the same way. They called a meeting of the parents and teachers at a small progressive elementary school nearby, and more than 50 people came.

To determine the community's needs and major areas for cooperation, they passed out interest sheets listing possible areas of cooperation. (See the community interest sheet on the next page, and the queries at the end of this chapter for "defining community" and for "People Starting a Community.") They decided to develop autonomous projects, such as cooking cooperatives, which, while serving the community,

COMMUNITY INTEREST SHEET

Your Name _____

Address _____

Phone Number _____

Please indicate your level of interest in any of the following projects by noting one of the below:

A. *Participant*—Interested in the idea, would use it if it developed.

B. *Worker*—Would be willing to work on it as it develops.

C. *Organizer*—Willing to help organize the original plans.

---

1. Sunday meeting   once a week_____ once a month_____
   Participant_____ Worker_____   Organizer_____

2. Food co-op
   Participant_____ Worker_____   Organizer_____

3. Services exchange
   Participant_____ Worker_____   Organizer_____

4. Goods exchange
   Participant_____ Worker_____   Organizer_____

5. Job referrals within the community
   Participant_____ Worker_____   Organizer_____

6. Community-oriented childcare
   Participant_____ Worker_____   Organizer_____

7. More shared parenting
   Full days_____ Weekends_____ Longer_____
   Participant_____ Worker_____   Organizer_____

8. Community garden

    Participant_____   Worker_____   Organizer_____

9. Political action/Discussion group

    Participant_____   Worker_____   Organizer_____

10. Cooking cooperatives

    Participant_____   Worker_____   Organizer_____

11. Drama group

    Participant_____   Worker_____   Organizer_____

12. Single parents discussion

    Participant_____   Worker_____   Organizer_____

13. Yoga

    Participant_____   Worker_____   Organizer_____

14. Medical

    Participant_____   Worker_____   Organizer_____

could be carried out by a nucleus of committed people.

After the interest sheets were compiled, each person who expressed interest in being an organizer met with those who had checked either the participant or worker category in a specific area. Together they made plans to implement their projects.

The community now comprises about 30 families and individuals. At first glance their homes seem typically middle-class, but they are different. The families interact with each other a great deal. Several cooking co-ops have developed, with three families in each co-op. Each family takes turns cooking one major meal a week and delivering it to the other two homes. In this way, the wives (or husbands) in each family spend less time cooking and have more time to pursue other interests. Similarly, children's afternoon play groups have been organized. The kids enjoy themselves and their parents can count on some time to themselves. A resource and skills exchange has been set up, and work days are organized at members' homes. A drama group meets once a week. A monthly "Sunday Meeting" has been started for people of all religious backgrounds for quiet and worship together. There is no dogma involved in the meetings. On the contrary, community members seek their own forms of worship those which are most alive for the community.

Most members have joined and helped develop the Briarpatch Market, a cooperative, nonprofit grocery store, where everyone works and the food is usually better and much cheaper than in most other stores. The market helps people keep their food budgets down and builds a sense of relatedness with other community-oriented people in Palo Alto.

According to one of the members, "The community is much more flexible than the first idealistic model we envisioned. It is more exciting and more vital. It has become a living vision of a number of people and is totally based on the needs of people in the group. We are always changing as we discover new ways to meet our mutual needs." Meeting one another's needs without the exchange of money had been one of the original purposes of the community. But an even greater need has turned out to be personal contact. Good will and a willingness to help each other at home, to cook for each other, and to meet each other's needs are the glue that holds this community together. No formal commitment is necessary to join, but "the only way to get much out of it is to participate."

How Communities Help People Meet Needs

Let's take a closer look at several existing communities to better understand how they have helped their members take charge of their lives. These communities focus on such things as simple living and resource sharing, resistance to the military, staying out of prison, and social change.

Community, Simple Living, and Resource Sharing—The Sharing Meeting

The Sharing Meeting is a group of Friends (Quakers) and others, largely in New York State, who were uncomfortable with their own life-styles and consumption in a world with so much need and who were concerned about using resources they had inherited or earned for constructive social change. Many of these Friends had been grappling with these issues for some time, but individually they had not made much progress. When several families and individuals realized a common desire for simplification and resource sharing, they called together others with the same concerns and decided to start a loosely organized support community, which they called a Sharing Meeting. They began coming together every three months to share the struggles and changes in their lives, and pooled the money they were no longer spending personally into a common sharing fund. Together, they decided to allocate these funds to people and groups involved in nonviolent social change.

Suggestions for resource sharing included tithing, turning over unearned income (interest or inheritance), and reducing their own consumption to halfway between their present standard of living and that of a poor American family of equivalent size. Nine months after its establishment, the Sharing Meeting had collected $120,894, which it disbursed to such groups as the Behrhorst Clinic in Guatemala, whose land reform program assists Indians buying land; the Black Development Fund, which underwrites various empowerment programs in New York State; the Schenectady, New York, People's Advisory Service; and several collectives associated with the Movement for a New Society. According to one member of the Sharing Meeting, "Far more than the dispersal of our liberated resources, discussion of our own questions and tensions concerning the implications of simplicity and sharing for our lives has commanded our greatest attention."

Community and Resistance to the Military

During the Vietnam War, many young men resisted the draft and faced prison. Alone, the decision to resist was a tough one to make, but with a support community, many men found they could handle it. The resistance communities supported them as they were making their decisions, while they were in jail, and after they were released. Jailed resisters also formed support groups inside prison.

Resistance support communities took many forms. Some simply got together for shared meals. Other resisters and their supporters formed households or living communities. Members in various groups played music together, started print shops together, and went to prison together. Many deep friendships developed. When trials and other difficult times came, supporters, many from far away, gathered together. Some men who resisted the draft but did not have support communities became overwhelmed and got burned out in the process. Many of the resisters who were lucky enough to have support communities have come out of the experience stronger people. As I spoke with people who had been members of these resistance communities, I got the sense that these men have taken charge of their lives. The government no longer controls them.

Tax Resistance Communities

Many Americans are now refusing to pay the amount of their taxes that goes into war and armaments (54.4 percent of their federal income tax and 6 percent of their telephone bill).[2] Some of these citizens are also forming support communities. Although refusing to pay war taxes does not usually mean risking prison, it is still hard for most people to act contrary to the way the government and society expect us to. Joining with other people struggling with the same issues helps us avoid feeling isolated. In Philadelphia, for example, the war tax resistance community comes together once a month for an informal supper and sharing together. They have formed a warm personal support community, contribute the money they refuse to pay for war taxes into a fund which they loan or give to community groups working for peace and justice, and give physical and financial support to one another when hardships do arise due to their tax refusal activities. There are similar communities in Boston, San Francisco, and other cities.

Community and Social Change

In a mass society, we are reduced in many ways to passive, irresponsible, unloving consumers. To counteract this tendency, a group of 13 people in Isla Vista, California, formed the Thomas Merton Unity Center, a living and working community that employs nonviolence as a way of personal and social change. The center sponsors speakers, study-action groups on a variety of topics, and publishes a newspaper each month. Member Scott Kennedy says, "In our community we are developing people who are active, who are responsible, who are loving, and who make choices instead of having choices made for them as is done in the marketplace. Community contradicts the form of mass society as well as the content. In a community we can become responsible, we can love those around us, and we can make decisions affecting our lives." [3]

Bruce Hamm, a member of a Seattle social change community that is developing a nonviolent direct action campaign to stop development of the Trident submarine, sees community as a base for long-term struggle for change in society. "By living in a social change community we embrace the concept of change as a process to be lived rather than an end to be achieved. Community is a deterrent to the well-known phenomenon of the 'burned-out radical' for in community we are with other activists who can identify with both the anguish and the joy of our struggles. Community is a base of support for the beliefs we have so we can actualize them and experiment with them in our lives." In community we can take charge of our lives and work to make our lives consistent with our beliefs and values. We learn cooperation and unlearn competition and the "me and mine" value system that is so prevalent in our society.

The United Farm Workers Union is a better-known example of a community that enables social change. As individuals, farm workers are powerless facing the Goliath of agribusiness. Together in the United Farm Workers Union, they are able to face the long struggle necessary to win justice and dignity. A feeling of community with other farm workers and others throughout the world who have supported their struggle by boycotting grapes, head lettuce, and Gallo wine keeps them going. They have a strong support community.

The United Farm Workers have formed living communities of farmworkers and others in UFW "boycott houses." Here the union takes care of the basic needs of boycott workers—food, shelter, and medical care plus five dollars a week per worker. These living communities have enabled the farm workers to continue their struggle with minimal financial resources. Alone they would long ago have been defeated. Together in community, they have survived and hope for real victories.

Community and Keeping Out of Prison— The Delancey Street Foundation

The Delancey Street Foundation in San Francisco is a community that helps its members kick the "crime habit." There are no bars and no guards. Most of Delancey Street's 320 members are former prisoners, half of whom are paroled to Delancey Street and half of whom come voluntarily. They are building a living community based on personal dignity, honesty, and hard work. All who come to Delancey Street agree to stay at least two years so they can become firmly grounded in their new life. A number of Delancey Street–operated businesses, including a restaurant, an auto repair garage, a construction and repair service, and a moving operation, offer work to members.

Members participate in ruthlessly honest small encounter group sessions three evenings a week. These sessions help them get all their feelings out in the open. They have a chance to see themselves as others see them. Together they get themselves out of the prison rut. As one community member said to me. "The supportive community of Delancey Street has made all the difference. We are all committed to building a new life. I have found something real to live for."

After a couple years most members "graduate" from

the foundation and are ready to get back into society. The community has an excellent record of members who have kicked "crime addiction." Says San Francisco Sheriff Richard Hongisto: "Delancey Street doesn't cost the taxpayers money and it's not bureaucratic. It is reasonably humane—it doesn't keep people locked up. And it has had a reasonable degree of success. Few rehabilitation programs do as well." [4]

The Philadelphia Life Center

The Philadelphia Life Center is a very special place to me because our family lived there during the life center's first two years, and because it is a place where people are living out many of the things we have talked about in this book. Our family still feels very committed to the concepts of the life center, and we are trying to build a similar community in San Francisco, where we now live in a household of twelve.

The life center began in 1970–71, as part of the Movement for a New Society—a national communication network of autonomous nonviolent training and action groups, of which the Philadelphia Life Center is still the largest single community. It developed around the idea that individuals and groups can and must take charge of their own lives in order for our society to become livable for all. Presently the MNS network across the United States is engaged in building caring communities of people trying to live *now* by the values they would like to see in a future society and working with each other in a many faceted struggle to build a new society. In short, they are working for nonviolent revolution. Two books are now available that explain in more detail the philosophy and strategy of the MNS—*Moving toward a New Society* and *Strategy for a Living Revolution*.

When the first life center houses were formed in West Philadelphia in the fall of 1971, our household, known as "Daybreak," consisted of six adults and four children. We four Hartsoughs had shared our home with others before, but this extension to a whole network of houses was a new experiment. Moreover, the life center community had a purpose beyond itself —to be a support base from which individuals and groups could engage in meaningful social change and political work. The Philadelphia Life Center community has now grown to over 100 people, including 19 in their fifties and sixties and at least 15 children, all living within an eight-block radius of each other. Although the 20 households are autonomous and vary in decision-making style, collective personality, and interests, they have a great deal in common. They are experimenting with simplified living styles, nonhierarchical structures, and communal living, as well as involvement in social change training programs and projects, including direct action campaigns, such as supporting Namibian independence from South Africa, working for public ownership of the local electric company, and challenging mainstream church groups on issues of global justice.

One has to enter into community with the assumption that conflict is normal, and we did; but we also believed it can be dealt with creatively. During the first two years we lived in the life center, we had a number of chances to test this belief. We found ourselves in a high-crime neighborhood; we had meetings that sometimes seemed to go on forever; and we were still tied into traditional men's and women's roles. There were personal conflicts within living communities; sometimes people just did not feel they were getting the support they needed, and a few eventually moved out of their houses or the whole life center community. Conflicts arose over how to deal with the children, and there were some adults who did not care to interact with children at all.

Over time, and with struggle, we found solutions to most of our problems. In response to crime in the neighborhood, we started doing block organizing so residents of the area grew to know each other better and felt safer seeing familiar faces on the streets. Everyone in the area was encouraged to carry pocket Freon horns, so if anyone was attacked or molested on the street they could blow their horn and everyone who heard it—in their houses or elsewhere—would come running blowing their horns. It became obvious that there were not isolated individuals walking on the street. The neighborhood started to become a community, and crime in the area decreased markedly.

After many long meetings, we learned a lot about group process and conflict resolution. Most life center households now have regular house meetings to talk things out and help prevent tensions from growing into big problems. One of the collectives in the life center has developed a whole repertoire of new group process techniques. Many of these are explored in the forthcoming book, *Resource Manual for a Living Revolution* (see bibliography). Some of the insights gained are shared at the end of this chapter; see the sections headed "Queries for Existing Communities" and "Making Decisions Collectively." We also decentralized our community so most of the decision making takes place in smaller groups, living collectives, and work collectives.

We have tried to liberate ourselves from traditional sex roles through consciously being aware of and working on the problem. Most of the men have cut back to part-time work so they can spend more time with children and do a lot more of the support functions. The more "front line" and exciting tasks are shared by all. Some of the struggles for us in the life center included discovering how to blend everyone's food wishes into new inexpensive recipes and finding a balance between personal needs for privacy, space, time, etc., and community needs.

A few people did not fit into the life center and thus some problems were considerably eased when they left. If people want to remain "secure" in the way they have always done things and not be challenged to new ways of approaching problems and life, community is probably not the place for them. Our family has found that living in community has strengthened our efforts to combat materialism and helped us to find new ways to live both joyfully and simply and to grow a whole lot in the process.

In the life center, men and women share housework and cooking. Every resident is expected to learn the skills needed in his or her particular household, whether it be making homemade bread or painting the living room. Women are learning traditional "men's" skills such as carpentry and household repair.

In our present household in San Francisco, as an example, we divide the cooking, cleanup after meals, and child care among all the adults in the house. The children take turns setting the table. We have developed a chart to help us all remember our other chores around the house. They are on two circles (pieces of paper), and as we rotate the outer circle

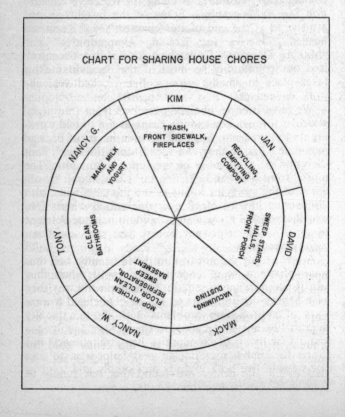

CHART FOR SHARING HOUSE CHORES

KIM — TRASH, FRONT SIDEWALK, FIREPLACES

JAN — RECYCLING, EMPTYING COMPOST

DAVID — SWEEP STAIRS, HALLS, FRONT PORCH

MACK — VACUUMING, DUSTING

NANCY W. — MOP KITCHEN FLOOR, CLEAN REFRIGERATOR, SWEEP BASEMENT

TONY — CLEAN BATHROOMS

NANCY G. — MAKE MILK AND YOGURT

with the names on it each month, we each have a new job. (See chart.)

When we lived in Philadelphia, the basement of our Daybreak House became the office for the Macro-analysis Collective—a life center group that has developed a politico-economic self-education course and is working to introduce and nurture study and action groups all around the country. Another house now contains the life center food co-op, which supplies fresh produce and staples at prices about 25 percent lower than local supermarkets offer. The purchase and distribution of food is handled cooperatively by all participants, and the co-op services are available to the wider neighborhood as well as life center houses.

A dental service has its headquarters in one life center house, and several training sessions in emergency medical care have been held to give people a sense of control over their own health care. Life center members have also developed such work activities as a printing shop, a home repair collective, and a block-organizing group that has focused on developing neighborhood communication and safety.

A central thrust of the life center is the training program to prepare people for long-term social-change organizing and struggle. Work in training for nonviolent social change has deep roots in the American peace and civil rights movements. In the 1970s it has broadened to include skills needed for long-term work and struggle for basic changes in this country and elsewhere. Building a nonviolent revolutionary movement requires people who can develop and share analysis, operate democratically and efficiently in groups, build campaigns and demonstrations, live simply and cooperatively, respond creatively to conflict situations, and celebrate together. The life center seeks to learn and share these skills. Both my wife, Jan, and I were part of the training program, and we continually use many of the skills we gained while living there. Doing training with groups outside the life center paid for some of our living expenses in Philadelphia. As part of the life center, we found that our family of four could live on less than $4,000 a year.

The need to hold full-time, "straight" jobs was eased considerably by the shared living arrangements and simplified life-style. We also did some income sharing in our household. Some people held regular jobs while others were freed up for specific projects such as training workshops, organizing demonstrations, or writing a book.

Growing, vibrant people celebrate. Life center folks gather informally to sing, to dance, and to play. Holidays find people decorating a tree in the park or caroling to the neighbors. At Thanksgiving one year, a band of bluegrass musicians from one house serenaded the other houses and picked up musicians and dancers as they went. Eventually about fifty people held a giant Virginia reel on the sidewalk near one of the houses. Neighbors and passersby watched or joined in.

Celebrations also took place in small prayer groups and in concerts by a member who shared her beautiful voice. There were informal community sings. We found that we were able to entertain ourselves inexpensively, creatively, and well.

My experience in the Philadelphia Life Center community has led me to believe that even within the confines of our present society, we can live cooperatively with each other, challenging each other to grow. We can be in charge of our own lives, life-style relationships, society, and environment.[5]

Queries for Communities and Notes on Collective Decision Making

Defining Community

People interested in building community, not just in the sense of living together but also in the sense of a bond among people that requires commitment of time and sharing, might start by asking themselves these questions, which are based on our experience and research.

1. How do we practice community right now?
2. What kinds of community exist around us?

3. How would community help us be the people we want to be and live the kinds of lives we want to live?

4. How can we begin to build community where we now live?

5. Are we close to people we would like to build a community with? What prevents us from moving ahead? Who are the people we trust? With whom do we have things in common? Does this help us define our community?

Questions for People Starting a Community

What will hold a community together? It could be a commitment to one religious or spiritual path, or a concern for living simply or for working for nonviolent social change. Or it might be a desire to live in a friendly neighborhood where people care about and cooperate with one another and where children can grow up in a healthy environment. Also important is the commitment people make to the community itself. Obviously, if people make little commitment, there will be little to hold them together. If they are willing to make a greater commitment—of time, energy, or money—the community will be stronger, and a more significant part of their lives. To help find out if there is a common understanding of this commitment by people interested in starting a community, try answering the following questions:

1. Do the people interested in forming a community like each other?

2. Would the members of your community share common principles, values, or spiritual beliefs (and practices)? What are they?

3. Would members share a common life-style or standard of living (vegetarianism, gardening, recycling, simple living, solar heating, doing without cars, abstinence from smoking, alcohol, or drugs)?

4. How would you make decisions? How would leadership roles be distributed?

5. Would members share any possessions? Which ones? Any special rules concerning possessions?

6. Would members share chores? How would you

meet the economic needs of the community? Would members share equally in meeting such needs? What portion of their time would be needed for work?

7. Is a certain location essential for your community? What qualities would this location need to have?

8. Would members share similar sexual attitudes? What would these be?

9. Would members share child rearing? Do you have common attitudes about it? What are they? How would you structure shared child rearing?

10. How much diversity of age, ethnic or socioeconomic background, and other characteristics would you seek or accept?

11. What commitments would the community ask of people seeking to join? What is your minimal expectation for the community (without which you leave, or it dissolves, or it is something different)? What is the community's minimal expectation of you?

12. What are the most important things for community members to agree on? Would you join the community as you have described it? If not, what else would you need?

Queries for Existing Communities

Here is a list of queries for those of us already involved in a community or group process, to help gauge the depth of group commitment and the effectiveness of group interaction.

1. How are people *feeling* about the community and group interaction?

2. To what extent is personal competitiveness among group members a problem?

3. To what extent has real cooperation become a reality?

4. Do you have a few "leaders" or does everyone pull his/her weight?

5. Do you often have meetings that are all talk and no action?

6. How well is the consensus process working? Or do a few people always get their way?

7. What constitutes status within the group?
8. How are differences of opinion and personal conflicts handled within the group?
9. How open can group members be about doubts, differences, personal feelings of weakness, etc.?
10. How much time do you spend on personal caring and sharing with one another in addition to project or work activity?
11. Do you find yourselves falling into specific roles within the group (crazy, workhorse, earth-mother, psychologist, politico, etc.) or are roles pretty well shared?

Making Decisions Collectively

In community, process is as important as product. The means we use are an integral part of the ends we are seeking. How do we relate to one another and how do we make decisions in our communities or in meetings in which we take part?

Decision making can easily become a time-wasting and frustrating drag for all concerned. This is especially true of collective styles of decision making. Particularly when concern is high and principled differences exist, we promote collective decision making, but we recognize that it is something that has to be learned and practiced in order to be done well. Personalities, emotions, and habits can often hamper the group's process unless members are ready to learn and use a few skills in dealing with them. Members also need to get to know and trust each other. How to use the skills each member brings and deal with problems and personality clashes is also important knowledge. In working toward successful collective decision-making processes, a number of groups involved in building community and in social change activities have found the following ideas helpful. These are discussed in more depth in *The Resource Manual for a Living Revolution,* by Coover et al. (see bibliography):

1. Start meetings with brief periods of "excitement sharing" in which members tell the group about something new or interesting that has occurred in their lives recently. People thus have a chance to

bring their attention to something new or interesting and the level of participation is raised.

2. Decide the agenda and how time is to be used at the beginning of the meeting. This avoids the classic situation in which the first item on the agenda—no matter how unimportant—takes up 40–70 percent of the meeting time.

3. Take care of each other. Ask someone to pay special attention to feelings that are involved in the discussion, and set aside regular times when the group can deal with the feelings toward one another and the group which develop in its work. We think better together if our heads are not all clogged up with old resentments, bad feelings, and uncertainties unrelated to the issue at hand. Members should try to be conscious of when they are being pushed by feelings rather than moved by thoughtful consideration. This is particularly true in situations of active confrontation. Those with the coolest heads are likely to be the most flexible and creative in their choice and use of alternatives.

4. When things start to drag or get bogged down, do something to get people's energy flowing again and raise the level of interest. A short but active game or jumping up and down and shouting some positive word or phrase can often do this. If a discussion gets really heavy and discordant, don't be afraid to call a break. People can often work things out informally in ways that can't be handled while a meeting is under way.

5. The facilitator/chairperson should see to it that everyone gets to participate in discussion—even those who initially feel they have little or nothing to contribute. Shy people often need to be encouraged and talky ones damped down. Often, especially if the topic is a hot one, it is a good idea to have an agreed time limit on each input. Particularly if a group is large, it is often helpful to break into smaller groups to discuss an issue. This gives more opportunity for input from everyone.

6. Switch roles from meeting to meeting. All members should get a chance to facilitate, take notes,

or process-observe. This can also help deal with any sexism or racism which might otherwise creep into role allocation and encourages everyone to learn these skills.

7. Have meeting evaluations. It is important for people to tell each other that they have done well; we give far too few compliments in this society. We also need to know where and how we can do better in the future.

8. Have fun together. People who do nothing but work together can easily get tired of each other's company. It's good to know that we can do more together than plan meetings, lick envelopes, and raise money.

9. Find ways of supporting one another outside of the area where you are working together. Taking time to listen to and enjoy each other is a good way to help build group solidarity and trust. This can pay great dividends when real difficulties develop.

10. Members should spend some time on personal growth and change. We all have had hang-ups, problems, and patterns laid into us which interfere with our flexibility and thinking. Many ways of working through these problems have become available over the last few years. Women's and men's support and consciousness-raising groups can also help us work on the sexism that we bring into political and social change work.

This is a very incomplete list, and none of these suggestions is a magic formula. They are simply a few ideas for working more effectively together in ways that emphasize our care for one another.

NOTES

1. "Religious Community: The Way of the Reba Place Fellowship." *Fellowship*, April 1975.
2. *FCNL Newsletter*, Friends Committee on National Legislation, April 1975.
3. *In the Tracks of the Dinosaur*, January–February 1975,

p. 3. Published by the Thomas Merton Unity Center, 892 Camino del Sur, Isla Vista CA 93017.

4. *Delancey Street Journal,* San Francisco, CA. 1975.

5. For more information about the Life Center or the Movement for a New Society, write MNS, 4722 Baltimore Avenue, Philadelphia PA 19143.

SOURCES OF FURTHER INFORMATION

(See also: Consuming Ourselves, Creative Simplicity, Personal Growth)

Books

American Communards. *Community Market's Cooperative Catalogue.* New York: Knopf, 1973.

Chapman, Paul. *Clusters: Life Style Alternatives for Families and Single People.* Stoughton, MA: Packard Manse, 1973. Available for $2.50 from Alternatives, 1924 E. Third St., Bloomington, Ind. 47401.

Coover, Virginia, et al. *Resource Manual for a Living Revolution.* For trainer/organizers in nonviolent social change. (To be published in 1977 by the Movement for a New Society, 4722 Baltimore Avenue, Philadelphia PA 19143.)

Duberman, Martin. *Black Mountain, An Exploration in Community.* New York: Dutton, 1972.

Gowan, Susanne, et al. *Moving toward a New Society.* Philadelphia: New Society Press, 1976.

Goodman, Paul. *Communitas: Means of Livelihood and Ways of Life.* New York: Vintage, 1960.

International Independence Institute. *The Community Land Trust: A Guide to a New Model for Land Tenure in America.* Cambridge, MA: Center for Community Economic Development, 1972.

Jackson, Dave, and Jackson, Neta. *Living Together in a World Falling Apart.* Available for $1.95 from Creating House, 499 Gunderson Drive, Carol Stream IL 60178.

Judson, Jerome. *Families of Eden, Communes and the New Anarchism.* New York: Seabury Press, 1974.

Kagan, Paul. *New World Utopias: A Photographic History.* New York: Penguin, 1975.

Kanter, Rosabeth Moss. *Commitment and Community:*

Communes and Utopias in Sociological Perspective.
Cambridge: Harvard University Press, 1972.

————. *Communes: Creating and Managing the Collective Life.* New York: Harper and Row, 1973.

Kriyananda, Swami. *Cooperative Communities: How to Start Them and Why.* Berkeley, CA: Ananda Publications, 1972. Available for $2 from Book People, 2940 Seventh Street, Berkeley CA 94710.

Lakey, George. *Strategy for a Living Revolution.* San Francisco: Freeman, 1973.

Morgan, Arthur. *The Community of the Future.* Available from Community Publications Cooperative, Box 426, Louisa VA 23093.

Movement for a New Society. *New Society Packet.* Available for 35¢ from MNS, 4722 Baltimore Avenue, Philadelphia PA 19143.

Whitney, Norman J. *Experiments in Community: Ephrata, Amish, Doukhobors, Shakers, Bruderhof, and Monteverde.* Wallingford, Pa.: Pendle Hill Publications, 1966.

Zablocki, Benjamin. *The Joyful Community.* New York: Penguin, 1972.

Periodicals

Communities. A Journal of Cooperative Living. c/o Twin Oaks, Box 426, Louisa Va 23093 (monthly).

Communities. 1975 Communities Directory, same address.

Dandelion. Newsletter of Movement for a New Society, 4722 Baltimore Avenue, Philadelphia PA 19143.

Delancey Street Journal. 3001 Pacific Avenue, San Francisco CA 94115.

Fellowship. Fellowship of Reconciliation, Box 271, Nyack NY 10960.

In the Tracks of the Dinosaur. 892 Camino del Sur, Isla Vista CA 93017.

6

Children Taking Charge

BY NANCY BURNETT AND JAN HARTSOUGH

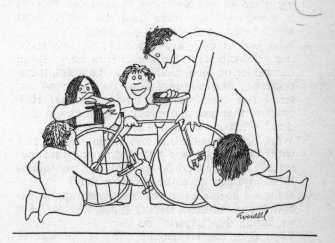

Queries

1. How welcome are children in our community? Who "pressures" us to have children and who discourages us? Why? How do we fell about adopting children? How do we feel about racially mixed families?
2. What are our goals for our children? What are our means? Are we on the right track?
3. Are we creating a home environment that helps people grow—children and adults alike? Is it a growing place (or as Brer Rabbit calls it, a "laughing place")? Are we trying to raise our children in a vacuum? Are there good role models from which parents and children can learn?
4. What do our daily lives teach our children about our responsibility in the world? How do we spend our money on food, clothing, entertainment, transportation, and housing? How do we spend our time? Are there ways to survive on less? How much of that time and money is spent on our children? What are we buying in the long run?
5. What kinds of games and toys do our children play with? What skills and values do our recreations teach? What materials go into the playthings? What toys can we make instead of buy?
6. Is there a program that welcomes parent participation in our children's school? If not, why not? Are we letting the "experts" do it?
7. What does our community offer in the way of broadly available day care, family counseling, and health services? What are we doing about making our community more responsive to the needs of children and families?
8. How do we divide labor in our homes? Are we extending our families—giving and receiving

help? Are we allowing enough unstructured time to just "be" together?

9. How do we deal with conflict in our homes? Do we express our feelings and ideas openly and work to resolve differences or find workable compromises?

10. Outside school, what activities involve most of our children's time? Are these activities active or passive?

Comments from Kids About Simple Living

The Cynics:
—"It's having your mom brainwash your dad into not buying comic books or records anymore."
—"Simple living is taking away the TV set."
—"Simple living. We never did start."
—"It's eating really healthy, awful stuff for a while, which nobody eats anyway except your parents. Then it's their breaking down and fixing hamburgers."
—"Simple living is feeding your cat dry cat food."
—"It's having Kelley's mouth zipped."

The Converts:
—"Simple living means our whole family in front of the fire instead of the TV."
—"It's playing games, or doing improvisational theater."
—"Christmas in the mountains instead of at Grandma's (we wish she'd come too)."
—"Simple living means not having crud to eat, like candy and sugary cereal."
—"It's the simplest problem . . . problems like figuring out how to make things."
—"We don't spend as much. Mom used to sort of butter us up."
—"It's doing it ourselves . . . like when we see advertisements on TV, it's making what I want myself instead."

—"Simple living is not having my mouth zipped. That's quiet living."

The Concept of Child Care

This chapter is not only for parents and children. It is written for all of us who have alive in ourselves the wonder and fear of our own "child-person."

This child-person is not the way you remember yourself as a child, but the way you are *now* when you are excited or creating something new and spontaneous, when you have abandoned your adult habituation and gone off to do something you've always wanted to do, or when you are angry and hurt. Most likely this child-person is who you are before you fall asleep at night, the quiet, feeling person who puts you back together again after a hard day or a hard lifetime of experience (even if your lifetime is only three years so far).

In childhood are the beginnings, the roots, of who each of us becomes. Yet the child-person is not a product, a has-been, but rather a being needing nurture, an ongoing process. We are all involved in "child care" whether we recognize it or not, as we care or fail to care for the child within day by day.

While everyone may be involved in child care, not everyone is a parent. Becoming a parent can now be largely a matter of choice. Many people are choosing not to be parents, for reasons such as population, professional involvement, or personal preference. Among those who are, some opt for adoption or caring for foster children. We know of people in communal living situations who have developed special part-time "godparent" relationships with children in their groups.

Yet, however much experimentation may be going on with its shape and function, the family still remains the basic social unit of our society. It is the first and most influential socializing institution in almost everyone's life. It is the preserver and transmitter of traditions and values—the place we came from, return to, or try to escape for a while. As they grow, children build relationships outwardly, one circle at a time: from parents to relatives, to people in the community, to the rest of the world.

Because of this key role, the American family is the centerpiece of the overdeveloped consumer society. Through media like television and the attention paid to them by parents, the attitudes of consumerism are taught to children often for as many hours a week as they spend in school. Families are also prime consumers of such things as food, clothes, automobiles, entertainment, and packaged recreation. Indeed, economists regard the number of new housing starts as one of the most sensitive indicators of the health of our economy, because with each new family dwelling will come a whole houseful of expensive manufactured goods—the upkeep, repair, and replacement of which keeps the families occupied and the whole system turning.

In this consumerist family setting, though, we believe much that is of value is lost: the family ceases to be a center of life and learning in its own right, and is turned instead into a receiver and consumer of values, mostly economically based, that come from institutions outside it and beyond its control. In addition, the solidarity of the members is eroded by their division into "market segments" by the media for the convenience of those with products to sell. How much of the much discussed "generation gap" is based in the fact that programming and advertising are aimed separately at children, teenagers, mothers, fathers, and older people in the home, and that they exploit the differences of outlook of each? We think a great deal. Beyond the specific messages, there is also a whole outlook on life being inculcated, one centered on novelty, the importance of packaging, and the idea that meaning and fun are to be found only in mass, passive activities.

For us, simple living in this setting means working to reclaim and reassert the centrality of the family itself, however structured, as a primary area for living and growing. In this reclaimed environment we are attempting to articulate, live out, and pass on to the children we nurture a set of values that is qualitatively different from those of the consumerist society around us; values stressing the importance of conservation and fair distribution of resources; self-reliance in work and play; cooperation with others across age and gender lines, in mutual assistance and constructive social action; and resistance to injustice and oppression, both near at hand and far away. Indeed, this whole effort can be seen as a form of resistance to the larger society's efforts to absorb us into itself by absorbing our families in passive consumption.

Different families have undertaken this task of reclamation and simplification in different ways. We will look at several of these experiments, but first let's look at sharing and extending family structures. Parents are finding many ways to pool and thus reinforce family resources and ease family burdens by cooperation—anything from renting a big old house and stocking it with toys, books, and buggies to settling into a neighborhood together. Nuclear families, too, can benefit from shared child care, co-op housekeeping and cooking, or weekends off occasionally. Choosing to be a parent doesn't really mean martyrdom or a life sentence to drudgery. On the following page is a chart we received at a women's weekend retreat which graphically illustrates what a relatively short time the so-called "dependent" years of childhood are. When parenting gets hectic, which it does, it can help to be aware that "this too shall pass away." The first eight to ten intense years need not be an exile from life.

The varieties of parental sharing are endless. Two women we interviewed have worked out an arrangement where one cares for their combined four small children three days a week while the other spends that undivided time developing her craft skill as a carpenter. The child-care mother participates with her friend's children as well as her own in a morning co-op nursery school. In the afternoons she takes all the children on errands, to the park, or on small excursions. She is a born educator who can take a child's

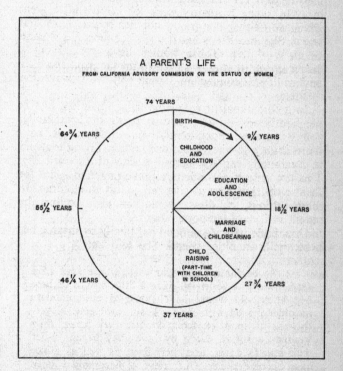

A PARENT'S LIFE

FROM: CALIFORNIA ADVISORY COMMISSION ON THE STATUS OF WOMEN

74 YEARS

BIRTH

9¼ YEARS

CHILDHOOD AND EDUCATION

EDUCATION AND ADOLESCENCE

18½ YEARS

MARRIAGE AND CHILDBEARING

CHILD RAISING (PART-TIME WITH CHILDREN IN SCHOOL)

27¾ YEARS

37 YEARS

46¼ YEARS

55½ YEARS

64¾ YEARS

simple "what if" and help him develop it into a day-long project or a playtime involving many different materials and friends. She is an expert at play, who truly appreciates that play is children's work. The other four days of the week both mothers spend special at-home time with their own children. The carpenter mother pays for her time without child-care responsibility by doing carpentry work for her friend, a great gift since neither her friend nor her spouse have that talent. She also keeps her friend's car tuned (a woman of many skills). These women have worked out a barter system that allows each to pursue what she likes best while still connecting to their children in ways that fit them.

In a communal or collective living situation, and in neighborhoods with a strong sense of community, young parents, nonparents, and children all have more chance to learn from each other. Living together in community can also permit sharing of responsibility. This not only allows adults to have time and space for themselves, but also to give full energy to children. In these settings, childless people can also explore the parent role on a temporary basis.

One single parent extended her family by sharing her home with an older friend. She told us:

> At the beginning, my four sons, whose ages span from twenty to fourteen, were a little unsure of how our household would be changed to accommodate an older person with serious health problems. Nevertheless, in spite of their doubts, they knew they wanted to try it. Little by little they began to let their guards down, and their lives, as well as mine, have become richer. Our friend is becoming a dear grandmother who enjoys and prizes their exploits and explorations. I have a companion who has a wealth of experience and who is willing to let us become part of her life. She enjoys the exchange of ideas with the boys, watching their active lives, meeting their friends.

Another small group that seems to be working hard

at building a new life-style for themselves consists of three single parents and their eight children.

We share an old house within walking distance from town. All but one of our children are pre-school or elementary school age. The younger kids bunk together. The older ones have converted huge walk-in closets into neat little private hangouts. The adults have a room that is a quiet room where we can read or carry on a conversation with a degree of coherence.

At first life was really chaotic with all of us. The kids fought over their toys, competed for adult attention, and refused to cooperate in the running of the house. As parents we found we had to make a lot of adjustments too. We had to get over the "She pinched *my* son," or "They broke *our* record player." We discovered that it is really important to work out a common set of expectations regarding child rearing. Even with some guidelines, our old images, habits, and patterns still can get in the way.

One of the things we did was set up a *nurturing schedule*. Each of us adults works with all the younger kids one day in rotation. The day might include reading stories, playing games, gardening, cooking, listening to multiplication tables or piano lessons, even sewing and weaving with them. The older children join in when they're interested, which they often are if using real tools and doing real things is part of the task. This nurturing schedule frees each adult to have two days we're not "on" with the kids. That's when we nurture ourselves. We may go out of the house, visit the day-care center where a couple of the little ones go, volunteer a few hours at our local peace center, or maybe just curl up somewhere with a good book.

There are other good things about living together aside from the shared work part. No one, child or adult, feels isolated anymore. And we do have truly *free* time now when someone else is taking care of things. By encouraging everyone to assume more responsibility, we all can be "mother" sometimes—

the kids too. We're learning to say what we need in a way that can be heard.

I've really come to respect how open kids are when we meet them halfway. They instinctively know what they need and their feelings are not easily hidden. As single parents we have found it easier to relate to those feelings with the support and help of other adults and children. I don't have to say in frustration, "I can't do everything!!" anymore. Instead I can say, "Ask Connie, she knows about animals," or "I can help you build it if Tom will help us figure out how much wood to buy."

If I had to sum up the feeling in our home in one sentence I think it would be, "We're all in this together, the crummy stuff as well as the good times." Sharing the joy is the best part. Not a day passes that somebody doesn't do something that jars us out of our rut and makes us laugh at the world or ourselves. The big problems look so much smaller when they're shared. The love is there for the asking and the giving. The thing I ask myself is "Why haven't we done this before?"

Facing Problems and Finding Solutions as a Family

Several families we visited use a "family meeting" process as their way to air and share feelings, set up work schedules, discuss money, and make plans together. These meetings are not just times to hear complaints, but regular get-togethers. Some begin with "excitement sharing," when individual family members tell about what happened that day or what's coming up. Then perhaps others will want to hear more about a new project or will begin discussing a controversial topic.

In some families, work assignments are decided by group process. All the jobs are written out on a big piece of paper. Depending on the list and the ages of the family members, each selects a job—the favorites on down to the least desirable ones. Then the bargaining begins. In addition, if someone doesn't know how to do something, someone else can trade in one job as payment for training him/her. Of course sometimes this system breaks down like any other. The problems that arise are opportunities to explore how and why things didn't work out, and to clear up faulty communications or hasty workmanship. It is very important to evaluate family meetings, and to remember that a failure once doesn't mean it can't work better the next time.

Meal Preparation Sharing Scheme

In one family of five, every person, even the seven-year-old, cooks dinner one night a week. The two unclaimed weeknights are "surprise" nights, when people either fend for themselves or elect to cook again. Fasting has also been tried! This family is exploring vegetarian cooking by having Monday night be rice night, Tuesday cheese, and Thursday beans. Wednesdays and Fridays are usually fish and chicken. The schedule goes for a month, so at the end of that time, each member has a repertoire of four or five dishes of a type. One Christmas each person received a card file (with a patchwork cover of his/her favorite old fabrics) in which to record some of the innovative recipes that each cooks up.

Sharing Finances

Another family sees their family finances as the arena to practice shared responsibility. They list all their sources of income, even the kids', and all the month's expenses. It's a real discipline to remember where all that small change goes. Keeping records allows the family to see how much they spend over several months' time. The kids like doing the arithmetic and finding out how much they're behind

or ahead. Usually any "surplus" money is earmarked
for the next month's expenses, like insurance. If there
is extra money at the end of the month, they talk about
how to use it. They feel that is a tremendous way to
find out what the family values are; when it's everybody's money, somehow each feels more responsible.
Everyone is aware of how much things cost to buy,
to maintain, and to get rid of (like the trash many of
us pay to have collected). It seems to take some of
the emotion out of money. Wanting something becomes
a matter of dollars and sense as well as desire.
Strangely, the kids seem more flexible in this respect
than the adults!

Another family used the family meeting as a way to
learn not only about their home economic picture, but
about world economics. After learning about world
hunger, they decided to have a meal of rice, tea, and
fruit one night a week, and to donate the money they
would have spent on the meal to UNICEF. A ten-
year-old suggested the project, so he takes care of the
money and mails a check off every month or two to
the UNICEF offices in New York.

Another family takes a portion of their income and
puts it into a fund with other families. They plan to
buy land eventually and set up a small community together.

Resolving Scheduling Conflicts

Weekend schedules are another area where conflict
seems to arise and where decisions need to be made.
People going in too many dirctions at once, the need
for baby-sitters, and transportation requests are a few
of the most common problems. One group has a giant
calendar in their kitchen where people write down
their plans. Children and adults sign up if they need
rides somewhere. Adults sometimes barter rides for
baby-sitting. At any rate, people can look at the
calendar and find out who is going where, and when.
Stay-at-home time is blocked in too, so there is time

for people just to be around and visit and hold down the fort.

What to Do for Recreation?

Families can learn to create a sense of joy in being together without depending on any outside helpers. Time spent watching television is *not* the same as time spent talking, reading, cooking, inventing something, sewing, gardening, playing hard outside, sitting around on the porch, *and* many more things that you, the reader, can think up. Moreover, television becomes a chief focus for entertainment only if we let it. If our children are watching it too much, perhaps we need to ask ourselves, and them, "What need is this fulfilling?" Are the children seeking security, or even community, in the TV world because their own world is too adult-oriented or too chaotic or too boring? Are the adults quietly ignoring the problem, choosing not to come to terms with it at all? Can we appreciate the good programming but also encourage our children to be discriminating?

What kind of activities could we involve our children in doing with us? How about helping prepare the next meal, planting some seeds, or doing some simple carpentry? Children like to feel useful and learn new skills. It gives them a sense of worth to be involved in "real" projects that benefit everyone in the family. The movement and excitement of a project is much healthier than the passive response that TV evokes. There are many idea books (see bibliography) available that give directions for making playthings and that outline educational projects. Making your own toys not only saves money, but can be fun. Biking not only saves gas, but can make you independent of a "chauffeur" and able to see and feel the world more directly. Sewing or redesigning old clothes not only saves resources, but is also more expressive of the individual's uniqueness.

Peer Pressures

If a family's efforts to simplify their life together mean that they have a different life from that of their friends, won't the children complain? Budgets, schedules, and consensus aside, don't kids resist doing work that other kids' moms do? Won't they be resentful of not buying a new back-to-school wardrobe, of not having a regular department-store Christmas, and of not buying into the American dream? Especially if they've had these things before, but even if they haven't —how do we convince our children that living simply, if it means giving up such things, is living better?

Peer pressure is not such an obvious challenge to the parents of small children. Because their world view is still quite narrow, they look to their parents to explain things. Interaction with other children and adults is limited. The family value system is not questioned severely. Depending on the neighborhood, everybody may seem pretty much alike. However, children learn early to spot the differences. "Because my daddy said so" soon yields to "Mark's dad lets him." Television, the nursery school or day-care center, church, the local grocery store, or the street corner offer opportunities for the preschooler to collect data that either support or challenge his world view.

Children seek to feel at home in the world—more than that, they seek some kind of mastery of it. Sometimes that means having a special, even magical, way to grasp it, to touch it, or to belong in it. Many of the clothes, cars, and houses that adults own or covet seem magical to children. Surely teenage fads reflect this desire for affiliation. The haircuts (or lack of them), the jeans, pop art T-shirts, expensive bicycles, and so on—these are valuable not only because they are functional or even beautiful but for what they symbolize—power and tribal identity. The same is true for young children. Their toys, clothes, and games can be a statement that they belong. Talking about what was on TV last night is like adults exchanging comments about the ballgames or the weather. It is all part of a common reality, and a sign of status. Children aren't the only people who confuse what a person *has* with what a person *is*.

If a family working to simplify their life begins cutting down on things and getting away from the television culture, at first they may feel as though they are handicapping themselves. Not buying can be like saying "you are different," not going to McDonald's like saying "you can't belong." There is no hard-and-fast rule about being different. It's more often *how* something is done than *what*. However, when a child's sense of worth seems to be involved, then it is important to be able to be flexible whenever possible, to be willing to bend, to negotiate. Simplifying our lives does not mean taking things away, but rather clearing away whatever is not of value in order to replace it with something that *is* truly valuable. It means finding better alternatives.

Sometimes people need to experience the cruddy TV show, the platform shoes that kill the feet, and the toy that breaks. Of course, it hits home harder if they have paid for these things themselves. Each person eventually develops his/her own value system. The point is not to resist all popular fashions or fads just because they're popular, but to learn to be *selective*. Know what you want and why—and then take the consequences. By being free to pick and choose, to go along with the crowd or not, we can show others what it is to be a responsible consumer and citizen.

The Simplification Process

In seeking to simplify our lives, we are not seeking to deny our children access to the twentieth century or to the way the world operates (or does not operate). If anything, we are trying to remove the confusion that comes from such denial. By learning to be creators as well as competitors, conservers as well as consumers, we are practicing the making of choices; sometimes saying yes, sometimes no; sometimes controlling, sometimes letting go of control. While learning to be more self-reliant, we are also learning to be more involved.

The simple life is not a life of convenience. It might be easier not to resist, to just go on eating poptarts and watching TV. And it is easier to say one thing and do another—for a while. Yet it all eventually catches up with most of us. If simple living means learning to be more self-reliant and less exploitative, it can take a lot of time. If a family agrees that their recipe for simple living should include sewing, carpentry, gardening, bread baking, even thrift shopping—these take not only know-how, energy, and time, but also a level of planning. Single or working parents may already feel stretched to the limit.

Furthermore, helping kids become more self-reliant is often very messy and frustrating. If your efforts at simplification involve important rearrangements in your household, it may mean living amid the clutter of half-done projects. Your nerves may be on edge while you are learning to do something you've never done before, making mistakes, taking the consequences, convincing others to help, resenting change. No longer able to just throw something away, you have to sort all that recyclable junk and store it somewhere. The compost heap needs attention—and the goat, if you've gone that far, needs milking.

Sure, it's easier to open a can of pineapple-grapefruit drink and a package of graham crackers for snack time than to help the kids bake zucchini bread from the zucchini they've planted and cared for themselves. Sometimes the bread doesn't even turn out (someone forgot the baking powder), but when it does, the satisfaction is truly wonderful. The bother, if it isn't always half the fun, is certainly half the point. Confrontation, not escape, is what this life is all about. Involvement, not comfort.

When we take time to do something ourselves or help our children do something for themselves, we affirm life. Not only do we say to them *it's* worthwhile, but *you* are worthwhile. *Efficiency is not our* primary goal and more than happiness is, although both may be side effects.

Being a parent is like being a twenty-four-hour-a-day teacher. We are the primary sources, the first reference, the givers of permission. Still, how many of us have yet to give ourselves that permission to be involved, to be different, to resist, to suffer even? How many of us say what we believe by the way we live our lives?

We can begin to live simply when we ask ourselves seriously what it is we want and need out of family life and how we can achieve our goals with minimal harm to ourselves, our children, and other people. For many of us, answering these questions may mean we will need to face up to the mess, recycle the bottles and cans, and repair and renovate old clothing, toys, and furniture. It may mean selecting food that is nourishing and economical and cutting down on our use of electrical energy and fossil fuels. It may mean involving ourselves in the mainstream of our community, participating in local politics, following through on what we believe whether we can win or not. Most of all, we live simply when we become aware of and responsible for our decisions, begin to model the behavior we expect of others, and approach each day ready to learn from ourselves and our children.

Pearl Buck, the American novelist who lived much of her young life in China, described the importance of her family experience in an address given at a joint session of the National Conference on Family Relations and the New York State Conference on Marriage and the Family:

We did not merely learn, we learned that we had something to do with all we learned—that nothing human was alien to us, because we, too, were human. We learned this not by hearing it said, but simply by seeing our parents deeply involved in action. They were so interested in what they did that they made themselves interesting to us. We were not left outside of their activities or left to ourselves while they came and went—we came and went too. Yes, we saw things and did things that many of us here would not consider suitable for children—I came to adulthood ready for life.

I believe the problems of the world must first be met in the home before we will have men and women sufficiently educated for the world, and that we do our children the most grave injustice when we do not fit them in the home for the world they will find waiting at their door when they step outside. If [the child's] home has shielded and denied him the knowledge and practice of life he will be terrified. The child prepared in the home through all the life of the home for the life of the world steps forward a self-confident and integrated creature. He will be afraid of nothing because he will say, "I know about this—I know what to do."

Some Tools for Introducing Kids to Simple Living

—A handcrank ice cream maker for honey ice cream, fruit sherbets.
—A foodgrinder to make your own peanut butter and potato pancakes, and even to grind your own wheat.
—Sturdy carpentry tools, real but child-size.
—Lumber.
—Nails, screws, nuts, and bolts.
—Sturdy gardening tools, real but child-size.
—Seeds, cuttings.
—Compost.
—Planters (might be made with sturdy carpentry tools).
—Old machines, junk.
—Old magazines, clippings, scraps of all kinds.
—Sewing supplies.
—Trunk filled with thrift-shop finery.
—Scarves, flimsy material for dancing, illusion, make-believe.

—Musical instruments, homemade as well as manufactured.

—Old sheets, blankets, clothespins.

—A cupboard at child level with cooking and clean-up supplies.

—Your child's own *tested* recipe file.

—Lots of cleaning stuff, child-safe, child-manageable.

—A bike and tools and oil to care for it.

—A bus schedule with well-used routes marked.

—Band-Aids and disinfectant.

Exercises for Children and Parents

1. Help your child make a family scrapbook. Include "familiar" people unrelated by marriage or blood. Exchange children for a weekend. Plan a neighborhood potluck. Celebrate a favorite holiday by including single people and people over fifty.
2. Make an inventory of what your child owns. Help your child develop the categories and system for accounting (you'll learn how she or he thinks). Are there things that are no longer used? Can your child think of someone who *would* use them? If they need repairs or mending, can you help your child restore these unused items before passing them on?
3. Do all the things your child owns have a place? How does your child order space? Are tools (crayons, clay, hammers, nails, and books) readily accessible? Can your child take charge independent of you? Using old boxes, pegboard, or similar materials, can you help her organize her space? (Be prepared, this may take days. Take long walks or water your yard when it gets too hairy.)
4. In a nonjudgmental way, discuss with your child what he wants for Christmas or his next birthday. How did this desire arise? How will the gift be used? Who makes it? Where do the materials come from? What happens to it when it gets broken or old?
5. Pack lunches and take an all-day walk around your

city or town. Take money for carfare home; you'll be surprised how the miles fly by. Share your feelings about what you see. What decisions have been made in your town or city about the use of space? Is there a "poor side of town"? Who has the most available recreation, transportation, libraries, clinics?

6. Check out your neighborhood thrift stores with your child. Take along a dollar each. Another day, compare what you bought with the retail prices of the same things new.

7. Try using the family meeting when a serious problem comes up. All members should have an opportunity to state their views and feelings *uninterrupted*. Resolution might not come in one meeting. Ask some member to state where things rest at the end of the time allotted. Appoint another time when you can all meet to continue your discussion.

8. Investigate what resources your city has available free or for very little cost—in entertainment, educational activities, health services, etc. Make your own people's yellow pages directory, including the people in your neighborhood to see about fixing a sink, planting a garden, flying a kite. Check out the libraries for story hours, puppet shows, records, and films. Find out where to buy recyclable paper, where to get throwaway paper for home art projects. Often these can be obtained just by inquiring and arranging to pick them up. Recycle your own stuff too.

SOURCES OF FURTHER INFORMATION

(See also: Community, Food, Personal Growth)

Background Books on Children and Family

Blessington, John P. *Let My Children Work*. New York: Doubleday/Anchor, 1975.

Breitbart, Vicki. *The Day Care Book—The Why, What and How of Community Day Care*. New York: Alfred A. Knopf, 1974.

Cohen, Dorothy H. *The Learning Child*. New York: Vintage/Random, 1973.

Dreikurs, Rudolf, M.D., and Soltz, Vicki, R.N. *Happy Children: A Challenge to Parents*. Great Britain: Collins/Fontana, 1964.

Erikson, Erik. *Childhood and Society*. New York: Norton, 1963.

Faber, Adele, and Mazlish, Elaine. *Liberated Parents, Liberated Children*. New York: Avon, 1975.

Farson, Richard. *Birth Rights*. New York: Macmillan, 1974.

Fraiberg, Selma H. *The Magic Years*. New York: Scribner's, 1959.

Gordon, Dr. Thomas. *P.E.T.: The Tested New Way to Raise Responsible Children*. New York: New American Library/Plume Book, 1970.

Hallett, Kathryn. *A Guide for Single Parents*. Millbrae, Calif.: Celestial Arts, 1974.

Moustakas, Clark E., and Perry, Cerela. *Learning to Be Free*. Englewood Cliffs, N.J.: Prentice-Hall, 1973.

Owens, Bill. *Suburbia*. New York: Simon and Schuster, 1971.

Satir, Virginia. *Peoplemaking*. Milbrae, Calif.: Celestial Arts, 1975.

Steinfels, Margaret O'Brien. *Who's Minding the Children: History and Politics of Daycare in America*. New York: Simon and Schuster, 1973.

Idea Books

Alternatives Collective. *Alternative Celebrations Catalogue*. Greensboro, N.C.: Alternatives, 1975 (third edition).

Caney, Steven. *Playbook*. New York: Workman Publ. Co., 1975.

Cardozo, Peter, *The Whole Kids Catalog*. New York: Bantam, 1975.

Carr, Rachel. *Be a Frog, Be a Bird, Be a Tree*. New York: Doubleday, 1973.

Gregg, Elizabeth, editor. Boston Children's Medical Center. *What to Do When There's Nothing to Do*. New York: Dell, 1967.

Kelly, Marguerite, and Parsons, Elia. *The Mothers Almanac*. New York: Doubleday, 1975.

Scargall, Jeanne. *10001 Ways to Have Fun with Children*. Toronto: Pagurian Press Ltd., 1975.

7
Work

BY LUCY ANDERSON

Queries

1. Do I enjoy my work?
2. Is my work personally fulfilling? Is it consistent with my values and simple living concerns? What changes would I like to make?
3. Is my physical and human environment positive and supportive? How well do I know the people I work with?
4. Does my work involve me as a whole human being, or do I leave at home important skills, abilities, and interests when I go to work?
5. Is there room for personal creative expression in my work?
6. In work situations, do I participate in decisions regarding myself?
7. Does my work harm others? Does it harm the earth?
8. What work do I do without pay? Would I like to be putting more or less time into these activities?
9. What do I do when I am unemployed involuntarily?
10. Is my work place an arena for self-growth?

Listen. Hear Our Many Voices

"Yes, it scares the shit out of me that I don't know where I will be working in September. There was a lot of security in my last job."
—Single mother of two children

"This is a homogeneous community here—we hire for eagerness and hard work. In exchange there is a steady supply of food, drink and friends."
—Coffee shop manager

"We work more than one-third of our waking life. Most people are here for more than pay—they want to be motivated, they want to take responsibility."
—Personnel manager for a large company

"People ask me why it is that they have to do 'shit work.' I tell them that they ask the wrong question—they look at the problem in the wrong way. There is no 'shit work'—all work is important."
—A local activist

"Simple living? There is no simple living around here—we work like hell!"
—United Farm Workers organizer

"What do you mean, do I like my work? It's work—everybody has to work. You gotta make money somehow."
—Baker, Whole Earth Bread Store, Palo Alto, California

"The difference is the conditions we work under. We want to be treated like people, not animals."
—Chuca and Ruiz, farm workers, Salinas, California

"Behold the turtle—he makes progress only when he sticks his neck out."
—Sign at a large factory

"After three months I quit my job—I felt like a cow in a herd."
—Former production line worker

"It is my responsibility to help people grow. People want to climb, get ahead. That is self-fulfillment."
—Production line area supervisor

"In 1973, after dialogue in a good discussion group, we made a conscious decision to refuse to give our lives to climbing the success ladder."
—Married couple, Belmont, California

"No, I don't like my job, but it's hard to change

jobs. I'm fifty now. There are certain things that my wife is used to and doesn't want to give up. If we were to make some changes together, then maybe it would be possible."

—Engineer

Our voices agree that work matters. It is important to feel a sense of dignity about our work. It is important that others respect our work and see it as a meaningful part of the whole functioning of society. Many people who are struggling to integrate their work and personal lives find themselves frustrated by unmet expectations, feelings of worthlessness, experiences of alienation, and painful conflicts of values. Some have resigned themselves to their work—"That's just how work is, you know"—while others have become aware of important changes that need to be made in the conditions, style, or places of their work.

What if starting today we were each to take control of our own work lives? What if we no longer allowed ourselves to be governed by voices that purport to know the road to success? What if our work became a place of self-expression and our success were no longer measured by promotion or pay raise but rather by personal growth? What if today we began to change harmful or distasteful conditions in our work places? What if, in fact, our work became the arena for mending our fragmented lives and becoming more whole individuals in harmony with the world around us?

What is work? How do we define it? Work is not just another name for employment. We all work, whether or not we are formally employed. Whether we drive a truck, clean and cook, paint canvases, go to school, or manage a team of researchers, we are working. Work is purposeful activity—it is a process, not a product. Our work is our contribution to society. Whether our work facilitates or hinders society's functioning and ability to meet all the people's needs is our choice.

What attitudes do we have toward our work? Some of us view employment as little more than a necessary evil. We just put in the hours and collect the paychecks, hurrying home to do our real living before and after hours. We are predisposed to think that employment cannot be enjoyable. Work is work—that is why you get paid for it. Doing what you want to do —leisure, entertainment—comes after work. We have grown to feel that doing what we want, whether frivolous or deeply spiritual, is personal and doesn't belong in the category of work. Right?

Wrong. At least, many of us who are exploring simple living choose to reject such an attitude. We approach work as if it mattered to us personally, as if we had some responsibility for our work, as if we deserved to be doing what we want, and as if this type of fulfilling job could still get the world's work done.

For others of us, work is the place where we channel all our striving and commitment and exercise our talents and skills in order to get ahead. It is a place of great pressures which we grow to feel is the ultimate proving ground for our worth as individuals. But what worth is there to prove? Perhaps we have compromised our own values in the process; abused our bodies from long hours of tedious work; or spent so much time away from home that we are no longer able to communicate our deepest questions, thoughts, and feelings with those people closest to us. And in the midst of this feverish pace we often become blind to the ends of our day-to-day work. It is hard for us to be objective about the patterns of work that we have established and followed over a long period of time. During a visit to a large electronics firm, I spoke to the personnel manager, who told me that his home and family were more important and meaningful to him than his work, although he really enjoyed his job. I asked whether he would like to have a four-day week every other week and whether it would be financially feasible. He said that he would love to have the extra day and that he made enough money so that it would be possible. Would he ever take action to bring about the change himself? He said no.

What are the ends of our day-to-day work? Will we wake to find that in all of our striving we have sacrificed the harmony between our personal and work lives and have become resigned to being tools for somebody else's goals or profits?

This is not the inevitable outcome. There is also a positive, creative attitude toward work. In the sixth century B.C., Buddha shared with his followers his philosophy of work, the principle of "right livelihood." For us today, the right livelihood concept means work that is more valuable than leisure and hardly less important to a sense of well-being than a good sound sleep. It is work consistent with our values and it does not harm others or our environment. It is a meaningful, valuable, and integral part of our lives. As E. F. Schumacher explains in chapter 4 of *Small Is Beautiful*, right livelihood means work that functions

—to give people a chance to develop and utilize their faculties

—to enable them to overcome their ego-centeredness by joining together with others in common tasks

—to bring forth the goods and services needed for a becoming existence.

Adopting Alternative Work Attitudes

Without stretching our traditional concepts of work and without honestly questioning our personal attitudes, we cannot move to change the conditions or styles of our work.

1. Evaluating What We Want to Do and Confronting the Obstacles to Doing It

What values do we want our work to reflect? What goals must we set in order to attain right livelihood? What skills must we develop in order to reach these goals? It is important that we think about what kind of work can be most fulfilling to us as individuals. But in determining our goals we cannot ignore the obstacles— whether family responsibilities, peer pressure, personal pressures of what we "ought to do," the need to acquire new skills, or our own fears associated with changing or finding work. It is easy to build our own obstacles around us, allowing ourselves to be intimidated by the mystique of the profession we would like to join but feel we could never qualify for or would prefer not to join but feel we "ought to" in order to be bona fide. We may feel too precarious or vulnerable to consider changing to work we really want to do: "I'm fifty and dissatisfied with my job. But I'm too old to change." Or "I just got out of school—no experience, no real skills. You think somebody's going to hand me the perfect job?" Or "I'm unemployed, I can't find any job, let alone something I would like to do."

These are real concerns. But many of us, particularly in the "unemployed or unemployable" situation, are beginning to discover that there is work available that suits our interests and abilities. There is, that is, if we are open to alternatives, willing to take some risks, and willing to explore the struggles and joys of simplifying our lives. Ideally, we will gain encouragement and support from our loved ones, from a simple living concern group, or from co-workers.

A couple with two children told me about their experience in simplifying their lives and confronting obstacles through group discussion and support. "Our vision and direction in life comes from our Christianity (we are Catholics), realized in community and dialogue with others. Our goal was a change in life-style. Now that we have reached that goal we have realized it is only the beginning of new directions, in terms of how we want to expend our time and energy, in a life of greater commitment and service."

2. Looking at Ourselves in Relation to the World Family

What values *does* our work reflect? Does our work harm others or the environment? When we look at ourselves in relationship to the world family, we realize that we are each a valuable part of that family and that we cannot individually attain our work goals at the expense of our neighbors. At the San Francisco American Friends Service Committee's Annual Meeting in 1975, Tyree Scott of the United Construction Workers Association cautioned:

In our quest to solve the problem of discrimination in employment, we have come to the realization that for every job won by a Third World person there is a job lost by a white worker. This is because the issue of discrimination in existing jobs is the only one that has been raised. We must now raise the issue that there cannot be a separate peace.

There is no separate peace—all our actions are part of an intricate weaving of events which enables our society and the world to function. Our actions can be either destructive or constructive, but the things we choose to do, our work, our way of life, will inevitably have an impact on others. Whether the effect we have on our neighbors and, ultimately, on the whole human family is positive or negative could be our choice.

On a summer day in front of the United Farm Workers (UFW) clinic in Salinas, California, Chuca and a friend and I stood talking while Chuca's wife was inside visiting the doctor. My Spanish is broken at best, and Chuca grinned at me as I wobbled out questions.

"Do I like my work? It's work—we all work," he said, but then without prodding he went on to explain how important it was to him that he was working for the union (UFW). Chuca said that everybody had to make some sacrifices, but that there was a real loving bond between the workers.

"There is a piece of bread," he said, as he held his hands out in front of him to indicate the size. "It's not a big piece of bread, but in the UFW we divide it in three—*uno para ella*" he motioned to my friend, "*uno para usted*" (he nodded at me), "*y uno para mi*" (he pointed to himself).

"Chuca," I said, "you speak about the sacrifices that you and your family have made, but it seems—" I groped for words I knew and finally said, "it really seems that you have a light within you."

"Oh yes," he beamed. "An enthusiasm for life. We all have it."

When we listen to the voice of the farm worker, it helps us to understand what it would be like to work cooperatively—contributing to the common good rather than striving for personal success—in an atmosphere in which tasks and decision making are shared.

Alternative Work Styles

So what are some of our alternatives if we choose to change or reevaluate our work conditions? Many new structures and styles of working are in existence already; others are still evolving. Some require creating a completely new type of employment while others involve revising and humanizing existing institutions we are already part of. I will mention only a few here. Many other options can be explored in our own locales.

1. Apprenticeship

School is not always the place to learn new employment skills. Especially if we have savings or other sources of income which we can use for a while, we might consider an apprenticeship. If we are willing to take on responsibilities and to make a time commitment, employers are often willing to take us on as an apprentice or volunteer worker. An apprenticeship can be an inexpensive and effective way to learn skills as well as a valuable experience which will aid us in finding or changing employment.

A very creative friend of mine decided that she wanted to become a weaver. School had always been an effort for her—not so much because it was difficult as because it did not challenge or meet her needs. Rather than go back to school, she investigated the weavers living in her area. Finally she found one who agreed to teach her to weave in exchange for five hours of carding and fleecing wool and ten dollars a week—a fraction of the cost of going to a weaving school. My friend is now an excellent weaver—dyeing, spinning, and weaving her own creations.

2. Income Sharing

Income sharing is another creative way to move toward an integration of work and life. Income sharing means equal distribution (or distribution according to need) of earnings within a family, an extended family, or an intentional community. It places the emphasis on quality and type of work by putting equal value on tasks, whether paid or unpaid. People in several community groups across the country are coming together to live simply and free their time and energy for social change, local community, and personal concerns. It is not unusual that one person in such a group may earn a great deal more than she or he needs. By sharing this income, others are able to engage in activities and experiences that may not always be found in an employment situation.

In the Philadelphia Life Center (see chapter 5), an intentional community of about one hundred people, income sharing is practiced. Each household deals with their finances autonomously. Within a household, income may be shared by pooling all earnings and redistributing them on a weekly or monthly basis or over longer periods of time. For example, one household member may put full-time effort into a six-month training program for social change activists, during which time she or he receives no income. Other household members will provide for that person's livelihood during the six months. When the program has terminated, the person involved will return to a paid job and free someone else to become active in a project that brings little or no income. If care is taken to work out mutually beneficial and just contracts or agreements, and if time is taken to talk out any anxieties that may arise, income sharing can create a positive and strong bond among the individuals involved.

3. Job Sharing

The notion of job sharing is rapidly spreading in the United States. Jobs that are ordinarily filled by one person are now divided and shared by two people.

With married couples, job sharing (whether with one another or with others in their separate places of employment) enables each partner to share in child care and household responsibilities as well as to pursue her or his own career.

Mark and Louise Zwick decided to change to a simpler way of life and began by acquiring part-time jobs. Louise now works at an environmental library, and Mark is a psychiatric social worker for a county children's mental health program. It was important to them to have time to care for their two children and share household tasks. They have worked it out so that on their separate days off they are responsible for child care. On the other days, Mark works afternoons and Louise works mornings. This arrangement permits each parent to be with the children and take responsibility for the home. It also frees weekends for special family projects.

Reflecting on the period of change, Louise says, "Practically speaking, since it was a gradual transition, the impact wasn't upsetting or unnerving, as it might have been. Half-time jobs were difficult to find and there was a temptation to take any job. But we had made a commitment to each other to work half-time, so it meant many job interviews." Now having made the transition, Mark says, "Working half-time allows me as a husband to have more energy to plan and do things with my wife and children. All of my best energy is no longer exploited by a job. I can now think about community involvement with my wife, writing, and being involved in my children's education." Mark adds that he feels free of the traditional role of father as breadwinner or provider, and can now explore what fatherhood means to him.

New Ways to Work, a community vocational resource center in Palo Alto, California, strongly advocates shared employment. Here are some of the advantages they cite. (1) the employer gets substantially more productivity from a four-to-six-hour than from an eight-hour-plus employee; (2) a viable alternative to layoffs is created, enabling employers to hold on the valuable workers; (3) single parents, "over-fifties," physically handicapped persons, and young graduates all have greater opportunity to gain experience and be employed; (4) the expanded labor market created by shared employment makes for healthier job competition.

New Ways to Work was instrumental in instigating job sharing in the city of Palo Alto. Several positions are now held and shared by two employees. According to a study undertaken by a group of Stanford University students, both employers and employees feel that there are numerous benefits to the program. A survey that the students conducted cites four main advantages to job sharing: (1) job creation: more jobs can be created and consequently more people can be employed; (2) diversity: there is opportunity for bringing more ideas, talents, skills, and thus creativity to a job than would otherwise be available; (3) productivity: a higher level of performance can be achieved due to shorter working hours, and thus less time is wasted on the job; (4) flexibility: employees can be scheduled for better coverage during "peak hours"; parents who have child-care responsibilities are able to work; and individuals who need on-the-job training are able to begin on a part-time basis.

What about wages, benefits, unions? These questions are answerable, but open-mindedness and honest grappling with the issues is needed as more people choose to do job sharing. Currently, in Palo Alto, wages are no different for sharers than for full-time employees of the same or equivalent position; they are simply paid for fewer hours. The city of Palo Alto has arranged to fully pay statutory benefits (social security, state disability insurance, and workman's compensation) and medical insurance. Other compensatory benefits (social security, state disability insurance, and workman's compensation) and medical insurance. Other compensatory benefits (paid vacation and holidays, sick leave, etc.) are prorated. This arrangement has been very successful, but it must be recognized that Palo Alto is a relatively affluent community. It is possible that other cities and programs might, for instance, need to investigate medical plans that are feasible for both employer and employee.

I talked with a spokesperson from the local union representing the Palo Alto employees and asked him how the union felt about part-time jobs. He responded that the union was the "moving party in negotiating" the jobs. He described the union's active support of part-time jobs and the variety of efforts to establish more flexible hours for employees. For example, he informed me that several Palo Alto city workers now had one three-day weekend each month. He said that the only real potential problem with job sharing is not one of employers' concern for payment of benefits or wages, but rather one of letting go of established concepts of work and employment. He mentioned as an example the issue of readjusting personnel staff to provide for administration of an increasing number of employees who are working more flexible hours or part-time. Such problems are not insurmountable, and changes will be made. Increasingly people are seeing the need and benefits of job sharing, and it is becoming a regular function of our communities.

4. Cooperatives and Collectives

Work cooperatives and collectives can either be profit-making or nonprofit-making organizations. Practically speaking, a cooperative or collective can be a group that operates to save money for the consumer without consumer participation—in other words, the consumer is not a worker. Cooperatives and collectives can also be a group of individuals working together to produce goods or services for themselves.

These days, low-price stores and markets such as consumer-oriented co-ops are a refuge from inflation, but in considering right livelihood we need to go beyond simple economizing. Worker- or producer-oriented collectives can nurture an atmosphere of cooperation in which both tasks and decision making are shared. In addition to dispensing services at low-profit or nonprofit rates, such collectives create a healthier atmosphere for workers. Work collectives enable workers to participate in the running of the business, from the menial jobs to finances to product selection. One such collective is the Briarpatch Cooperative Market in Menlo Park, California. In this instance, the workers are the consumers as well. Each member works two hours a month, stocking, packaging, labeling, helping with inventory selection and ordering, working the cash register, or updating the books. Prices are kept low by keeping the overhead low. The members run the store themselves with the help of two paid managers. Each member pays what is called a "direct charge" of two dollars a month (regardless of how much she or he purchases) to cover operating costs. Let's look at what the Briarpatch Market has to say about its operating philosophy:

> We will endeavor to supply our needs as inexpensively as possible. We will keep our overhead to a minimum by using only low-cost functional space and equipment and avoiding merchandising methods whose only purpose is to sell. We will know our store's policy because we will make it. The books will be open and members encouraged to use them. Decisions will be made openly and democratically in ways which encourage meaningful participation by the membership. We will include in our activities a program of product information reflecting a concern for nutrition, ecology, and economy. We refer here not only to personal economy but also to the fact that as consumers we are the ultimate object of the economy at large.

The market has established several channels, such as discussion groups and a bulletin board, to help educate members to meet their food needs in an ecologically and economically sound manner. In doing so, they have simultaneously built a stronger sense of community among the participants. Members feel a sense of pride and concern for the market, and it is not unusual for them to volunteer to share their skills.

Defining work, clarifying our values, evaluating our skills—these are all necessary components to finding work that is right for us. We can explore alternative attitudes toward work and alternative work styles. We will come to recognize that some of these alternatives are clearly not for us; they do not meet our needs or concerns. We will find that other alternative work styles and life-styles will challenge us in affirming and creative ways and make our lives more fulfilling.

It is spring now, as I finish writing this chapter on work. For many of us it is time for preparing the gardens that will provide us with food. We find working our gardens nurturing, meaningful work. The days are longer now, the wild flowers have begun to bloom, and in the garden the seeds that were planted in the flats only days ago have begun to show signs of life. The soil is turned, the compost spread, and soon the small sprouts will be carefully transplanted into the rich bed of soil. Then come weeks of mindful watering and gentle constant care. By the end of summer, the sunflower stalks will be eight feet high; there will be strawberries and strawberry jam; and tomatoes, carrots, and cauliflower will be bountiful—more than enough for family and friends. The work that goes into making our gardens is a slow, nurturing process that we do with love and care. As simple livers we can take this same approach in regard to our own personal growth and thus to all our work. As in Kahlil Gibran wrote in *The Prophet*: "You work that you may keep pace with the earth and the soul of the earth."

What You Can Do

1. To clarify your personal and vocational goals, make a list of what you would like to do in your lifetime or write your own *Who's Who* entry as if it were written about you at age 70. Be imaginative and complimentary. What do you really want to do? Please dream! You may want to revise this list or story from time to time, because career and life planning is an ongoing process. Having described what you want to do, examine what skills,

abilities, and experiences you have or need to carry out your vision.

2. Skills. Make an inventory of the skills you presently have—things you do well and enjoy. Write an autobiography describing the activities, both paid and unpaid, in which you have participated. Include in your description what you did and did not like about each activity. Be thoughtful and take some time with this. Were some of the activities for which you were not paid more meaningful than some for which you were paid?

   After identifying your long-range and short-range personal and vocational goals and inventorying your skills, try to identify what new skills you will need to achieve your goals. Again, making lists can be helpful. Assess each new skill according to the time and effort it involves. Research and discover the most resourceful way to acquire the needed skills.

3. As we consider making changes in our employment, it is important that we take time to evaluate our present situations.

   a. Family obligations. Most people who consider changing their places of work must first assess their financial and personal responsibilities to themselves and to those whom they support. In confronting and attempting to reduce obstacles, ask yourself the following:

   —Is my housing excessive?

   —Are my utility bills excessive because I waste energy?

   —Am I increasing my food expenditures by eating too high on the food chain? (For information about food chain, see Food chapter.)

   —Are my clothing needs artificially expanded by fashion?

   —Could I do without my automobile? If I have two, would one be plenty?

   —What ways can I find to enjoy my leisure hours more and spend less money while doing so?

These questions will help determine your economic priorities. While it is unrealistic to ignore money in determining vocational alternatives, much can be done to reduce your need for money and hence the obstacle money can present to taking responsibility for your own employment.

b. Conditions of employment. Determine what changes you would like to make in your employment situation. Consider yourself an active agent who has the ability to form the present and future environment. Construct a chart like the one below:

What I Can Control		What I Cannot Control
1. Conditions I can improve by changing my work place	2. Conditions I can change in my present situation without changing employment	1. Present conditions I cannot control

4. Investigate job and income sharing. In a family this can be accomplished by the husband and wife working together at one job or at separate part-time jobs. Responsibility for income can be shared year by year or day by day. Job and income sharing permit time and energy to be freed for personal growth, family, and social concerns.

5. Create or invent your own work if the work you want to do cannot be found. Many communities need day-care centers, legal aid, honest car repair, and a variety of other services you might enjoy performing.

6. If your job happens to pay more than you feel comfortable spending, consider establishing a foundation to put the surplus to some constructive use. Your excess income could help finance health clinics, free schools, a small business, and many other creative enterprises.

7. Peer pressure. Invite a group of friends to your home for a potluck. Include people who are in traditional vocations as well as some who are exploring alternatives. Discuss alternative approaches

to work. Let people express their fears and excitement, their disapproval and approval. Perhaps this group will want to continue to meet to work out its differences.

8. Become aware of times when home and work are integrated. Do dinner conversations often reflect concerns that have arisen at work? For a week or two, keep a list of the times and places when home and work feel comfortably integrated.

9. Just quit? Just fired? Before you start searching for new employment, stop and think, clarify your values, evaluate your skills. Take at least one day to dream, to discover what you would most like to do with your work and life in the days ahead. Decide how many hours each day you will put into "job hunting." Leave yourself some free hours. Choose and involve yourself in one (or two) projects you have wanted to do but have not had enough time for—e.g., making a chair, painting the kitchen, stitching a quilt, working with the local affirmative action group, getting involved with the local tenants union, etc. These projects will help to keep morale up during unemployment and possibly give you insights into the type of work you find most enjoyable.

10. The income game, a group activity. Divide into small groups of four or five. Each group is assigned a different annual income. If there are four groups, for instance, each member brings the following amount of money to the group: Group 1, $2,000 per year; Group 2, $4,000 per year; Group 3, $6,000 per year, and Group 4, $8,000 per year. Thus, if there are four players in each group, Group 1 will have $8,000, Group 2 $16,000, and so on.

   The groups are then asked to figure out how they could live on this income. Will each family live separately or will all live communally? What resources will be shared? Members must calculate as part of the group's expenses all dependents they actually have. Property individuals already own (such as a house) can be kept for their own use or shared by the group, but they cannot be sold or rented to give the group additional money. No other capital assets from real life are available to the group. The groups are asked to try to live simply and draw up their budget accordingly. They are encouraged to try to have some money left over and decide as a group what they will do with the excess.

After the groups meet for about an hour to decide how they will adjust to their new circumstances, everyone comes back together. One reporter from each group describes their annual budget and what happened in their group. What did people learn from the experience? Was the difference in group income of any importance? Did the differences in income produce a difference in values?

SOURCES OF FURTHER INFORMATION

(See also: Community, Consuming Ourselves)

Bolles, Richard. *What Color Is Your Parachute: A Practical Manual for Job Hunters and Career Changers*. Berkeley: Ten Speed Press/Bookpeople, 1974.

New Vocations Project, AFSC of San Francisco. *Working Loose*. New York: Random House, 1972.
A book about finding work you want to do.

Terkel, Studs. *Working: People Talk About What They Do All Day and How They Feel About What They Do*. New York: Pantheon, 1972.
An interesting account of people in a wide variety of occupations; reflections on how workers feel about their jobs.

Vocations for Social Change: VSC programs have been established in several states. This group helps individuals consider alternative work styles that are geared for social change. Local VSCs also publish the *People's Yellow Pages*, an excellent source of possible alternative work places and of groups working for social change. West Coast address: 5951 Canning Street, Oakland CA 94609. East Coast address: 353 Broadway, Cambridge MA 02139.

8

Creative Simplicity

BY LUCY ANDERSON AND SUSAN LEE

Queries

1. How do we express creativity in our everyday lives?
2. Do we assume that living simply means having a drab environment? Or do our surroundings express the richness of our lives?
3. Can we trust our own esthetic tastes, or do we allow professionals and advertisers to dictate to us?
4. Do we regard creativity as a primarily feminine activity? How do we involve all people—men, women, and children—in the creative process?
5. Do we celebrate seasonal life cycles such as the summer or winter solstice? Are we aware of weekly, monthly, or yearly cycles or patterns in our own lives?
6. Are there important and meaningful events in our lives for which there are no rituals or celebrations? How could we begin to develop them?
7. What traditional rituals and personal experiences hold special symbolic meaning for me?
8. Do phrases like "centering" or "getting in touch with myself" mean anything to me? Do I take time regularly to meditate or sit quietly?

> What if . . .
> . . . stars were turnips
> . . . the moon was a ball of yarn
> . . . we could drink the Milky Way
> . . . I was a flute
> . . . I was a garden snail
> . . . we shrank instead of grew
> . . . purple were blue
> . . . I could write with my finger
> . . . sunflowers wore hats
> . . . windmills were caterpillars
> —*Lucy Anderson and Debbie Leland*

"Lucy, play a game with me," Debbie, my seven-year-old friend, pleaded.

I am sure it's not what she had in mind, but I said, "Okay, let's write a poem." So here is our poem, full of special memories of a summer romping in the garden amidst strawberries and sunflowers. Debbie wrote it out on a piece of notebook paper. We both feel that it is very special. It is our poem. We wrote a poem!

All of us are creative. Remember when you were a child? Didn't you draw pictures for your mother or father? Didn't you weave tall fantasies for yourself or your friends? When you heard a story, couldn't you picture the action and the characters in vivid detail? All these endeavors are creative.

Look around your home; look at the place where you work; look at your clothes. Do you know anyone else who has exactly the same thing in every particular? Our tastes and possessions may be similar to those of other people, but the way each of us puts them together reflects our creativity and is unique.

Expressing this creativity is, we believe, a basic human need, one that comes to the surface once immediate survival needs are met. It is one of the ways we make life worth living. Through creative expressions we make our own unique and self-contained statements about ourselves, our life experiences, and our values.

In preindustrial society, people's creative urges were often expressed in their work. People made their own houses, clothes, food, and so on. While patterns of custom and fashion shaped the making, no two of these were alike; without mass production, they couldn't be. Today we live in a unique historical situation: as Marx put it, people are for the first time alienated from their labor. No longer, for instance, are most lace products produced at home by expert lace makers; they come from factories run largely by computers. Very seldom anymore do people gather round an elderly storyteller to hear the tales and legends of their group or culture; most nights nowadays we gather round a television set.

Moreover, making things "by hand" is now a big

business in America; factories crank out a cornucopia of predesigned and prepackaged kits, the purchase and assembly of which is supposed to display our creativity. But what kind of statements do these objects make? How much do they express our own individuality, as distinct from that of a corporation's marketing experts? Do they help develop a sense of uniqueness, or are they primarily another example of the consumerist rat race?

An important part of simple living is an effort to reclaim ourselves and our creativity from commercialism. We want to make our own songs, dances, recipes, stories, crafts, ideas, humor; we want to fulfill our creative needs ourselves, and do so in ways that express our own set of values. This reclamation of ourselves and our capacity to make our own statements is what we mean by creative simplicity.

Of course, it is obviously impractical, if not impossible, for most of us to create everything we do and use instead of buying it. We live, after all, in the latter half of the twentieth century in postindustrial America. The practical options we have to express our creativity depend upon the sort of life each of us leads. For example, the two of us—Lucy and Susan—incorporate creative simplicity in our lives in different ways.

Susan: I am a mother, a student training for my career, a suburbanite, a sometime social/political activist, and a very busy woman in the process of becoming a more complete and integrated person. Creative simplicity for me means mainly little things, yet it is an important part of my life. It is a process which helps me keep my identity and the values I hold intact. For instance, I spend some days rushing from class to meeting to grocery store to baby-sitter's in a frantic whirlwind of activity. As I collapse on the couch in the evening, after having put my daughter to bed, with all the necessary glasses of water and good-night kisses; after I have done the dinner dishes, read the mail, and worried about the bills— after all this, I begin wondering what my life is about.

It is at this point that by doing something creative, be it mending a toy, thinking up a special birthday idea for someone, singing a song, or just plain meditating, I get back in touch with myself and my life begins to fall back into perspective. I begin to feel like a unique and valuable person again instead of a machine programmed to accomplish a set number of tasks in a given period of time. Creative simplicity is a way for me to recapture the joy of who I am.

Lucy: I graduated from Stanford in 1974. I majored in religious studies and then went on to do graduate work at Harvard Divinity School in religion and social change. I left graduate school after one semester, because I was tired of school and at that time it was the practical, not the theoretical, work of social change that I wanted to become involved with. Now I am living in a semirural area where we grow most of the food we eat. Usually I spend my weekends with the other people I live with, at home building a third dome so we can expand our community, or constructing a solar dryer, or simply working in the garden. We all try to live simply and be respectful of natural resources and careful with our personal use of them. During the week, I now put most of my time into organizing a cooperative housing project for low-income people.

Sometimes I really struggle with simple living; other times it is just naturally the way I live my life. Creative simplicity to me means self-expressions such as our domes and garden, but it also reflects the attitude with which I approach life. When I am frustrated and impatient, feeling that I have to change the world—tomorrow!—creative simplicity helps me to slow down and remember that process is as important as ends. I then take time to work in the garden, to dance, to read, or simply to have some quiet time. Creative simplicity helps me see that my political actions are integrally bound up with how I live my personal life; and it helps me as I strive to find a balance between the two.

Creative Simplicity and Gift Giving

Gift giving is a form of personal expression that almost everyone participates in. Most of us, however, usually head for a store when we want to get a gift; a large part of our economy depends on this gift-buying habit. But how often do these purchased gifts make a statement that is genuinely personal, showing thoughtful consideration of the recipient's personality and interests, as well as being truly expressive of values we want to uphold—values like utility, conservation, cooperation, and community? Here creative simplicity means giving a part of ourselves to others as an expression of love and caring. It reminds us that our greatest gift is the gift of ourselves—our time, energy, concern, and thoughts. We are giving when we accept a gift with openness and genuine attention. Creative simplicity can inspire us to find or make meaningful gifts for those we care about.

Susan: Every year my grandparents ask for their favorite Christmas gift from me—homemade preserves. Preserves are inexpensive and relatively easy to make, yet my grandparents appreciate them much more than the gifts I used to buy after hours of wracking my brains for things they did not already have.

A close friend of mine, whose hobby is photography, gave me a lovely gift last year—a sitting for a portrait. I gave him three hours' worth of clothes mending and had great fun patching his blue jeans. A nice housewarming gift given to me once was a small plant grown from a cutting off a plant I had admired at my friend's house.

Lucy: I remember when Heidi, then nine years old, came to me with a dragonfly wing. It was her gift to me. She was fascinated by the intricate and transparent nature of the tiny wing, and I was captured by her world. Another very special form of giving is storytelling and make-believe. Through them, families and small groups can come together and jointly create a poem, a song, a myth. The work created can make a traditional holiday more meaningful and personal. It can also be a gift to one particular person on a special occasion, such as a birthday, baptism, or wedding.

Susan: A bachelor friend of mine, who has three pre-school children, had a birthday. Several mutual friends and I wanted to give him something special. After warning him, eight of us descended on his house. While one person took all the kids to the play-ground, the rest of us, armed with mops, brooms, cleansers, floor wax, and the like, spent the day cleaning his house from one end to the other. By the time we were done, the place sparkled. We cele-brated with a musical jam session and an inexpensive bottle of champagne. He said it was one of the best gifts he had received in years.

Lucy: I have struggled with the issue of gift giving and the monetary value of the gift. I have at times felt that having fun or doing something nice for someone else requires spending money—going out to dinner or a movie, buying a gift. Sometimes it seems easier to go to the dinner or the movie if I just don't have the energy to be creative about an-other activity. But often these purchased experi-ences or gifts fall short of expressing my real feelings.

Probably the best resource for simple-living-oriented gift-giving ideas is *The Alternative Celebration Cata-logue* (see bibliography). In its opening pages, the authors set out their philosophy of giving. These guide-lines for gift giving are important ones for me:

Simply put, the philosophy affirms that we are to:
1. Be sensitively aware of the effects of our giving or nongiving on people and the Earth and insist that they be life-supporting and conserving.
2. Commit ourselves to simplified living, which makes more of our income available for giving.
3. Rediscover that creating gifts with our hands (in-

stead of depending on machines) makes us and the gifts more humane.

4. Remember that our purpose of celebrating and gift giving should be the enrichment of human relationships, a process that requires more than something material: the most important ingredient is the investment of self.

5. Experience the power of our purchases to produce justice.

When traditional gifts end up costing more money than we would like and when they don't express our real feelings, we want to be able to use our imagination to find alternative gifts which make our statement creatively and with simplicity. Sharing the love we feel for ourselves, our families, and our friends by giving gifts that are part of us is an expression of love.

Rituals and Celebrations

Through creative simplicity we can also begin to rediscover our collective imagination when we gather in groups for celebration. Too many people today have such hectic, transient lives that many rituals have become locked into a particular form, with little remaining sense of meaning; they are simply done the way everyone has always done them. Yet most rituals originated when people gathered to say something special to one another. They are a collective way of making a statement about ourselves, our lives in relation to others, and our values.

Susan: At the time my uncle died, I strongly believed that funerals and the surrounding rituals served only to line the morticians' pockets and provide a spectacle to prove to the community how important and popular the person was. My uncle's funeral changed those ideas. It seemed that each new step of the process was right in phase with my emotional condition. The rituals—from callers bringing condo-

lences and casseroles to the gathering after the inter-
ment—all gave reality to the fact that he was dead.
It helped, even encouraged, me to grieve openly and
come to terms with his death. The symbols became
important ways to make my passage through that
time.

Funerals exemplify some of the issues involved in
rituals and celebrations very well. As rituals, funerals
are very important, but the average funeral in America
costs $2,000, and costs of $5,000 to $10,000 are not
unusual. In this sense, suspicions about profiteering
in the funeral industry were more than justified.
Funeral costs often become a financial disaster for the
family involved, however psychologically helpful the
ritual may have been.

Fortunately, there are alternatives available. More
than 150 nonprofit funeral and memorial societies
exist in this country through which one can obtain
dignified, simple, and economical burial arrangements.
These societies encourage people to arrange for their
funerals in advance, so mourning families can avoid
financial pitfalls and the need to make decisions while
in the throes of mourning. A small fee is charged for
membership in an association (the Peninsula Funeral
Society in Palo Alto, where the authors live, asks $10
from individuals and $15 from families for a life-
time membership), and local societies have reciprocal
arrangements with each other through the Continental
Association of Funeral and Memorial Societies, 1828
L St., N.W. Washington DC 20036.

What is true of funerals is true in different ways for
most artistic, religious, cultural, and athletic rituals
in our society. To simplify our lives, we are working
to reclaim our rituals from consumerism and to give
them back to ourselves.

The same point applies to holidays. Holidays are
meant to be times for celebration, and today we buy
most of our celebrations ready-made and prepackaged
off the shelf of a store. Christmas epitomizes holiday
commercialism; we all know about that. The same

phenomenon figures, albeit less intensively, for other holidays as well.

Lucy: Early one Easter morning, three of us drove across the Golden Gate Bridge to Mount Tamalpais. Easter is special to me—it means new life; it means it is okay to start over again when I have screwed up; it means rebirth . . . and birthdays of understanding what this thing of living is all about. As Lynette and Michael and I crossed the bridge, the sun was just beginning to soften the sky with light pinks and yellows. Soon the sun was beginning to feel warm on our backs, as we hiked along the hillside to a spot which opens up to a sloping valley and then leads down to the sea. The night before we had decided that we wanted to do something different, something special for one another. We chose to give each other a gift of words—our own or someone else's—and an image. Michael read to me:

My Gift

I have come to sing,
The song of life.
I know not, how to teach.

I have come to love,
The diversity of life.
I know not, how to preach.

I have come to live,
A sane, healthy life.
I know not, how to lead.

I have come to enjoy
The perfume of life.
I have no message for you.

My heart is a lotus,
These words are petals.
This is my gift unto you.

So we exchanged our words and thoughts. Ah, and then it was time for an Easter brunch—chi, biscuits, and cheese. We sat, talked, munched, and laughed. By the end of the day, we were drowsy from a day in the warm sun and we returned, each rather mellow and quiet with our own thoughts. I realized we had created a ritual of our own.

Susan: In years past, my friends and I usually celebrated the Fourth of July by piling into cars with food, drinks, and fireworks. In a race with thousands of other people, we would head for the beach, driving over congested highways layered in smog, lined with franchised fast-food outlets, and dotted with traffic accidents. On arriving, we would compete with everyone else for enough space to enjoy ourselves. These ventures would be expensive, too, when we added up the cost of gasoline, paper supplies, food, fireworks, and the rest of the paraphernalia.

Last year a group of us associated with the Palo Alto Friends Meeting decided to celebrate in a different, and for us more meaningful, way. We planned a party to celebrate "Interdependence Day," a recognition of our conviction that we as a people and as a nation are interdependent. We are members of one world family. Everyone was invited to the party, and those who came ranged in age from just under two to seventy-nine. Each family brought food and an activity to share. With scraps of material she had on hand, one woman delivered a quick course on designing and making patchwork. Another family brought an old-fashioned, hand-operated ice-cream maker and supervised the children while they turned the handle. Many quarts of ice cream were made and eaten. One group sang madrigals, and others brought guitars. People played games, shared gossip, and enjoyed one another's company. The potluck dinner, spread across the buffet table, featured special dishes from each household.

As darkness came, the group gathered around a huge bonfire that had been built during the afternoon. The musicians brought out their guitars for a round of folk songs, which evoked images of the forty-niners heading for California in search of gold and the laborers who built the nation's railroads. We sang of other peoples, too, who had similar pioneering histories. Later we shared our thoughts about this country and what the celebration of Interdependence Day meant for each of us. The evening ended as each person lit a candle and we all sang "Let There Be Peace on Earth." The beautiful lyrics, of how peace on earth must begin with each of us, summed up the feelings we had in common. Celebrations like this have special meaning for me, for they come from ourselves and our creativity.

Celebrations need not be confined to traditional holidays; they can acknowledge other meaningful events in our lives. We know of women who have created puberty rites for their daughters. When their daughters begin menstruating, they mark the occasion in some special way. However they do it, what is important is the personal expression of a significant event in their lives.

Since we are celebrating something important to us in our ceremonies, doesn't it make sense to do it in a manner that has the most significance to us? Rites and rituals can be such exciting times, for when people are jointly involved in celebration, the whole becomes greater than the sum of the parts. The group attains a life and creative dynamic that goes beyond the collective members.

What if windmills were caterpillars? What if we really gave ourselves the opportunity to explore our creativity and imaginations? And explore it in a manner which reinforced our values and reflected our concern for the earth and for the world family? Letting go of prefabricated, consumption-centered forms of creativity and allowing our uniqueness to push through and express itself can be a very freeing process. The gifts we give, the rituals and celebrations we join and create—all these can enrich our lives at the same time they help simplify them.

Projects

1. Collect percussion instruments (especially home-made ones, such as two sticks, a pot and lid, bells, etc.) and other instruments. While playing or sing-

ing a song (either live or recorded), have everyone join in with the various instruments and create variations on the beat. Make a real jam session out of it, even if thigh-slapping is what you feel most comfortable with.

2. On a roll of paper or a large wall blocked into squares, have everyone draw something in whatever style he likes. Encourage cooperation. Such murals make great decorations in meeting rooms, children's bedrooms, doctors' offices, and the like.

3. Try some improvisational theater work. Imagine a scene a group would like acted out. Each person takes a part (inanimate objects can be played by people too), and the script is improvised. Players should interact with each other, responding to ideas and generating new ones. For some scenarios, mutual trust and support can be very important.

4. Make a collage that expresses some of your in-interests and concerns. Using magazine and other pictures, create a piece that reflects your unique personality.

5. Using craft books and magazines as guides, try making toys for children; for example, rag dolls, cars made out of orange juice cans, etc.

6. An alternative type of gift giving is the exchange of a thought, a picture, a poem, or a dance. In groups of four or five, have each person select an image or poem for each of the others. In larger groups, each person can draw the name of a person to whom he will give a gift. Concentrate on what is special to you about the other person and what uniqueness in them you wish to acknowledge. Perhaps you will recognize some new aspect of his or her personality that you have not seen before.

SOURCES OF FURTHER INFORMATION

(See also: Clothing, Food, Children, Work)

Alternatives. *The Alternative Christmas Catalogue* (2nd edition) and *Alternative Celebration Catalogue* (3rd edition). For copies write to: 701 North Eugene St., Greensboro NC 27401.

Two great catalogues with many ideas for celebrating.

Cadwallader, Sharon. *In Celebration of Small Things*. Boston: Houghton Mifflin, 1974.
She talks mostly about around-the-house projects, especially in the kitchen.

Callenbach, Ernest. *Living Poor with Style*. New York: Bantam, 1970.
This book gives many suggestions for living a creative, yet inexpensive, life. It is very detailed, with many examples of how to make things.

Community Market, Inc. *The Community Market Cooperative Catalogue*. New York: Alfred A. Knopf, 1973.
A handbook on community craft cooperatives throughout the United States, with information about what they make or do.

Hennessey, James, and Papnek, Victor. *Nomadic Furniture I & II*. New York: Random House, 1973.
"How to build and where to buy lightweight furniture that folds, inflates, knocks down, stacks, or is disposable and can be recycled."

Koch, Kenneth. *Wishes, Lies and Dreams: Teaching Children to Write Poetry*. New York: Vintage, 1970.

Laurel, Alicia Bay. *Living on the Earth*. New York: Random House, 1971.
A fun book with many do-it-yourself ideas.

Morgan, Ernest. *A Manual of Death Education and Simple Burial*. Burnsville, N.C.: The Celo Press, 1975.

Poriss, Martin. *How to Live Cheap but Good*. New York: Dell, 1974.
This how-to-do-it book includes sections on furnishings, housing, clothes, food, health, and repairs.

Sunset Books puts out several books on different crafts—some for children—according to topic. Examples are *Crafts for Children, Gifts You Can Make, Sculpture with Simple Materials, Macrame,* and *Quilting and Patchwork*. These books can be obtained in most bookstores or by writing Lane Magazine and Book Company, Willow Road, Menlo Park CA 94025.

Thomas, Marlo, and Ms. Foundation, Inc. *Free to Be You and Me*. New York: McGraw-Hill Book Co., 1974.
"A book of stories and poems and songs that would

help boys and girls feel free to be who they are and who they want to be."

Young, Jean. *Woodstock Craftsman's Manual*. New York: Praeger Publishers, 1972.

How-to's on a variety of arts and crafts.

————. *Woodstock Kid's Crafts*. New York: Bobbs-Merrill, 1974.

Instructions for crafts: tie-dyeing, weaving, and street theater for children.

9
Clothing
BY SUSAN LEE

Queries

1. How do my clothes contribute to my well-being?
2. Do I think about what is used in the production of my clothes? What technology produces the fabrics I wear? Who makes the cloth and clothing and under what labor conditions?
3. How do my clothes reflect my attitudes towards health, practicality, personal expression, and style? In what ways is style important or unimportant to me? How do my clothes express the uniqueness of my personality and my creativity?
4. Do I need new clothes, or could secondhand garments from garage sales, thrift stores, and "free" stores provide me with a wardrobe?
5. What is my usual frame of mind when I set out to buy clothes? Do I go clothes shopping because I am not feeling good about myself and therefore need an ego boost? Do I shop when I am bored and need something to do? What else could I do to feel better or active, rather than buying clothes I may not really want?
6. What impression do I try to convey about myself through clothes? How do I judge others by their dress? Do these attitudes hold up when I actually get to know someone? How important is "dressing the part"?

During my periodic house clean-outs, when I sort out all my closets, shelves, and drawers and get rid of unwanted clutter, I end up looking at my wardrobe in sheer revulsion. Weeding out unwanted clothes is the most laborious and anxiety-ridden task I face during these housecleaning sprees. While my closet and drawers are relatively full, I certainly don't feel as if I'm a well-dressed woman. As I go over each item,

I wonder if this outfit will hold up another season. I must decide if that style dress, bought three years ago and hopelessly out of date, is worth keeping in case it comes into fashion again. It was upsetting when I finally got rid of six pairs of spiked heels and pointy-toed shoes, for they were in good condition. It always seems like such a waste of money—not to mention the effort I put into the shopping trips—to have my clothes become inadequate and useless so quickly.

The rest of the American public and I spend $60 billion a year on clothes, according to Callenbach in *Living Poor with Style*. This is enough, it would seem, to drape the earth. As Thoreau wrote in *Walden,* "As far as I have heard or observed, the principal object is, not that mankind be well and honestly clad, but, unquestionably, that the corporations may be enriched." Obviously all the clothing we buy is not absolutely necessary to protect our bodies. Much is the result of our response to fashion, but this is not entirely the consumer's fault. The fashion industry uses, as its production maxim, planned obsolescence. Planned obsolescence means that products are designed and manufactured with the express purpose of either wearing out or looking shoddy after a few years or becoming undesirable before the life of the product is ended. Fashion falls in the latter category, i.e., a suit is designed to be out-of-date by the following year so that we consumers will need to buy another, even though the first one is in perfectly good condition. Vance Packard, in his book *The Waste Makers* (New York: David McKay Co., Inc., 1960), devotes an entire chapter to planned obsolescence and uses the woman's fashion industry as his prime example. He cites B. Earl Puckett, chairman of Allied Stores, as saying that basic utility "cannot be the foundation of a prosperous apparel industry. . . . We must accelerate obsolescence. . . . It is our job to make women unhappy with what they have. . . ." (p. 72). (While these remarks are aimed at women, they are applicable to men as well. Perhaps one of the unfortunate results of the sexual equality movement is that the men's clothing industry now rivals the women's. Today's men are as subject to fashion's planned obsolescence as women have been traditionally.)

Mr. Puckett's message has certainly been heard and made note of by the garment industry. Not only do styles change fast enough to make it expensive and difficult for consumers to keep up, but the quality of many garments has steadily decreased. In my experience, for example, seams are often so poorly sewn together that the threads have broken after just a few times through the washing machine. I'm continually appalled when I look at the inside of a garment hanging on a store rack and see the hanging threads and raw seams, sure signs that the garment will not hold up long.

All these thoughts race around in my head while I look at my clothes and wonder how I can cope with the situation. I want to be able to wear what I want to wear, what looks good on me, what feels comfortable, what won't fall apart in just a few months. I want my wardrobe to require little of my time and energy, but without looking as if it were thrown together with no thought. How do I achieve this?

It is in answering this question that a model, used often by those involved in simple living, becomes very useful. This model entails imagining how you would like to be in the best of all possible worlds, looking at where you are now, and finding the process and alternatives to direct yourself toward the goal.

Clothes are important not only because we need to protect our bodies but because they are a primary extension of our personalities. Nothing tells others more about us more immediately than clothes, for they are the visual message that we offer the world about who we are.

In my ideal world, I would like to have a wardrobe of simple, free-flowing clothes that allow my entire body to move without restriction, to flow with grace. I would like the lines of my clothing to be compatible with the lines of my body, so that we work in unison.

When we wear clothing that binds or leaves red marks on our skin, we restrict our cardiovascular system so that blood cannot circulate as it should. Doctors have long known, for example, that girdles contribute to varicose veins, swollen ankles, and other leg and foot ailments. Tight-fitting underwear and pants on men can lead to impotency and reduced sperm production. It's no accident that men often remove their ties, unbutton their collars, and loosen their belts a notch or two when they sit down to relax. Women's clothing is often equally ridiculous. Recently popular platform shoes have caused endless foot and ankle injuries; in addition they are awkward to walk in and are highly impractical.

I would like to be unconcerned about my figure. Most of us dress to make our bodies fit some preconceived ideal model. It's a shame we cannot accept every human body as a beautiful creation—broad hips, narrow shoulders, paunch, and all. We have been so bombarded with the beautiful models who peer at us from fashion magazines and advertisements that anything other than a perfect, long, bony shape seems unacceptable. I want my body to be a source of joy whatever its shape; for example, in the invigorating feeling of using our muscles in strenuous activity, or the serenity of moving gracefully and naturally. Our clothes should be designed to reflect and enhance this joy.

I would like my clothes to reflect my personality, my uniqueness. I would like to use my own resources and creativity in the things I wear.

In short, my ideal wardrobe would feel comfortable, would complement my body, would reflect my personality by being uniquely my own rather than subject to the capricious whims of fashion designers, and would not be a source of wealth to the clothing industry at my own financial expense.

Unfortunately, I do not own my ideal wardrobe, which is why I become so exasperated and distressed when cleaning out my closet. My clothes are reasonably comfortable, but the waistbands are on the snug side. I have been trying to make my figure appear closer to the hourglass shape than it is. I have neither the time nor the skills at this point to create or alter everything I wear. There are only one or two unique extensions of my personality in my wardrobe, and that number is not likely to increase in the near future. Although I'm not eager to fatten the wallets of the garment industry by reducing the size of my own wallet, I do it anyway. It's easier to go to my local department store for a couple of hours than to expend twice that time thinking up what alternatives I have. In addition to all of this, there are some real restrictions placed on what I can wear by the jobs that I do. I cannot go to the office in a muumuu or caftan, and I'm not going to garden or wash the car in my hand-embroidered pants.

But the fact remains that there are methods that can take me closer to the ideal, methods that still are compatible with the real world I have to live in. I believe this is true for most of us.

If our clothes are not allowing our bodies to move and function as they should, perhaps we can change our bodies so that they more accurately express what we want them to say about us. This task we must each face individually. If we want to lose weight or shape up our muscles, we have to do it in a manner suited to our situation. I'm trying to face the fact that I was handed a thicker-than-a-model's waist when I was born. Diets and exercises haven't changed that; and wearing clothes that cinch my poor torso in two doesn't help the situation. The lithe bodies that peer out of advertisements are not my body and never will be. One alternative is to wear clothes that don't emphasize my waist, a relatively simple task. Caftans, muumuus, and the loose pajama like clothes popular in India come into fashion with regularity.

Of course, we can get a perfect fit in terms of size and style by learning how to sew. And learning to use a sewing machine is a simpler matter than you may realize. A machine that stitches only forward and backward is more than adequate for making even elaborate garments. The extra zigzag features that modern sewing machines boast are used primarily for decorative stitching. They allow the sewer to monogram or top-stitch colorful designs—a nice thing to have, but certainly not fundamental. If Simplicity, Butterick, or Vogue patterns make you feel stupid and all thumbs, several books are available that make clothing construction an elementary matter. Two such books are *Hassle-Free Sewing* and *Son of Hassle-Free Sewing* (San Francisco: Straight Arrow Books). Both teach the reader how to design simple, straightforward clothes that require little ingenuity.

If sewing is not going to work for you, you can barter with friends who do know how to sew. I made two shirts for a friend in return for his baby-sitting my daughter. One was a blue work shirt that he bought and I embroidered; the other I put together from material and a pattern. He now owns two shirts that are distinctive, and we both saved money.

Saving money and reducing high consumption in our wardrobes can be done by utilizing alternative methods of obtaining clothes. Swapping skills, as my friend and I did, is one method. Swapping the actual clothes is another. When I want or need to overhaul my closet, some friends and I get together and trade. All of us who wear about the same size bring the clothes we no longer want to wear to one of our houses and spend a few hours picking and sorting. We have a lot of fun, and we get the added bonus of a free new wardrobe.

Swapping can be very useful with children's clothes, especially teen-agers. Most adolescents are extremely conscious of their appearance, and the pressure on parents to assuage their children's needs to be well dressed is very intense. By promoting the idea of co-operation instead of competition, you can encourage teen-agers to share and trade clothes. Younger children are usually so pleased about getting something to wear that they don't mind, and often don't notice whether the clothes are store-bought or hand-me-downs. Secondhand stores become especially useful for the purpose of children's clothes, since most kids outgrow their belongings long before they outwear them.

For those clothes that can no longer be worn in their present condition, recycling may be the answer.

A friend of mine does a marvelous job of creating her own clothes while at the same time recycling material. She cuts out the good fabric from clothes, sheets, or curtains that are worn and no longer serviceable and uses it to make clothes for herself and her family. She made a beautiful pair of slacks from bright floral curtains that her mother-in-law intended to throw away. Around the bottom of each pant leg, she embroidered and highlighted the outline of the flowers, creating a distinctive touch. (She gave the slacks to her mother-in-law.) When her or her husband's clothes wear out, she opens all the seams and recycles the fabric to make clothing for her children.

Recently I complimented another friend of mine on the lovely sweater she was wearing. It was covered with beautifully embroidered flowers. She said, "It's an old sweater that was full of moth holes. I didn't want to throw it away because I've enjoyed wearing it so much. So I decided to plug the holes up as best I could and this is the result." Not only had my friend rescued and recycled a favorite sweater, but she had given it added value by creating something artistic.

Secondhand stores and thrift shops can be invaluable sources of inexpensive, but well-constructed, clothing. Despite the fact that these establishments can exist only because someone else has done the initial buying, they are great places to obtain inexpensive, recycled clothing. As long as some people are purchasing new clothes at high prices, the thrift shops benefit those of us who do not want to participate in direct buying. They have the advantage, too, of giving income to needy organizations and individuals rather than to the large and wealthy clothing industry.

Ernest Callenbach, in his book *Living Poor with Style,* gives extensive advice and information on secondhand purchases. He writes in detail about what to look for in a garment, how to judge good fabric, and so on. Although it is often convenient to buy new clothes at the local store, it may be a luxury we cannot afford. If we follow the principles of simple living which stress reducing high consumption, we must rethink where and how to obtain our clothing. As a friend of mine put it:

> One of the ways in which my efforts toward simple living has affected my life is that I now find shopping in secondhand stores much more satisfying than regular stores. Secondhand stores are full of life, each item has its own story, people are looking for basics rather than frills, and the price is right. If I don't find what I want there first, I might go then to a regular store where now I find I feel oppressed by all the newness, bigness, busyness, advertising, and high prices. By this time I often decide I don't really need the item after all. After going through this a number of times, I find that I need less and less, and I rarely go shopping anymore. Advertising is no longer tempting.

In spite of these suggestions, there are those of us who need to wear clothing that conforms to the standard required by our employers. Some companies, such as IBM, have dress codes, which all employees are required to "dress up" to. Since we don't live in the best of all possible worlds, we need to be able to modify our ideal to fit reality. A well-made, coordinated suit, consisting of three pairs of pants, two jackets, and one or two vests, could be arranged and rearranged into twelve or more different outfits by mixing and matching the separate pieces. If it is in basic, neutral colors (browns, tans, blacks, grays, blues) and has a classic cut, the suit can be appropriate for a large variety of occasions, both formal and informal.

On the other hand, I have noticed that some companies are more flexible about the appearance of their employees than many people realize. When the employee is a hard-working, valuable part of the company, his (or her) "eccentricities" in dress are sometimes overlooked. These eccentricities can also be turned into a positive factor by drawing a new clientele to the firm. An example of this occurred in a law group I know of. The lawyers dressed in the conservative, pin-striped suits traditional to their profession. After hiring a promising young lawyer, they discreetly applied pressure to have him give up his levis and work shirts and conform to their standards. The young man resisted. Meanwhile, prospective clients began to appear, asking for the new lawyer; clients who were of the "hippie" genre who were starting new businesses or buying communal land. Because of the lawyer's dress, these new clients felt comfortable dealing with him. At the same time they brought new business to the firm.

We often have more alternatives in things such as clothing than we realize. When we dress in a manner that is comfortable for our states of mind and reflects our interests, we can often remain engaged in our work or other activities without impediment.

Not only do we need to be mindful of who dictates the style in which we dress and the manner in which we obtain our clothes, but also we must be concerned with maintaining the clothes we have. Dry cleaning, spot removers, detergents, fabric softeners—all these are expensive and time consuming. Synthetic fabrics require less maintenance than natural fabrics, because many synthetics are treated so that they require no ironing, repel spots and stains, and don't need dry cleaning. Hence, the consumer needs to put little energy or money into maintaining synthetic items. Yet, by using petroleum-derived materials of this nature, we are eating up precious resources that the earth cannot provide indefinitely. The production of synthetics is very costly in terms of energy, and disposal of these materials adds to the pollution burden. Each of us needs to find the balance between the use of natural fibers and the use of synthetics.

As I continue the overhaul on my wardrobe, I run across two shirts that are almost identical. I purchased the first one because I honestly needed it. The second I acquired for psychological reasons. I remember the day I bought it. Everything seemed to be going wrong for me. I slept through my alarm, I had a quiz in a class I had forgotten to prepare for, the telephone company threatened to cut off my phone unless I paid my bill immediately, and so on. When I finally made it to the laundromat, several hours behind schedule. I decided to relax and window-shop while the clothes were washing. The boutique next door announced a grand clearance sale, and the sale table was placed right by the window. I couldn't resist. (Of course, by placing the table by the window, the store management counted heavily on my being lured into the store on impulse.) I assuaged my conscience by noting that the shirt I wanted was on sale and that I was therefore being economical. On arriving home, I hung my newly acquired reward for a rotten day right next to the shirt I had bought just a few months before. The two shirts were disturbingly similar. Since the second shirt had been bought on sale, it could not be returned. Now when I go clothes shopping, I sternly ask myself if I honestly need what I'm considering buying, and I never go shopping when my ego is at low ebb.

A hitchhiking trip I made through Europe showed me how little clothing I really need to get by. I am no glutton for discomfort, so since I was carrying everything on my back, I packed with great concern for efficiency and versatility. I found that one good dress, one casual skirt, two pairs of jeans, four tops, one sweater, one coat, two pairs of shoes, four changes of underwear, one swimsuit, and assorted scarves and jewelry were plenty. Now I stand in front of the closet, completing the weeding out process, and recall how few possessions I needed then and how easy their care was. Maybe I'll go back and live out of my knapsack. Now, *that's* simple living!

Projects

1. Make an inventory of the clothes you own. Consider how many pants, coats, shoes, socks, shirts, and suits you have. Which ones have you worn in the last year? In the last two years? Can you determine how they contribute to your well-being. Might your unused clothing be given, traded, or sold at low cost to others?

2. Try to find out who is getting your money when you buy blue jeans at a local department store. Investigate secondhand stores and garage sales. What are the advantages and disadvantages of shopping this way? What attitudes do you notice in yourself as a consumer in a local department store and in a thrift shop?

3. Look at the clothes you are wearing. What took the least labor to put together? If you have never made clothes, perhaps it would be worthwhile to learn to sew. If you know how, do you also know how to minimize waste of fabric? Can you design clothes that minimize work? Have you tried to patch worn clothing?

4. Inform yourself about the structure and practices of the clothing industry. Find out what a runaway shop is. You can start by checking the *Reader's Guide to Periodical Literature* in your local library for magazine articles on the subject.

10

Health Care

BY JAN HARTSOUGH

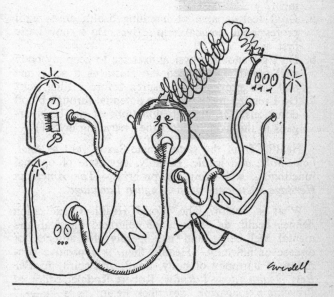

Queries

1. How can we begin to take charge of our own physical and mental health? Are there ways to challenge the health-care system's control over us?
2. How well are my family and I covered in case of sickness? Have any of us needed medical care but done without because of the cost? Does anyone presently need it?
3. How do I choose the medicine I take?
4. Do I ask the doctor to explain all advice and treatment?
5. Do I feel capable of handling health crises until professional medical help arrives. Do I know basic first aid?
6. Do I get enough physical exercise to keep my body well toned? Do I heed the messages it sends me and take preventive measures before getting sick?
7. Do I realize my life-sharing potential through blood donations? Or through donations of my body organs to the living when I die (recycling myself)?

Health: from the same Anglo-Saxon root as *heal, hale, holy, and whole.* Broadly, any state of optimal functioning, well-being, or progress.—*The American Heritage Dictionary of the English Language*

What is health? The World Health Organization defines health as "a state of complete physical and mental well-being and not merely the absence of disease or infirmity." Health, then, is a positive condition of harmony of body, mind, and spirit. In *The Best Health Ideas I Know,* Robert Rodale, editor of *Prevention* magazine, describes health as a "talent" that we can develop in ourselves through study, practice, and effort. A key factor in this process is our attitude toward health. Do we expect the doctor to cure us or do we assume responsibility for our own well-being? Do we have the desire to be healthy? According to Richard Carlson, author of *The End of Medicine,* "health is a dynamic state, one the individual can actively pursue." How actively are we pursuing better health for ourselves?

Environment is a major determinant of health. A life in balance with nature is a healthy life. Our lives depend on nature. Therefore, preserving and enhancing the environment are very important health-related tasks. Among the environmental problems that concern our health are contamination of food, air, and water; excess noise and congestion; and substandard housing. In addition, the sheer complexity of our modern lives and the overabundance of choices and opportunities that we face today often lead to stress and confusion. Alvin Toffler coined the term "future shock" to describe the shattering stress and disorientation induced in people subjected to too much change in too short a time. These anxieties and frustrations trigger chemical changes in our bodies, which accumulate just as external pollutants do and which are equally detrimental to our health. If we don't improve our environment and simplify our external lives, we shall remain sick individuals in a sick society.

Individual and group activities are as important to health as the environment: our diets; whether we exercise or smoke; the safety of our driving habits; how much stress is generated by earning and spending our money; how we relate to our family, neighbors, community. We can consciously work to create a more healthful "inner environment." Some aspects, such as diet, are within our immediate control; others, such as employment and community, involve a longer process. It is healthier to choose the kinds of changes we want to make than to be overwhelmed by the stress of external, seemingly uncontrollable, changes. A commitment to simple living will lead to sounder nutrition (junk food is expensive) and healthier recreation (exercise and celebration don't cost much). Furthermore, as living costs continue to rise, we will *have* to examine our dependence on expensive forms of health care.

The Politics of Health

> Among the Western industrialized nations, twenty-six
> have a longer [than the U.S.] life expectancy for men,
> eleven a longer life expectancy for women, and four-
> teen have lower infant death rate.—*1971 Statistical
> Yearbook of the United Nations*

America's health-care system focuses on treating
disease rather than promoting health. It could be more
correctly called a "disease-care system," for it emphasizes illness, drugs, and surgery at the expense of
primary and preventive care. Comparatively little time,
effort, and money are allocated to teaching people
how to maintain good health. Instead, health care has
become a commodity one buys rather than something
one does. Overtreatment and "iatrogenic disease" (disease introduced by the medical-care system itself, such
as the birth defects produced by the inadequately
tested tranquilizing drug thalidomide in 1962) use
up much of our medical resources. In his newest book,
Medical Nemesis: The Expropriation of Health, Ivan
Illich argues persuasively that modern medicine sick-
ens more than it cures, and that the medical establishment is a major threat to health.

Another dubious distinction of our health-care system is specialization. The general practitioner is a
dying breed, replaced by a confusing array of specialists offering fragmented and costly services. No longer
does the family doctor deliver babies, make house
calls, counsel us, and care for our everyday health
needs. Instead, we frequently get shunted from specialist to specialist, feeling more like objects than human
beings as we pass down the assembly line, paying a
fee-for-service at each stop. Since over half the doctors
in the country today are specialists, it's hard to find
alternatives. Another important factor here is that
hospitals have become the major location for providing
medical care. The fact that most insurance plans pay

only for in-hospital care, along with the increasing sophistication of medical procedures, has reinforced this central role of hospitals.

How has this unhealthy situation come about? Health care is big business in America. Our profit-motivated "medical-industrial complex," composed of doctors, hospitals, insurance companies, and drug and hospitals have become the major location for providing enormous concentration of wealth and power, rivaling that of the defense industry. Hospitals and medical schools have joined forces to pursue teaching and research, often focused on unusual or advanced symptoms of disease, while common diseases and public-health problems get less attention. Hospital and drug suppliers and private insurance companies have all allied themselves with the big hospitals in order to look after each other's business interests.

> From the outset, the aim of the health industry—the private companies which supply, equip, finance, build for, and (sometimes) manage the health delivery system—is not to promote the general well being, but to exploit existing profitable markets and create new ones. Its emphasis, then, is not on products and services which would improve basic health care for the great mass of consumers, but on what are essentially luxury items: electronic thermometers, hyperbaric chambers, hospitals which specialize in elective surgery for the rich, expensive combination drugs.[1]

Power, money, and decision making in our medical-industrial complex operate in a pyramid from the top down, leaving little room for participation by the one most immediately affected by health care—the patient.

People with money can pay for any medical care they need or want, including cosmetic treatment arising from our culture's emphasis on beauty and youth (such as face-lifting or breast enlargement). These luxury services use up valuable medical resources that most Americans can't afford. Is this the way to get best value for the health dollar? At some point, we believe our society is going to have to choose between allowing expensive and exotic treatments to be available to some people and making less expensive basic facilities available to everyone.

Health care in this country is very expensive. The average American works about one month out of every year to cover the family's medical bills. Most health care is financed by insurance, either private (such as Blue Cross, Blue Shield, and other commercial companies) or public (Medicare for the aged and Medicaid for the poor). At the same time, about 24 million people in this country have no medical insurance of any kind. It's not surprising, then, that medical bills are the number one cause of bankruptcy in the United States today!

Among the world's major industrial nations, only the United States has thus far failed to devise some kind of national program that either provides or subsidizes comprehensive health care. Britain has had a national health plan since 1948, and both Sweden and Norway adopted theirs in the 1950s. Proposals for national health insurance continue to appear on the American horizon. Yet none of them would change the health-care picture very much. They remain grounded in a partnership between the federal government and the private insurance companies, aimed at putting the financing of medical care on a sounder basis. The more basic issues of priorities and power in the health-care delivery system are left unresolved, and the real costs in terms of money and health fall back on the consumers.

Many of these plans feature the formation of health maintenance organizations (HMOs), groups of doctors who provide comprehensive services (preventive, diagnostic, outpatient, and hospital) for a fixed amount, paid in advance. HMOs allegedly streamline the system for us. Because the HMO collects a fixed fee, it correspondingly makes more money the fewer procedures its doctors prescribe—the opposite of the fee-for-service system. This provides a good incentive to keep costs down by keeping you healthy and out of the hospital. Still, the motivation remains profit, which grows out of quantity rather than quality of service. "We can well imagine a string of HMO's being developed and franchised around the country, like McDonald's hamburgers, for the benefit of the profit-motivated HMO management, and with the government underwriting the cost." [2] If a national health-insurance program is ever instituted, we can hope it will at least establish the right of health care for all and stimulate debate and public concern.

Steps Toward Health

The greatest potential for improving the health of the American people is not to be found in increasing the number of physicians or in forcing them into groups, or even increasing hospital productivity, but is to be found in what people do and don't do to and for themselves. —Victor R. Fuchs, *Medical Economics,* February 5, 1968.

1. Find Out About Yourself

Traditionally, doctors have had the aura of magicians. A first step toward breaking this spell is to educate ourselves about our own bodies. Medical students spend years learning the secrets of medicine, and their knowledge is power. We believe that to simplify and take charge of our lives, we must learn how to keep our bodies healthy and we must know what the healing process is once they get sick. We must take responsibility for healing ourselves and view health workers as our assistants rather than our healers.

A wide range of self-help health books are becoming available. A popular example is *The Well Body Book* (Samuels and Bennett), which gives advice on how to keep our bodies in good working order and develop a personal system of preventive medicine. It advocates treating the *causes* of common diseases rather than the *effects*. It includes a physical self-examination and basic diagnostic questions to assist the reader in determining what ailments really require outside medical attention. Along with the growth in feminist consciousness has come an increase in women's self-help health resources. For example, the Boston Women's Health Book Collective published *Our Bodies, Ourselves* to help women learn practical health information and skills from the personal experiences of other women. Information on feminine medical problems, the United States health-care system, and the changes needed to make the system more just for everyone are clearly presented.

Another self-help approach is to enroll in an adult education course that seeks to share medical knowledge beyond the confines of medical school. Dr. Lowell Levin of Yale's School of Public Health believes that doctors will be happier with a "self-care competent population of patients." He claims that at present doctors have to give attention to a lot of cases that do not call for professional expertise. People are so imbued with the necessity to call the doctor that they don't do things for themselves that they could do. Dr. Levin advocates the concept of "activated medicine," which teaches people the basics of primary care and gives them a greater sense of self-confidence.

Georgetown University's Center for Continuing Health Education in Maryland offers a course entitled "The Activated Patient," which attempts to demystify medical information and make it available to non-medical students.[3] The three goals of this course are first, to teach patients to save money by educating them in more effective use of health-care resources; second, to give patients a better understanding of self-help and preventive medicine; and third, to train them to do certain easy procedures and make better observations of clinical events in minor illnesses and emergencies. The course is taught by an interdisciplinary team composed of doctors, nurses, dieticians, pharmacists, and others involved in health education. The emphasis is clearly on prevention, not diagnosis. The purpose is to encourage patients to become active, rather than passive, partners in their own health care.

In San Francisco, a people's medical school has been set up by lay people for lay people, with advice from medical personnel. Such a program could be set up in your community with the help of sympathetic doctors. As patient knowledge and skills are increased, physicians will be forced to interact differently when their patients demand to participate in their own treatment.

Many people are beginning to feel the need to integrate Western medical technology with other healing concepts into a broader health-care picture. The San Andreas Health Council (SAHC) of Palo Alto, California, hopes to further this holistic approach by providing a structure for interdisciplinary health education.[4] The Council offers a diverse quarterly program of workshops and lecture-demonstrations to both health professionals and the general public, covering such topics as nutrition, pregnancy, relaxation and meditation, body care and movement, and emotional well-being. Medical doctors practice in their building and serve on their board, providing a clear link between traditional medicine and the alternative practices the Council offers.

Susan Harman Stuart, the community organizer who founded SAHC, told me she feels that there are many health problems, either stress-related or with a strong stress component (such as migraine and tension headaches, insomnia, pain, asthma, etc.), which traditional medicine can control but has had little success in curing. With the help of SAHC programs, people have come to understand more fully why they are in poor health, and have learned how to prevent health problems in the future.

One participant in the SAHC program shared this story about her personal search for better health. A woman in her sixties, she had been bothered for several years with metabolic problems and feelings of extreme tiredness. Last spring her condition worsened, and she developed hand tremors of increasing severity. She sought medical advice and was told by her doctor that the only possible cure was reduction in tension, for which he had no program to propose other than offering tranquilizer pills.

A long-time believer in the holistic approach to

health problems, and realizing that most of us learn very early to separate mind and body, she decided to try to get in touch with her body through exercise. She began to participate in yoga sessions at the San Andreas Health Council and was amazed to find that within two weeks all traces of the tremor were gone. Since then she has continued to participate in a comprehensive program for older people called Passage, which involves deep relaxation techniques, biofeedback training for stress reduction, graduated exercise, music therapy, and the study of diet. The Passage program has helped her to keep the tremor stabilized and has provided an opportunity to continue growing in awareness about herself. When she returned recently to her doctor for a checkup, he was delighted and much encouraged with the changes in her health status. Needless to say, she is too!

2. Learn About Medicines

If we are to help ourselves and save money, we need to become informed about drug usage. We live in a drug-oriented society. Drugs are overprescribed, overconsumed, often useless, and sometimes dangerous. According to the Health Policy Advisory Center study:

> For the last ten years, the drug industry has held either first, second or third place among all United States industries in terms of profitability, outdistancing such obvious money makers as the cosmetics, aerospace, recreation, and entertainment industries.[5]

Drug companies bombard doctors with millions of dollars' worth of advertising for their drugs each year. For every dollar brought in by drug sales, about twenty-five cents goes toward advertising expenses and ten cents goes into research. Medical journals are supported by drug-company advertising, which aims at so familiarizing doctors with the brand names of the advertisers that prescribing them will become an automatic response. And the process works: nine out of ten doctors prescribe brand-name drugs, producing high profits for the manufacturers and an avoidable expense for the consumer.

What can we do when we get a prescription from a doctor? Ask him to prescribe a generic formula. Prescription drugs generally have two names—a brand name popularized by advertising and a *generic* name giving the drug's chemical identity. According to the Food and Drug Administration, generic drugs are generally cheaper (sometimes very much so) and comparable in quality and strength to their more expensive brand-name counterparts.

Most drugs carry a seventeen-year patent or copyright, and only after it expires can another company make the same drug without the patent owner's permission. Companies often extend the patent by issuing new dosage forms (chewable rather than liquid, for example), by making minor molecular changes in the drug's chemical structure, or by offering it in combination with other drugs. Detailed information about drug prices, composition, side effects, and comparative efficacy is available in Richard Burack's *New Handbook of Prescription Drugs*.

By requesting prescriptions by generic name from our doctors and pharmacists, we can hope to save a great deal of money.

It is important to build up a relationship of trust with your pharmacist and to keep careful records of all drug purchases and your reactions, if any, to the drugs. Be suspicious if your doctor prescribes a drug for every ailment. Always ask that the drug's name, correct dosage, and indication of usage be recorded on the container. Drug companies are required to include a labeling leaflet for each drug they produce. Ask for this leaflet, which includes a full chemical description of the drug and the hazards, if any, involved in its use. It is important to cross-check your prescriptions for drug combinations that might be antagonistic to each other when taken simultaneously.

We are even more susceptible to manipulation when buying nonprescription, or over-the-counter, drugs. Looser control of these drugs make them potentially more dangerous to consumers. The same is true for herbal medicines, which are increasing in popularity. There is currently virtually no quality control or monitoring of herbal remedies sold commercially.

Along with the movement toward natural foods and simpler living, there seems to be a revival of interest in the "tried and true" home remedies some of us recall our grandparents using to heal us—for example, hot apple cider vinegar and honey tea to soothe sore throats or camomile tea to calm one's tummy. Some people feel that many health problems created by synthetic drugs could be eliminated by relearning and relying more upon these old folk remedies. This is a field that is worth exploring.

3. Stick Up for Your Rights

We have the right to have explained to us the cause, prevention, and treatment of our medical complaints in words we can understand. Often doctors use "medi-code" to explain things to us, hoping to intimidate us and discourage us from asking further questions. We should insist on seeing our medical records and being included in decision making about our health care. Doctors and hospitals are supposed to serve the people; they have an obligation to help their patients. Health care is, after all, a basic human right.

As a patient, you should insist on "informed consent"; no doctor or hospital can perform a surgical procedure or medical treatment on you without your consent. Before you say yes or no, you have a right to know what treatment the doctor wants to use and why, what other treatments are possible and why this is the best one, whether this is for *your* benefit or for research, how risky it will be, how much it will cost, and whatever else you need to know to make a considered, informed, uncoerced decision.

Confidentiality is also a patient's right. Your medical records are strictly private, and the doctor or hospital cannot legally release them without your consent. Likewise, you have a right to privacy while you are in a hospital. You have a right to know who is the person responsible for taking care of you, and you needn't put up with medical students or other onlookers. Hospital workers should treat you with respect and dignity. Unfortunately, doctors and nurses may forget your personal needs and treat you impersonally. You must insist on being treated properly, which is often difficult when you are sick, because energy levels are low. One way of getting around this problem would be to have patient advocates in every hospital, whose job would cover explaining, supporting, and enforcing the above-mentioned rights and acting as a liaison between patients, doctors, nurses, and hospital workers.

4. Investigate Local Health-Care Services

The wide range of medical services currently available extends from individual practices to single or multispecialty group practices, prepaid group plans, and community clinics. Taking a careful look at what's available in your community will help you be an informed consumer. An area where patients can gain some power is in evaluating the services of existing doctors. There is now a guidebook available on how to develop a consumer's directory of doctors for any local community.[6] Some areas of concern covered in such a directory are fees; emergency arrangements, including housecalls; affiliation with local hospitals; and prescription policies.

Another way for lay people to have influence is in challenging a hospital's accreditation standing.[7] Hospital funding often goes towards prestigious and "professionally interesting" specialties rather than into the basic needs of community people. Consumers from the area that a hospital serves have the right to testify at public hearings held biannually by the Joint Commission on Accreditation of Hospitals. All hospitals are very concerned about their accreditation, because interns and residents who are training to be doctors may not get credit for their work unless the hospital is approved. Also without accreditation the hospital cannot receive money from Medicare. Citizen participation in a JCAH hearing provides valuable information for all parties, regardless of the outcome.

5. Support Alternative Health Systems

Many communities now have neighborhood-based health centers controlled by the patients and workers who use them. These alternative clinics are attempting to radically restructure the health-care delivery system in this country and reorient us toward community health care. Most community clinics seek to combine crisis intervention and primary care with health maintenence concepts into a balanced, inexpensive, and responsive system. Often they operate on shoestring budgets with all volunteer labor, under considerable pressure from the medical establishment. Yet to us they represent important beginnings. The fact that increasing numbers of people are being seen by alternative clinics indicates the continuing need for them and shows that their base of service has broadened to include senior citizens, families affected by unemployment, minorities, etc., as well as the street people they were often first created to serve. The two major problems they face are fund raising and recruiting volunteer medical staff. One study of several community-based free clinics indicated that a particular organizational structure, centered on a paid administrator responsible for securing funds and staff, increased the survival potential of such facilities.[8]

The Country Doctor Community Clinic in Seattle, Washington, is an example of a local, nonprofit health-care center that offers primary care with a preventive focus.[9] Begun in 1971, it was founded on the belief that health care is a human right, not the privilege of the wealthy. "Country Doc," as it is called by the local people, is financed primarily by donations from the people who are treated at the clinic—about a thousand patients a month. They have a suggested fee schedule posted for the various treatments they offer, but no one is turned away for lack of funds. Considerable funds have also been raised by church and community groups in the surrounding Capitol Hill neighborhood it serves. Patients of all ages can get medical help at Country Doc. Daily from noon to five, a "continuity clinic" is held for people who need care on an ongoing basis—

children, those with chronic problems, and the elderly. One morning a week is devoted to nutrition; one afternoon is especially focused on people over forty. The clinic is open five nights a week—three nights for everyone, one for pediatric care, and one for women.

The Country Doctor clinic places a high value on transferring medical skills. The clinic's paid staff consists of a nonhierarchical collective of twenty-two members, plus over a hundred volunteers. Two medical doctors work full-time. One of them is licensed in acupuncture. Working with them are three certified physician-assistants, and four more in training. Many other doctors volunteer their time at the clinic whenever possible. The rest of the staff and many of the volunteers have been trained as patient advocates, who help patients understand the treatment procedures performed at the clinic and who ensure follow-up and referral if necessary. Often an advocate will accompany a patient to a hospital appointment or help make the necessary arrangements for Medicare or Medicaid.

Country Doctor's facilities, in a former fire station, include consultation and treatment rooms, a fully stocked pharmacy, and even a medical library. The clinic has also published a book called *Healing Yourself,* explaining how to use herbs, vitamins, and other home remedies, not as a substitute for good doctoring but as a preventive measure. One of the clinic staff reported to me, "The success of the clinic shows that alternatives can be found if people don't like existing structures. Country Doctor helps people, and is effective for just that reason."

There is an ancient Chinese practice of paying a physician to keep you well, and not paying him if you become sick, because this represents a failure of care on his part. Dr. John Travis of Mill Valley, California, has opened a Wellness Resource Center, based on this notion of maintaining wellness.[10] "High-level wellness," he says, "means giving good care to your physical self, using your mind constructively, expressing your emotions, being creatively involved with those around you, being aware of your physical and psychological environment." He contends that there are no patients in well medicine, only clients. Patients tend to wait for their doctor to *do* something *for them*. Clients, on the other hand, take responsibility for themselves and their health, using health resource consultants to further their own evolution.

Wellness is not a static state. Most of us still think in terms of illness and assume that its absence indicates wellness. But there are different degrees of wellness just as there are different degrees of sickness. Many people, though they lack obvious physical symptoms of illness, are bored, depressed, tense, anxious, or generally unhappy with their lives. These emotional states often lead to physical disease through the lowering of the body's resistance. The same feelings can lead to abuse of the body through smoking, drinking, and overeating. The Wellness Resource Center's program seeks to address the various levels of sickness and wellness in our lives and help us along the path to high-level wellness. Through a series of questionnaires—a health hazard appraisal, a wellness inventory, a nutritional survey, and several others—data are collected about a person, from which a plan of action can be drawn up. This might be training in relaxation using biofeedback machines, or group work on improving how we relate to others and express our feelings, or programs in physical fitness and nutritional awareness. How we proceed on the journey toward wellness is up to us!

Wellness and alternatives to conventional health insurance are major concerns of a small group in Philadelphia called the Mountain Thyme Health-Caring Group, who describe themselves as a support community offering each other mutual aid of many kinds.[11] Living simply and having very little money, most of them had no medical insurance before developing their own alternative plan several years ago. Presently numbering about twenty people, between the ages of twenty and forty, each contributes fifty dollars a year to a cumulative community fund available to group members for three specific purposes. First, it is available to cover medical costs in the range of $100 to $1,000. Anything under that is handled by the individual. The group is too small to cover catastrophic medical bills, and it intends to stay small. Second, the fund is used to help members gain skill and knowledge in paramedical work, nutrition, and other health-related areas, primarily by financing participation in health conferences and training programs. Third, it is loaned out as financial support to groups working to bring about change in our medical system. Since most members of the group have been healthy so far, the bulk of the money has not been disbursed for individual needs. It is currently on loan at no interest to a Mennonite medical clinic working with poor people in Appalachia and is returnable on demand.

The Mountain Thyme Health-Caring Group members share many common values and assumptions— among them, a major interest in preventive medicine. Members have developed a lending library of health-related materials, and they share skills and experiences of alternative health and healing methods. When a community member is sick, other members offer support via letters, visits, prayer, advocacy during medical appointments, and home nursing. As one group member told me, "For fifty dollars a year I have help in meeting my medical expenses *and* a supportive group of people who will help me keep well and sustain me if I do get sick. And I don't have to support the big insurance companies in the process!"

From the perspective of simple living, we can say that we seek a health-care system that strives towards wellness and emphasizes health rather than sickness. We seek to encourage the growth of alternative and small-scale health institutions like Country Doctor Community Clinic and the Wellness Resource Center. At the same time, we need to be challenging existing institutions and making them more responsive to our needs. We need to work toward a healthier society, too, in which nutritious food is available for everyone, pollution is controlled, consumer products are made safe, and drugs and cigarettes are not pushed by advertising. Most of all, we need informed consumers of health care, who can take care of themselves as much as possible and demand quality care if they need it.

From the WELLNESS INVENTORY
Wellness Resource Center, Mill Valley, California

This questionnaire will help give you an idea about where you presently are on the wellness scale. It is not intended to be all-inclusive, but rather a representative sampling of ideas.

PRODUCTIVITY, RELAXATION, SLEEP

- [ ] I usually enjoy my work.
- [ ] I seldom feel tired and rundown (except after strenuous work).
- [ ] I fall asleep easily at bedtime.
- [ ] I usually get a full night's sleep.
- [ ] If awakened, it is usually easy for me to go to sleep again.
- [ ] I rarely bite or pick at my nails.
- [ ] Rather than worrying, I can temporarily shelve my problems and enjoy myself at times when I can do nothing about solving them immediately.
- [ ] I feel financially secure.
- [ ] I am content with my sexual life.
- [ ] I meditate or center myself for 15 to 20 minutes at least once a day.

PERSONAL CARE AND HOME SAFETY

- [ ] I take measures to protect my living space from fire and safety hazards (including improper sized fuses and storage of volatile chemicals).
- [ ] I have a dry chemical fire extinguisher in my kitchen and at least one other extinguisher elsewhere in my living quarters. (If very small apartment, kitchen extinguisher alone is adequate).
- [ ] I regularly use dental floss and a soft toothbrush.
- [ ] I smoke less than one pack of cigarets or equivalent cigars or pipes per week.
- [ ] I don't smoke at all (if this statement is true, mark item above true as well).
- [ ] I keep an up-to-date record of my immunizations.
- [ ] I have fewer than three colds per year.
- [ ] I minimize my exposure to sprays, chemical fumes or exhaust gases.
- [ ] I avoid extremely noisy areas (or wear protective ear plugs).
- [ ] I am aware of changes in my physical or mental state and seek professional advice about any which seem unusual.

NUTRITIONAL AWARENESS

☐ I eat at least one uncooked fruit or vegetable each day.
☐ I have less than three alcoholic drinks (including beers) per week.
☐ I rarely take medications, including prescription drugs.
☐ I drink less than five soft drinks per week.
☐ I avoid eating many refined foods or foods with sugar added.
☐ I add litle salt to my food.
☐ I read the labels for the ingredients of the foods I buy.
☐ I usually eat nutritionally balanced meals.
☐ I drink less than three cups of coffee or tea (with the exception of herbal teas) a day.
☐ I have a good appetite and maintain a weight within 15% of my ideal weight.

PHYSICAL ACTIVITY

☐ I climb stairs rather than ride elevators.
☐ My daily activities include moderate physical effort (such as raising young children, gardening, scrubbing floors or factory work which involves being on my feet, etc.).
☐ My daily activities include vigorous physical effort (such as heavy construction work, farming, moving heavy objects by hand, etc.).
☐ I jog at least one mile twice a week (or equivalent aerobic exercise).
☐ I jog at least one mile four times a week or equivalent (if this statement is true, mark the item above true as well).
☐ I regularly walk or ride a bike for exercise.
☐ I participate in a strenuous sport at least once a week.
☐ I participate in a strenuous sport more than once a week (if this statement is true, mark the item above as well).
☐ I do yoga or some form of stretching-limbering exercise for 15 to 20 minutes at least twice per week.
☐ I do yoga or some form of stretching exercise for 15 to 20 minutes at least four times per week (if this statement is true, mark the item above true as well).

EMOTIONAL MATURITY AND EXPRESSION OF FEELINGS

- ☐ I am frequently happy.
- ☐ I think it is OK to feel angry, afraid, joyful or sad.
- ☐ I do not deny my anger, fear, joy or sadness, but instead find constructive ways to express these feelings most of the time.
- ☐ I am able to say "no" to people without feeling guilty.
- ☐ It is easy for me to laugh.
- ☐ I like getting compliments and recognition from other people.
- ☐ I feel OK about crying, and allow myself to do so.
- ☐ I listen to and think about constructive criticism rather than react defensively.
- ☐ I would seek help from friends or professional counselors if needed.
- ☐ It is easy for me to give other people sincere compliments and recognition.

COMMUNITY INVOLVEMENT

- ☐ I keep informed of local, national and world events.
- ☐ I vote regularly.
- ☐ I take interest in community, national and world events and work to support issues and people of my choice. (If this statement is true, mark both items above true as well.)
- ☐ When I am able, I contribute time or money to worthy causes.
- ☐ I make an attempt to know my neighbors and be on good terms with them.
- ☐ I would at least call the police if I saw a crime being committed.
- ☐ If I saw a broken bottle lying in the road, or on the sidewalk, I would remove it.
- ☐ When driving, I am considerate of pedestrians and other drivers.
- ☐ If I saw a car with faulty lights, leaking gasoline or another dangerous condition, I would attempt to inform the driver.
- ☐ I am a member of one or more community organizations (social change group, singing group, club, church or political group).

CREATIVITY, SELF EXPRESSION

☐ I enjoy expressing myself through art, dance, music, drama, sports, etc.

☐ I enjoy spending some time without planned or structured activities.

☐ I usually meet several people a month who I would like to get to know better.

☐ I enjoy touching other people.

☐ I enjoy being touched by other people.

☐ I have at least five close friends.

☐ At times I like to be alone.

☐ I like myself and look forward to the future.

☐ I look forward to living to be at least 75.

☐ I find it easy to express concern, love and warmth to those I care about.

(The complete Wellness Inventory contains over 100 items, including sections on Environmental Awareness, Automobile Safety, and Parenting.)

NOTES

1. Barbara Ehrenreich and John Ehrenreich, *The American Health Empire: Power, Profits and Politics* (New York: Random House, 1970), p. 97.

2. Testimony of Melvin Glasser, U.A.W., before the Senate Subcommittee on Health, July 21, 1971.

3. For further information on this course, write Keith W. Sehnert, M.D., Course for the Activated Patient, Center for Continuing Health Education, Georgetown University, Washington DC 20057; or John H. Renner, M.D., Chairman, Department of Family Medicine and Practice, 777 South Mills Street, Madison WI 53715 (formerly at Georgetown).

4. The San Andreas Health Council is located at 531 Cowper Street, Palo Alto CA 94301.

5. Ehrenreich and Ehrenreich *op. cit.*, p. 99.

6. *A Guide for Compiling a Consumer's Directory of Doctors* is available from Public Citizen's Health Research Group, 2000 P Street N.W., Dept. D., Room 708, Washington DC 20036.

7. *The Accreditation of Hospitals: A Guide for Health Consumers and Workers* is available from the Health

Law Project, University of Pennsylvania Law School, 133 South 36th, Philadelphia PA 19104.

8. Forest S. Tennant and Carmel M. Day, "Survival Potential and Quality of Care Among Free Clinics," an article in the November-December 1974 issue of *Public Health Reports,* vol. 89, no. 6.

9. Country Doctor is located at 402 15th East, Seattle, WA 98112.

10. Dr. John Travis and the Wellness Resource Center are located at 42 Miller Avenue, Mill Valley, CA 94941.

11. Requests for information about this group should be sent to The Mountain Thyme Health-Caring Group, c/o Donna Lord, 1006 South 46th St., Philadelphia PA 19143.

SOURCES OF FURTHER INFORMATION

Books About the System

Bodenheimer, Tom; Cummings, Steve; and Harding, Elizabeth (editors). *Billions for Bandaids.* San Francisco: Bay Area Chapter, Medical Committee for Human Rights, 1972.

Carlson, Richard J. *The End of Medicine.* New York: John Wiley and Sons, 1975.

Ehrenreich, Barbara, and Ehrenreich, John. *The American Health Empire: Power, Profits, and Politics.* New York: Random House, 1970.

Illich, Ivan. *Medical Nemesis: The Expropriation of Health.* New York: Random House, 1976.

Placere, Morris N., and Marwick, Charles S. *How You Can Get Better Medical Care for Less Money.* New York: Walker and Co., 1973.

Somers, Anne R. *Health Care in Transition: Directions for the Future.* Chicago: Hospital Research and Education Trust, 1971.

Source Collective. *Organizing for Health Care: A Tool for Change.* Boston: Beacon Press, 1974.

Self-help Resources

Bairachi-Levy, Juliette. *Common Herbs for Natural Health.* New York: Schocken, 1974.

Boston Women's Health Book Collective. *Our Bodies,*

Ourselves: A Book by and for Women. New York: Simon and Schuster, 1971.

Burack, Richard, M.D. *The New Handbook of Prescription Drugs*. New York: Ballantine Books, 1970.

Clark, Linda. *Know Your Nutrition*. New Canaan, Conn.: Keats, 1973.

Consumer Reports (editors). *The Medicine Show*. New York: Pantheon Books, 1974.

Cooper, Kenneth H. *The New Aerobics*. New York: Bantam, 1970.

Frank, Arthur, and Frank, Stuart. *People's Handbook of Medical Care*. New York: Vintage, 1972.

Luce, Gay Gaer. *Body Time: Physiological Rhythms and Social Stress*. New York: Bantam, 1971.

McCamey, John C., M.D., and Presley, James. *Human Life Styling: Keeping Whole in the Twentieth Century*. New York: Harper and Row, 1975.

McGuire, Thomas, D.D.S. *The Tooth Trip*. New York: Random House/Bookworks, 1972.

McQuade, Walter, and Aikman, Ann. *Stress*. New York: Bantam, 1974.

Muramoto, Naboru. *Healing Ourselves*. New York: Avon Books, 1973.

Oyle, Irving. *The Healing Mind*. Millbrae, Calif.: Celestial Arts, 1974.

Prensky, Joyce (editor). *Healing Yourself*. Seattle, Wash.: Country Doctor Community Clinic, 1975.

Public Citizen's Health Research Group. *A Guide for Compiling a Consumer's Directory of Doctors*. Washington, D.C.: Public Citizen's Health Research Group, 1974.

Rodale, Robert. *The Best Health Ideas I Know*. New York: Avon Books, 1974.

Samuels, Mike, M.D., and Bennett, Hal. *The Well Body Book*. New York: Random House/Bookworks, 1973.

Shiller, Jack G. *Childhood Illness: A Common Sense Approach*. New York: Stein and Day, 1974.

Sobel, David Stuart, and Hombacher, Faith Louise. *An Everyday Guide to Your Health*. New York: Grossman, 1973.

11

Using Energy and Living Simply

BY JACK STUART

everdell

Civilization in this country, according to some, would be inconceivable if we used only, say, half as much electricity as now. But that is what we did use in 1963, when we were at least half as civilized as now.[1]

— *Amory B. Lovins*

Queries

1. Do I still think of energy as being available in unlimited amounts, or am I moving toward understanding it as a limited set of resources to be used carefully and conserved? Do I have some control over the energy-consumption level in our society, or is it the result of social and corporate policies that I had little or no part in setting?

2. Even if energy were available at a reasonable price, would continued increases in our society's use of it really benefit me and society? Or would it produce social and psychological problems in much the same way that it now produces physical problems such as pollution of the environment?

3. If the energy companies in my area are privately owned, do I know how their rates compare with those charged by publicly owned utilities of similar size? Would municipal or cooperative ownership reduce my electric and fuel bills? Could such changes in ownership and control help America become an energy-conserving society?

4. Does public transportation in my area provide a real alternative to automobile travel? If not, what changes in tax and other public policies would make possible the building of a regional public transit system that could actually meet the day-to-day needs of the people?

5. Do I know what portion of the national energy we use goes for military purposes such as keeping SAC bombers in the air around the clock, conducting

military exercises, and maintaining our forces around the world? Can I think of more efficient and peace-promoting ways to use these resoruces?

How can we satisfy our growing appetite for energy? Though this question is often asked, it is hard to answer. The energy issue isn't just a matter of finding, developing, and applying new sources of power to replace the ones that are disappearing or damaging the environment. Instead, it involves a complex of interrelated processes that profoundly affect the way we live. In our discussion of energy, we have to consider all these processes—economic, technological, political, social, and environmental. From the perspective of simple living, a better question to ask might be, How can we move toward using our fair share of energy with due regard to all the consequences of doing so?

Growth of Energy Consumption

Today Americans use up more energy per person than anyone else on earth. Until recently, the only constraint on consumption was its immediate cost. Even now, with more frequent shortages and higher prices, most of us act as if there were no limit to the amount of energy we can consume. With only 6 percent of the world's population, we use more than 60 percent of the natural gas, 35 percent of the petroleum, and 30 percent of most other energy resources.[2] On the average, we consume energy at twice the rate of Western Europe, where the way of life can be considered modern and similar to our own.[3]

West Germany is a case in point. Many German industrial plants generate some of their own electricity instead of buying it all from public utilities. "Waste" heat, often left to dissipate in the United States, is piped into homes, offices, hospitals, schools, and apartment buildings. West German houses and rooms are smaller than ours, and Germans often leave parts of the house, such as bedrooms, cold. Germans heat hot water with small devices at the point of use, e.g., above kitchen taps, rather than maintain large hot-water tanks.[4] These examples suggest that it may be possible for Americans to lower their present energy use significantly.

Today, with a population four times what it was a century ago, we use twelve times as much energy as we did then. How did we get to this point? For one thing, population and per-capita consumption have a multiplier effect; together they raise energy use more than either factor would by itself. Not only do more people use more energy, but the more money they have the more they buy and the more energy-intensive technology goes into the goods they buy.

Table 1 shows the startling increases since World War II in the use of various items that require large quantities of energy to manufacture. Note that, although most of us think gasoline consumption has gone up a lot since the war, it appears near the bottom

Table 1
Consumption Growth Since World War II[5]

Item	% Increase
Nonreturnable bottles	53,000
Synthetic fibers	5,980
Air conditioner compressor units	2,850
Plastics	1,960
Fertilizer nitrogen	1,050
Electric housewares	1,040
Synthetic organic chemicals	950
Aluminum	680
Electric power	530
Pesticides	390
Wood pulp	313
Truck freight	222
Consumer electronics	217
Motor fuel consumption	190
Cement	150

of the list. Other things we now consider necessary or at least ubiquitous have increased much more, such as electric appliances (how many did your parents or grandparents have forty years ago?), plastics, synthetic fibers (how many things you wear don't have polyester in them?), and especially disposable bottles and cans. These throwaway containers use up the energy equivalent of millions of barrels of oil yearly. One observer has estimated that by not recycling two aluminum beer cans, we waste more energy than each person in the poorest third of the world's people uses daily.[6]

Though farming has supposedly become more efficient, the energy involved in producing food has grown too. In 1910 it took an average of one calorie of energy to produce, prepare, and put on the table one calorie of food in the United States. It now takes an average of ten calories of energy to put one calorie of food on the table.[7] This astounding figure is attributed mainly to the energy now devoted to fertilizer production, manufacture and use of farm machinery, long-distance transportation, and food-processing technology.

The growth of the military since 1940 has also contributed to our increased energy diet. Before 1940 we had no large standing army during peacetime, but since World War II and the Cold War, things have changed. Now we maintain a vast arsenal and garrison all over the world. A larger percentage of the government's tax revenues goes into the *development* and *procurement* of weapons than into any other single item.[8] Even without the vast amounts of waste that have been reported, military spending would require prodigious quantities of energy. And this spending is unproductive in economic as well as social terms, because all that hardware is not used to produce anything. Military production robs the economy of valuable resources, the hardware in turn lies idle, and thus the inflation rate rises.

Recent trends in the transportation industry, which uses about a quarter of the U.S. energy budget, are also significant. Transportation depends on petroleum, and the transportation, petroleum, and petrochemical industries are dominated by twenty major corporations which have together determined how this resource would be used. Our transportation system in the last thirty years has systematically eliminated the most efficient modes of freight and passenger traffic—the railroads and intercity trolleys—and replaced them with

trucks and cars, which require much more fuel and
capital and which have a much more devastating effect
on the environment. Further, passenger cars have
changed from relatively low-speed, low-compression
engines to high-speed, high-compression engines which
use more gas and produce more pollutants. The charge
is frequently made that U.S. companies have favored
inefficient transportation because cars and trucks are
more profitable than trolleys and trains.[9]

In the area of industrial manufacturing, other important changes have taken place. Shirts and dresses
are now often made of synthetics rather than cotton;
shoes, luggage, and purses are made of plastic instead
of leather; food and consumer goods are more packaged, and the packaging is made of plastic rather than
paper, wood, or cloth; people and freight move by
plane, trucks, and large cars instead of by train and
low-powered cars; people travel farther between their
homes and their jobs. All of these changes have required more energy and done more damage to the
environment. They have also meant increased profits
for the manufacturers.

It is clear that the trend of increasing energy use
cannot continue, even if we want it to. Our main
sources of energy have been the fossil fuels—coal,
petroleum, and natural gas—developed over millions
of years from the remains of prehistoric plants and
animals buried under layers of sedimentary rock. These
hydrocarbon fuels have been valuable because long,
slow chemical change has concentrated great energy
in a relatively small volume of material. They have also
been abundant and readily obtained. But these fuels
are not renewable, and we are running out of them.
Assuming major new deposits are not found, it appears
we will run out of natural gas and oil before the end
of this century and coal by the end of the next century.[10]
As these fuels become more scarce, it becomes more
expensive to obtain them, both economically and environmentally. Higher costs will result in increased
centralization of the energy industry and greater pollution.

Our other great source of power—hydroelectricity—

has reached the limit of its development. Nearly all potentially useful and economically feasible dam sites have been exploited over the last several decades. The high costs of building new hydroelectric plants in this country probably outweigh the value of the energy that could be derived from them.[11]

Most new sources of energy are still being developed or debated. Because of the government's and industry's emphasis on nuclear energy and new methods of fossil fuel extraction, none of the most promising possibilities, such as solar power, have more than gotten off the ground. But even if all possible sources of energy were being developed to their full potential, there would be a finite limit to the amount of energy that could be consumed on this planet without raising the temperature of the atmosphere to unacceptable levels and thereby altering the biosphere. It has been estimated that an average increase worldwide of only a few degrees could radically change climate, agriculture, the level of the oceans, and life as we know it.

Such finite limits on the use of energy have implications for economic growth. Economic growth is usually equated with industrial development, higher production, greater consumption of goods and services, long-distance transportation, centralization, and so on. All of these things require more energy. Obviously, if energy is limited, economic growth must be limited too. Moving from this growth orientation to a steady-state economy (one in which there is no net growth, but where growth in one sector is matched by cutbacks in another) is going to be one of the major challenges of the next decades.

Net Energy

It takes energy to make energy. Research, exploration, development, delivery, and cleanup all require an investment of energy. The coal has to be mined, shipped to the power plant (which itself has to be built, the end of another energy chain), converted by furnaces and generators to electricity, carried along power lines to substations, and distributed to the consumer, who must have his own capital plant (wiring, switches, appliances, and so on) to be able to use it. To have any meaning, the productivity and efficiency of any energy source must be expressed in terms of *net* energy—the amount of energy delivered minus the amount of energy used to produce it and get it there. If the energy cost of delivering one kilowatt of electricity is one kilowatt, then we're like a squirrel on a treadmill—getting nowhere.

The concept of net energy is essential for evaluating the future of our energy resources, because as oil, coal, uranium, and other nonrenewable fuels become scarcer, we have to work harder and use more energy to get them, whether by offshore drilling, extracting oil from shale, strip-mining coal (which also involves restoring the land after the coal has been taken out), or developing energy-intensive ways of recycling uranium. It's not just our own gas or electric bill we should be concerned about; it's also the amount of energy the power company has to use to get it to us, and how that amount affects the whole energy picture.

Another way of expressing the relationship between the energy we use and the energy the power company uses to produce it is by means of the important concept of efficiency. Efficiency is simply the ratio of the useful energy we get from a power source to the energy we put into it, usually written as a percentage (for example, conventional power plants are said to be around 35-percent efficient). Physicists and chemists like to talk about efficiency in terms of what they call thermodynamics, or the conversion of heat energy into mechanical motion, or work. The First Law of Thermodynamics (called a law because it has never been shown to be wrong) states that when one form of energy is converted into another, such as when the chemical energy of coal is converted to heat, no energy is gained or lost—it is only changed in form. That is, energy is always conserved. What this means is that if only 35 percent of the energy in coal comes out as electricity, the other 65 percent doesn't just disappear. It has to go somewhere, and it is usually dissipated to the environment as waste heat. The heat given off by a light bulb, an automobile engine, or a power plant is waste heat. If present in large enough quantity, waste heat can change climate, harm wildlife, and otherwise degrade the environment. But if waste heat can be captured and used to perform other tasks, such as heating a building, then efficiency is increased.

The value of energy is, obviously, its capacity for doing work—boiling water, spinning a turbine, running a motor—when it is converted from one form into another. The Second Law of Thermodynamics states that whenever energy is transferred from one system to another (or converted from one form to another), such as from a boiler to a turbine, the amount of it that is actually available for doing work is diminished. This principle doesn't contradict the First Law; the missing energy isn't destroyed, it is simply lost to the system (boiler, turbine, motor), usually as waste heat or motion (exhaust, friction, vibration).

From these two principles we can see that the farther energy flows from its original source through a series of transfer steps, the less of it will be available at the end of the chain to do the work we intend it to do. We can also begin to see the advantages of having a decentralized energy distribution system; not only do we have more control over our energy use, but also the energy is used more efficiently, because it doesn't have as far to travel.

Similarly, the bigger the difference between the total potential energy of the source and the energy required to perform the needed task, the lower the efficiency of that kind of energy for that task. An efficient system is one in which the energy source closely matches the work to be done. A blast furnace would be an inefficient way to toast a marshmallow, because most of the heat would be wasted. It can also be said that a nuclear reactor is an inefficient way to produce electricity, because only a small amount of the heat generated is needed to convert water into steam. Only by matching low-energy tasks with low-level energy and high-energy tasks with high-level energy can we have efficient energy use; only in this way can we get our money's— and our energy's—worth.

Nuclear Power

For two decades the government and the power companies have been committed to the development of nuclear power as the answer to our need for a continuous source of energy. Nuclear power plants produce electricity the same way conventional power plants do—by spinning the turbines of generators which convert mechanical energy into electrical energy. In nuclear plants, these turbines are spun by the steam that results when water is heated by the splitting of uranium nuclei. This reaction is a controlled version of the same chain reaction that produced the atomic bomb. In conventional plants the water is heated by burning coal or oil. Hydroelectric plants use the force of falling water to spin their turbines. Because there is more potential energy in a gram of uranium than in a gram of coal, it takes much less fuel to power a nuclear plant than a conventional one.

One of the supposed advantages of nuclear power plants is that they can produce less expensive electricity than coal—or oil-burning plants as long as there is a readily mined source of uranium ore. But U.S. reserves of this ore are limited, with only enough to fuel the reactors we already have until the end of this century. If the construction of nuclear power plants continues, however, the industry will be compelled to travel outside of this country to find the necessary uranium ore. As dependence on foreign sources grows and uranium prices increase yearly, it is important to recognize that unilateral price hikes by the ore-producing nations (which includes South Africa), or even uranium embargoes, could develop. The attendant economic and political crises, similar to the ones resulting from OPEC policies of the recent past, are formidable indeed.

But the government and the power companies have

refused to take these factors into account, and continue to promote the development of nuclear power. So billions of dollars have been poured into the development of the "breeder" reactor, which, as its name suggests, would produce more fuel than it used up. The fuel is plutonium—every time two plutonium nuclei split, three new plutonium atoms are created. But the breeder reactor has not advanced much beyond the experimental stage.

Nuclear power advocates also claim their energy is environmentally safe—it doesn't add smoke, hydrocarbons, or sulphur compounds to the environment like coal and petroleum do. However, these arguments dangerously overlook the fact that nuclear fuel, either uranium or plutonium-239, and their by-products, in the form of radiation, are potentially the most harmful substances on earth.

Plutonium-239 is the most poisonous element ever handled in quantity by man, and its half-life is 24,400 years. It has been estimated that one pound of this enormously toxic substance has the potential for *nine billion* human cancer doses.[12] Given the energy industry's pursuit of plutonium-based breeder reactors, "the annual handling of plutonium-239 in a fully developed nuclear power economy will be in the one-hundred-ton category, or some 200,000 pounds annually. Comparing this with the one pound that can provide an intolerable potential lung cancer burden, we estimate that better than 99.999 percent containment of plutonium-239 is hardly good enough to avert disaster. . . . Who can guarantee the requisite containment of plutonium-239 will be achieved?"[13]

The problem continues with the storage of radioactive wastes and the containment of its radiation. Each nuclear power reactor produces toxic radioactive waste similar to fallout from atomic bombs. The energy companies and the federal government continue to pursue a policy of nuclear energy development, even though a thoroughly safe method of disposal has *not* been found, nor has a permanent waste-disposal site been established. At present, there are 100 million gallons of radioactive waste stored at various sites across the United States. In the state of Washington, the Hanford storage site has leaked half a million gallons of radioactive waste, caused by the corrosion of containers and resulting in permanent contamination.

Plans for the future call for solidification of all commercial wastes and their shipment to a "Federal Interim Storage Facility." Plans for permanent storage do not exist, since no truly safe depositories have been located. A reliance on nuclear fission power is thus, in Alvin Weinberg's words, a " 'Faustian bargain,' in which the safety, health, and freedom of future generations are traded for ample and cheap power for ourselves."[14]

Supporters of nuclear power development claim that so many safeguards have been engineered into the system that the likelihood of serious accidents is very small. Some careful research shatters this initial contention, and raises even more serious problems. If reactor technology is so safe, why have the energy and insurance companies persistently refused to pay for any damages resulting from accidents? Rather than directing business to share the burden of economic readjustment in the event of damage, the federal government has shifted responsibility entirely onto the taxpayers. The result is a $560 million insurance bill paid completely by the public. This is a staggering sum of money, yet wholly inadequate to cover the *billions* in property damage that could result from even one serious accident.

Even if safeguards could insure technological stability in the nuclear power industry, they would not address themselves to the problems of war and terrorism. It must never be forgotten that the "peaceful" atom is actually the hand-maiden of nuclear armaments. Advancement in plutonium research will surely be transferred to the military for incorporation into nuclear warfare. Each improvement in nuclear energy technology, every political guarantee given to the energy companies and government agencies such as the Energy Research and Development Agency will result in a strengthening of a military that can already destroy the world fourteen times over.

Political terrorism and blackmail also become much more dangerous as nuclear power proliferates. Plutonium fuel is used in the production of nuclear bombs (about 20 pounds of plutonium fuel can make an atom bomb), and bomb technology can easily be found in physics books or encyclopedias. At present, nine countries possess nuclear armaments capability. "By 1980, fifty countries will have enough plutonium from nuclear power and research reactors to make several thousand atom bombs. Just a one-percent diversion of this plutonium per year into atom bombs would make a farce out of the Nuclear Non-Proliferation Treaty" and endanger the lives of all of us. Attempts to cope with the threat of stolen plutonium and sabotaged nuclear facilities could lead to a police state. In 1975 the Nuclear Regulatory Commission commissioned the "Barton Paper" which raised the possibility of a special police force empowered to conduct domestic surveillance without a court order, detain nuclear critics and dissident scientists without filing charges, and under certain circumstances to torture suspected nuclear terrorists.[16]

The nuclear power industry also shares the same "public relations" bed with the armaments industry and the military. The desire is to increase employment, and nuclear power advocates maintain that a program of reactor development will do just that. However, nuclear power plant development is a *capital-intensive* project; an operating plant requires only 125–150 workers, and most of them would be highly trained technicians. In addition, nuclear facilities attract only businesses that need large amounts of electricity; these generally are firms that are highly automated, and employ few workers.

The cost of nuclear plant construction is also a vital factor in the economics of power. The price tag on proposed plutonium-enriched breeder reactors has increased greatly in recent years. "Total costs for the breeder program are now estimated at $10 billion, up from original estimates of less than half that amount. Cost estimates for a breeder prototype have gone from $700 million to $1.95 billion. A breeder facility in Washington state now is to cost $933 million up from $87 million."[17] The inflationary aspects of the diminishing supply of uranium ore, and in the basic construction of nuclear power plants are in evidence. Our currently troubled economy can ill afford to develop and maintain such a program.

If all the problems associated with nuclear power were somehow to be solved, what would the effect of "unlimited power" on society and the environment be? We know from our earlier discussion that the amount of energy that can be used from any source is limited by the fact that our biosphere is a closed system; the waste heat given off by energy consumption would build up inside the system, unable to dissipate beyond the atmosphere, until radical and eventually harmful changes took place. But short of such drastic consequences, there would be subtler, more quickly felt changes. The trends of the last thirty years would continue. Power and wealth would continue to be concentrated in the hands of fewer and fewer large corporations, military spending would increase, industry and agriculture would use more synthetic materials and higher technology, waste and pollution would be encouraged, consumption of consumer goods would rise along with inflation and unemployment, and government and commerce would be increasingly centralized. In short, life would be anything but simple, and we would have very little control over our own lives. Simple living requires more than a "nonpolluting" replacement for conventional sources of energy. It requires a whole new approach to the development and use of energy.

New Approaches to Energy

Part of any new approach to the production and use of energy is coming face to face with the necessity of "de-development" and widespread decreases in our total energy consumption. Even if we can find the "perfect" renewable energy source, we won't be able to use it at the profligate rate we have been burning fossil fuels. Since any truly renewable energy source represents the energy that is available right now (from the sun, for example) rather than the energy stored up over millions of years (in coal, for example), a system based on such sources would have a built-in control: we couldn't use any more energy than was currently available (renewable energy can be stored, too, but not on nearly the scale as, say, the chemical energy in coal). As society shifts its reliance from petroleum-based energy to renewable energy sources, energy conservation measures in both public policy and private life will become more important; the level of consumption of goods and resources—especially nonessentials—will decline. A recent Ford Foundation study[12] concludes that energy consumption in the United States could level off between 1985 and 2000—without nuclear power and with Americans still maintaining a comfortable life-style—by incorporating substantial conservation measures in day-to-day life.

With conventional energy sources becoming more expensive, polluting, and difficult to obtain, and with nuclear power in serious doubt as well as dangerous, it makes sense to explore the problems and promise of developing alternatives on a large scale and making them economically feasible. Our research and public-policy priorities on energy need to be reordered. One of the most difficult obstacles to achieving this—and to simple living—is our dependence on large, monopolistic, privately owned corporations for the power to heat and light our homes, cook our food, run our appliances, and fuel our transportation. These corporations have tended to treat energy as a profitable commodity rather than a social need and, with the cooperation of government agencies, have made decisions largely on the basis of profitability. Because of this orientation toward profit, centralization, and expansion they, along with government and industry, have been unable and unwilling to meet the essential social requirements of renewable and non-polluting energy sources and agricultural, manufacturing, and transportation systems that use energy efficiently and with minimal environmental impact.

In spite of government regulation, we have little say in where our power comes from, how it is generated, how much it costs, what it is used for, and how it affects us and our surroundings. No matter how much we are personnally committed to the practice of simple living, no matter how little energy we use from day to day, our individual action cannot change the basic flaws in our energy system. To begin to make such changes, we must get to the roots of the energy issue. We need to explore the possibilities of creating an energy system that serves social needs rather than making profits and is controlled by the many who depend on it rather than by the few who dispense it. And further, the product of this system, the energy itself, must be evaluated by the efficiency and impact of its use.

So what *are* our alternatives? There are the so-called biofuels: wood, cornhusks, wheat chaff for burning; alcohol fermented from fruits and grain and distilled into fuel; methane gas, both a fuel and a raw material, generated from organic wastes and sewage. Geothermal energy, which takes advantage of the earth's internal heat by tapping natural geysers of steam to produce electricity, is another alternative. But many of these alternatives could produce power on only a small scale, and others share an important drawback with fossil fuels, which is that they are not renewable.[13]

Solar Energy

The only truly renewable energy source is the sun, which has been rising and setting for billions of years and will continue to do so. Solar energy is any energy that comes from the sun, directly or indirectly. This includes photosynthesis, by which green plants use sunlight to convert water and carbon dioxide to oxygen and carbohydrate; wind, which is generated when air heated by the sun rises and cooler air rushes in to replace it; and the water in lakes and streams, which gets there after having been evaporated from the oceans and condensed as rain. Solar energy even includes the difference in temperature between the surface and the depths in tropical waters.

As Barry Commoner has said, "solar energy is the richest resource on earth, and the least used."[19] It is diffuse, but it can be concentrated. It is concentrated naturally by winds and rivers; windmills, waterwheels, and hydroelectric plants take advantage of this natural concentration. Windmills and waterwheels have long been used to drive pumps and millstones, and hydroelectric plants generate electricity from the kinetic energy of water stored behind dams. Heat engines can float on the sea and produce electrical power from tropical water temperature gradients. Solar energy can also be concentrated by solar collectors, photovoltaic cells, and parabolic mirrors.

Solar collectors are black, heat-absorbent plates with transparent covers and space in between. A series of such collectors can heat a continuous stream of air or water, which then enters a storage tank to be distributed or stored for later use in providing space heat and hot water to houses or communities. Sunlight can also be used directly to produce electricity by means of a photovoltaic cell. Similar to a transistor in structure and operation, a cell is a thin wafer of ultrapure silicon crystal sandwiched between two electrodes. When sunlight strikes one of the electrodes, it causes an electrical current to flow through the silicon. Hooked together in large numbers, these cells can be a significant source of energy. Their principal raw material, silicon, is abundant. It is the second most abundant element in the earth's crust, and as silicon dioxide is the main constituent of sand.

There are ways of storing solar energy, too, for times of darkness or bad weather. Solar-generated electricity can be used to manufacture hydrogen by splitting water molecules; the hydrogen can be stored as hydrogen fuel and reconverted to electricity as needed by fuel cells. Fuel cells use hydrogen and oxygen to produce electricity; water is the only by-product; there are no moving parts, and fuel cells are more efficient than conventional systems for converting fuel into electricity. Because they are more efficient, they don't have to be built on as large a scale as conventional power plants. Small-scale power plants mean more flexibility and more community control in the energy system. Other means of storing solar energy once it has been converted into electricity include pumping water to a height and using its gravitational force as needed, compressing large volumes of air and later using the pressure, and turning giant flywheels.

Solar energy has been shown to work; it can heat, generate electricity, and be stored. If so, why hasn't it been developed more by now? For one thing, the myths that it is too diffuse, too impractical in bad weather, and too expensive are persistent. Further, until now the fossil fuels have been inexpensive and easily obtained, and environmental costs have been of secondary concern. Solar energy has not been considered a profitable venture by the power companies. In 1975 the federal government spent $1.5 billion on nuclear power research and $38 million on solar energy.[20] This bias against solar energy extends to the local and personal level. Solar energy equipment is still hard to find and expensive. Architects and contractors are often reluctant to work on solar-related projects because they consider them unproven and risky. Banks are unwilling to make loans for the same reasons. And motivated by profitability, the power companies have assigned low priority to solar energy research, contending that its use as a major energy source is many years off.[21]

Until recently, solar energy has been dismissed as a quixotic hope, unattainable for now and therefore irrelevant to our present needs and problems. If we look at it fairly, however, with a willingness to abandon long-held assumptions and consider the consequences of our present energy habits, we can see that solar energy has the potential to take the place of conventional fuels, reduce environmental pollution and economic inflation, and produce power efficiently. The diffuseness of solar energy is its main advantage in terms of efficiency, economy, environmental impact, and community accessibility. Recall that thermodynamic efficiency depends on matching the power source to the task. Solar energy can be used in relatively unconcentrated form to perform low-temperature tasks such as space and water heating with little waste heat. In concentrated form, it can be matched suitably to high-temperature tasks. Because of this flexibility, the net energy derived from solar energy is higher than that derived from conventional sources.

To paraphrase Barry Commoner, the sun is nearly the ideal energy source. It is renewable, available everywhere, and nonpolluting. It can be used in conjunction with conventional energy. Because it is available everywhere and its net energy is high, it is ideal for local and regional development. No giant monopoly can control its supply or dictate its uses. There are not significant advantages to large solar power plants over small ones. Solar energy could be used effectively to meet the needs of a household or a whole community. With a commitment by government, industry, and communities, solar energy could help us move toward simple and healthy living.

Projects

1. Try playing the Energy Game. This game can help us move toward simpler living by enabling us to recognize consciously which of the things we do and own are most necessary and meaningful to us. To play the game, make a list of the things you use each day which consume energy. Consider the energy needed in the original production of the item as well as the energy needed for its continued use. Next, cross out the items on your list which you could do without fairly easily. Then go through the

list again and circle all the things you could do
without only if you were to simplify your life drastically. Next to the circled items write down something that could be substituted. For example, if
you circled "automobile," you might replace it with
a bicycle or public transportation. Try this process
in a small group; have everyone share their lists,
including what was crossed out, what was circled,
and what has been substituted for what was given

Who Exerts Control Over My Energy Consumption?

Categories	Subcategories	I control	I do or might have some influence
My home	a. heating/cooling b. food used c. food storage, preparation d. lighting e. clothing f. garden g. other		
My transportation	a. walking b. bicycle c. public d. auto e. other		
My work	a. machine use b. temperature c. facilities d. cafeteria e. stairs/elevator f. other		
My recreation	a. transportation b. items consumed c. other		
Regional and national systems	a. food preparation and delivery b. transportation c. consumer items d. communication e. military		

up. Perhaps you can also decide whether this has helped you see some changes you can make in real life.

2. The Energy Addict's Calorie Counter (see chapter 12) is a useful tool to help us become more aware of our energy consumption. Use it to keep track of the energy you use in a day or week, and see how your consumption level compares to those of

| | Control exerted by others | | | |
Industry	Local gov.	State gov.	Federal gov.	Other

other Americans and of people elsewhere in the world.

3. Pay a few visits to meetings of your local public planning body. Does it seem to be making energy-wise decisions? Is it paying attention to development of parks and other facilities that provide recreation without expending great amounts of energy, or is it concentrating on public buildings with lots of glass, airconditioning, and big parking lots? How could you make your influence felt in the direction of energy-conserving policymaking?

4. Using the chart, try to figure out who really controls the energy you use and the prices you pay for it. Identify the areas where you have some control and those where you have little or none. Can you think of ways in which you and your community could increase your share of control?

5. Read up on the proposals being made to increase participation in energy decision-making and speed development of new, nondepleting energy sources such as solar, tidal, and wind power. Then write your state and federal representatives, expressing support for those proposals that seem wisest and most practical.

NOTES

1. Amory B. Lovins, "Energy Strategy: The Road Not Taken?" *Not Man Apart*, November 1976 (Friends of the Earth, 529 Commercial Street, San Francisco CA).

2. Dennis Pirages and Paul Ehrlich, *Ark II* (San Francisco: W. H. Freeman. 1974).

3. *The Christian Science Monitor*, Western ed., Feb. 19, 1976.

4. Ibid.

5. Barry Commoner, *The Closing Circle* (New York: Bantam Books, 1972).

6. *National Enquirer*, Dec. 24, 1974.

7. Eric Hirst, "Food-Related Energy Requirements," *Science*, Vol. 184, No. 4134, April 19, 1974.

8. Barry Commoner, "A Reporter at Large: Energy," *The New Yorker*, Feb. 2, 9, 16, 1976.

9. Gil Friend and David Morris, *Kilowatt Counter* (Alternative Sources of Energy, Rt. 2, Box 90A, Milaca MN 56353, 1975).
10. Barry Commoner, "A Reporter at Large: Energy," *The New Yorker,* Feb. 2, 9, 16, 1976.
11. Ibid.
12. John Goffman, in *The Case for a Nuclear Moratorium* (Washington D.C.: Environmental Action Foundation, 1972), p. 3.
13. Ibid., pp. 3–4.
14. "Friends Committee on National Legislation's Energy Policy," *Congressional Record,* February 26, 1976.
15. Sen. Mike Gravel, in *The Case for a Nuclear Moratorium,* p. 8.
16. Howard Kohn, "The Case of Karen Silkwood," *Rolling Stone,* January 13, 1977, pp. 38–39.
17. Public letter from Sen. Mike Gravel, July 1, 1976.
18. Friend and Morris, *op. cit.*
19. Barry Commoner, "A Reporter at Large: Energy," *The New Yorker,* Feb. 2, 9, 16, 1976.
20. Ibid.
21. Pacific Gas and Electricity advertisement, *San Francisco Chronicle,* March 1976.

SOURCES OF FURTHER INFORMATION

Books

Berger, John J. *Nuclear Power: The Unviable Option.* Palo Alto, CA: Ramparts, 1976.

The Case for a Nuclear Moratorium. Washington, D.C.: Environmental Action Foundation, 1974.

Clark, Peter, and Landfield, Judy. *Natural Energy Workbook.* Box 996, Berkeley, CA: Visual Purple, 1976.

Commoner, Barry. *The Closing Circle.* New York: Bantam, 1972.

Darrow, Ken, and Pam, Rick. *Appropriate Technology Sources.* Stanford: Volunteers in Asia Press, 1975.

Freeman, et al. *Exploring Energy Choices.* New York: Ford Foundation, 1974.

Fritsch, Albert, and Castleman, Barry. *Lifestyle Index.* Washington, D.C.: Center for Science in the Public Interest, 1974.

Fuller, John G. *We Almost Lost Detroit*. New York: Ballantine, 1975.

Gage, T., et al. *Energy Primer*. Menlo Park, CA: Portola Institute, 1974.

Holdren, John P. *Energy*. New York: Sierra Club, 1974.

Illich, Ivan. *Energy and Equity*. New York: Harper and Row, 1974.

Illich, Ivan. *Tools for Conviviality*. New York: Harper and Row, 1973.

Kash, D. E., et al. *Energy Under the Ocean*. Norman, Oklahoma: University of Oklahoma Press, 1973.

Lovins, Amory B. "Energy Strategy: The Road Not Taken?" *Not Man Apart,* November, 1976. Friends of the Earth, 529 Commercial Street, San Francisco, CA.

————, and Price, John. *Nonnuclear Futures: The Case of an Ethical Energy Strategy*. Cambridge, MS: Ballinger, 1975.

Lovins, Amory B., et al. *Soft Energy Paths: Toward a Durable Peace*. Cambridge, MS: Ballinger, 1977.

Morgan, Richard, and Jerabek, Sandra. *How to Challenge Your Local Utility: A Citizen's Guide to the Power Industry*. Dupont Circle Building, Washington, D.C.: Environmental Action Foundation, 1974.

Olson, McKinley C. *Unacceptable Risk, The Nuclear Power Controversy*. New York: Bantam, 1976.

Patterson, Walter C. *Nuclear Power*. New York: Penguin, 1976.

Pirages, D., and Ehrlich, P. *ARK II*. San Francisco, CA: W. H. Freeman, 1974.

Rifas, Leonard. *All Atomic Comics*. Box 40246, San Francisco, CA: Educomics, 1976.

Scientific American, September 1971. (Entire issue devoted to energy.)

Scortia, Thomas N., and Robinson, Frank M. *The Prometheus Crisis*. New York: Bantam, 1976.

Spectrum: An Alternate Technology Equipment Directory. Mulaca, New Mexico: Alternate Sources of Energy, 1974.

Steinhart, Carol E., and Steinhart, John S. *Energy— Sources, Use, and Role in Human Affairs*. North Scituate, Mass.: Duxbury Press, 1974.

Taking Charge: A New Look at Public Power. Washington, D.C.: Environmental Action Foundation, 1976.

Terry, Mark, and Witt, Paul. *Energy and Order: A High School Teaching Sequence.* San Francisco, CA: Friends of the Earth, 1976. Thomas Alva Edison Foundation. *Energy Conservation, Experiments You Can Do . . . From Edison.* Southfield, Mich.: Thomas Alva Edison Foundation, 1974.

Warren, Betty, and Cushman, Debbie. *Energy Bibliography.* San Francisco, CA: Friends of the Earth, 1977.

Periodicals and Newsletters

Critical Mass, P.O. Box 1538, Washington, D.C. 20013.

Ears Catalogue of Nuclear and Alternative Energy Information, Ears, 2239 East Colfax, Denver, Colorado 80206.

Not Man Apart, Friends of the Earth, 529 Commercial Street, San Francisco, CA 94111.

Nuclear Opponents, Citizens Energy Council, Box 285, Allendale, N.J. 07401

People and Energy, Center for Science in the Public Interest, 1757 S Street N.W., Washington, D.C. 20009.

Monthly Information Bulletin, Office of Senator Gravel, 3317 Dirksen Bldg, U.S. Senate, Washington, D.C. 20510.

Rain, Environmental Education Center, Portland State University, Portland, OR 97221.

Common Ground, Crossroads Research Center, 2314 Elliot Ave. So., Minneapolis, MN 55404. (See especially issue No. 7 Winter 1976.)

12

The Energy Addict's Calorie Counter [1]

BY BETH COLLISON AND ALAN STRAIN

Energy, a Common Denominator

What we do, what we consume, and what we own can all be measured in terms of energy use. A calorie counter can help us better understand the significance of our way of life as members of a global village. It attempts to bring together and clarify information we need to make informed energy choices—choices we hope will help us to live more simply, justly, and joyfully.

What Do You Mean, "Addict"?

One medical encyclopedia describes addiction as "the state of feeling *compelled* to take certain food or drugs." It notes that while physically dependent, the addict also becomes psychologically dependent on the addiction for comfort or escape. In this sense, most of us are energy addicts. We are dependent upon our possessions and conveniences, both physically and psychologically. To break this addiction, like any other, requires finding new ways to meet our needs as human beings. This is difficult to do alone, but working with fellow or former addicts makes changes more possible.

What Is a Calorie?

A calorie is a unit of heat energy. There are small-*c* calories and large-*C* calories. A small-*c* calorie is defined as the heat required under standard conditions to raise the temperature of one gram of water one degree Centigrade. A large-*C* calorie is one thousand times larger: the amount of heat required to raise the temperature of one kilogram of water one degree Centigrade. Since most people are more familiar with food Calories, which are large-C Calories, this is the energy unit we will use to measure the total amount of daily energy we consume.

Why Count Calories?

First, because no matter what our income level, many of us find little satisfaction in what we own and consume. Our lives are often complicated and cluttered by our conditioned habits of consumption. We hope that by counting all the Calories we use, we may discover ways our daily lives can be both simplified and enriched.

Second, counting Calories may help us see more clearly our relationship to others who share the planet Earth and its resources. It may help us understand the personal and social changes needed to build a world whose resources are more equitably shared by all its people.

Energy Slaves

Before commercial energy was widely available, the well-to-do had slaves or servants to multiply their work and comfort for them. Today, in the "developed" parts of the world, human slaves have been replaced largely by "energy slaves."

Viewing ourselves as energy slaveholders is one way of gaining a more concrete grasp on our total energy use. But to do that, we must first distinguish between two kinds of Calories that are available to us.

First, there are food Calories, which maintain our bodies and give us the energy to live and work and play. We will call these *Personal Energy Calories*.

In addition, we also use a large amount of commercial energy. This greatly extends what we can do on our own, increasing our freedom to travel, our ability to stay warm and comfortable, to work, and to play. These commercial energy Calories we will call *Multiplier Calories;* they multiply what we can do with our own metabolic energy.

Dividing our total Multiplier Calories by our Personal Energy Calories yields the number of times our commercial energy use potentially multiplies our own efforts: that is, the number of *energy slaves* we have at our command.

In the energy-slave calculations that follow, we have arbitrarily chosen 2,500 Personal Energy Calories as the average daily figure for a healthy human being. This is well above the Caloric intake of most people in the world today, but less than the average for most Americans.

The World Spectrum of Energy Use

The "average" person in the world now uses approximately 43,000 Calories per day, which translates into 17 energy slaves.[2] However, there are few "average" people in the world. Some people use far more energy than that, while most use far less.

An average citizen of the so-called "developed" countries uses 136,000 Calories each day (54½ energy slaves). However, more than two-thirds of the world's people live in the "developing" areas, where the average person uses only 8,200 Calories of nonmetabolic energy daily (3½ energy slaves).[3]

The ends of the spectrum, however, show the full range of energy use more clearly. The average American now uses over 250,000 Calories per day (101 energy slaves), while the average inhabitant of Burundi uses only 250 Calories per day (1/10 of a slave). But even this range of 1,000 to 1 is not the full story. Active, "successful" people in highly developed areas—

people in business, government, and the professions, who travel frequently by jet airplane—often average well over *one million* Calories per day (roughly 500 energy slaves). So the actual range in individual energy use is more like 5,000 to 1.

Such vast differences are hard to comprehend. They may be easier to understand if we think about how people live in countries we have visited or know about. The following chart shows the average per-capita energy consumed in selected regions and countries.

AREA OR COUNTRY	Multiplier Calories	Personal Energy Calories	Energy Slaves (MC ÷ PEC)
WORLD	43,000	2,500	17
Developed	136,000	"	54½
Developing (over ⅔ of world's people)	8,200	"	3½
REGIONS			
North America (developed)	249,000	"	100
Western Europe	89,000	"	35½
North and South America (developing)	16,000	"	6½
Africa	8,800	"	3½
COUNTRIES			
U.S.A.	252,000	"	101
Australia	123,000	"	49
Sweden	115,000	"	46
England	112,000	"	45
U.S.S.R.	107,000	"	43
France	97,000	"	39
Japan	74,000	"	29½
Argentina	36,000	"	14½
Mexico	30,000	"	12
China	14,000	"	5½
Brazil	12,000	"	5
Egypt	9,200	"	3½
Philippines	6,900	"	3
Congo	4,600	"	2
India	3,800	"	1½
Ethiopia	870	"	½
Berundi	250	"	⅒

Cutting Calories and Kicking the Habit

While it is important to understand the realities of our world, dwelling too long on the world's predicament can lead to despair and paralysis. We can make changes in our lives now. The Calorie Counter is for those of us who know we're addicts and want to begin to break the addiction.

How can we begin to change our daily patterns, alone or working with fellow addicts? Here are a few general suggestions for starters.

Set a goal (but don't expect miracles). First you may want to set a goal for an "energy diet"—perhaps the average level of energy use in the developed world or in a particular country such as Sweden, England, or France. Or perhaps a less stringent diet. Whatever diet you choose, don't expect miracles. There are just too many things beyond our immediate control, which is why we have to organize for larger changes as we go along. The energy required to collect and store and treat drinking water and to transport it hundreds of miles and pump it to a tap in a big city apartment is vastly greater than that required by a farmer or peasant who gets water from a stream or well. Moreover, like it or not, many of us must depend upon cars and freeways to go about our daily work. And although we may want to use a watch for a lifetime, the economics of a throwaway culture condemn us to replace the watch we can't afford to repair. The web in which we are caught is a tangled one indeed, not easily undone. But we need not wait for society to change; we can make changes now. There is no assurance that social and political reorganization will follow, but we believe personal change is a necessary part of creating new institutions.

Many of these possible personal changes can be summed up in three words: *paring, sharing,* and *caring.*

Paring empty Calories and unneeded needs. One of the first things to look for are empty Calories which add nothing to our lives—possessions that are a worry rather than a joy, labor-saving devices that don't save labor, things that are larger or more than we need. How many electrical conveniences, from clocks and toothbrushes to dishwashers and pencil sharpeners, do we own that could be replaced with simpler mechanical devices? Is my car or house larger than I really want? What *are* my real needs and how many of the things I buy and want would disappear from my life if they were not advertised?

Of course the answers to such questions will vary. People's needs vary, and not everyone has the luxury of choice. If I am poor and need a car, I may only be able to afford the secondhand gas eater that has depreciated rapidly to a bargain price.

Caring for what we own and use. An obvious way to invest less in material things is to care for them so that the energy investment they represent is spread over as long a time as possible. If I *must* own a car, careful maintenance can extend its life by up to ten years and spread the energy costs accordingly. So it is important to cherish and care for the things we buy and use.

Sharing. Sharing ownership or use of things with others can also help spread energy costs. And, as a hidden benefit, sharing may help overcome one cause of addiction to possessions—the lack of mutually satisfying and interdependent relationships with others. Car pools can substantially reduce the energy spent on personal transportation and also help us get to know our fellow riders. The co-ownership of tools, garden implements, recreational equipment, and so on— especially of things we use infrequently—eliminates unnecessary duplication of possessions among friends and neighbors. A small use-fee can build repair and replacement funds and eliminate hassles. (See "Another View of Economics" for a fuller description of such an arrangement.)

Many other specific suggestions for eliminating empty Calories, caring for the things we own, and sharing their ownership and use can be found elsewhere in this book.

Using the Energy Addict's Calorie Counter

The Calorie Counter is laid out in worksheet form to make it easier to figure both "ownership" and "use" Calories, and to calculate the number of "energy slaves" at one's command. To calculate your own daily energy use:

1. Estimate your daily intake of food Calories and record this figure under "Personal Energy Calories." (It may help to count your food Calories carefully for a few days to find out just how much food energy you use each day.) Your Personal Energy Calories provide a constant standard by which you can measure your use of commercial energy, or "Multiplier Calories."

2. Estimate the "ownership" Calories for each item you own, including those things you rent or lease. If ownership costs are shared, enter the total number of joint owners under "Sharing Factor." Now divide the ownership Calories by the Sharing Factor to find your share of the Calories.

3. To find your daily "use" Calories, first enter under "Amount Factor" the number of minutes, hours, days, or miles each item was used. Then multiply the "use" Calories by this amount to get total use Calories. Again, if use was shared, enter the number who shared under "Sharing Factor" and divide "Total Use Calories Per Day" by that number to find your own use Calories.

4. Add your personal use and ownership Calories for each item and enter the result in the column headed "Multiplier Calories."

5. Finally, divide your "Total Daily Multiplier Calories" for each item by your "Personal Energy Calories" to find the number of energy slaves you use each day for each item.

6. Spaces are provided to record subtotals and a grand total for each category of Calorie and for energy slaves. You may wish to compare your total energy use and energy slaves with the figures in the table on page 251 and begin to plan your own energy diet.

The Energy Addict's
Calorie Counter
(Some selected items)

Personal Energy Calories

On the average, how many Calories of food do you consume each day? _____.

Enter this figure at the top of the column headed "Personal Energy Calories."

The energy we get from the food we eat is used at varying rates during sleep and waking activities. A few selected activities suggesting the range of normal Calorie use are listed below. You may wish to divide an average 24-hour day into the approximate amounts of time you spend on activities that use about these varying amounts of Calories. The total Calories you use should approximately equal the Calories in the food you consume.

ACTIVITY	CALORIES PER HOUR[4]	NUMBER OF HOURS	TOTAL CALORIES
Sleeping	60	X _____	= _____
Lying down	80	X _____	= _____
Sitting (reading, desk work, eating, etc.)	100	X _____	= _____
Driving	120	X _____	= _____
Standing	140	X _____	= _____
Light housework	180	X _____	= _____
Walking (2½ mph)	200	X _____	= _____
Bicycling (5 mph)	200	X _____	= _____
Gardening	250	X _____	= _____
Walking (3¾ mph)	300	X _____	= _____
Heavy Housework	300	X _____	= _____
Tennis	420	X _____	= _____
Bicycling (10 mph)	450	X _____	= _____
Swimming (1 mph)	500	X _____	= _____
Heavy Sustained Work or Exercise	500	X _____	= _____
Bicycling (15 mph)	700	X _____	= _____
Running (10 mph)	900	X _____	= _____
	TOTAL:	_____	_____

Multiplier Calories (Commercial Energy)

Item	"Ownership" Calories Per Day 5 (Owning or renting)	Sharing Factor	My "Ownership" Calories	"Use" Calories Per Mile, Hour, Day, Etc.	Amount Factor	Total "Use" Calories Per Day	Sharing Factor	My Daily "Use" Calories	Total Daily Multiplier Calories (Ownership plus use)	Personal Energy Calories	Energy Slaves (Multiplier Calories Divided by Personal Energy Calories)
TRANSPORTATION 6											
Automobile Full-size, American luxury ($8,000, 10 mpg)	96,800	÷	=	5,200 per mile	×	=	÷	=	+	÷	=
Full-size American ($6,000, 14 mpg)	72,600	÷	=	3,700 per mile	×	=	÷	=	+	÷	=
Mid-size American ($5,000, 18 mpg)	60,500	÷	=	2,900 per mile	×	=	÷	=	+	÷	=
Compact ($4,000, 23 mpg)	48,400	÷	=	2,200 per mile	×	=	÷	=	+	÷	=
Subcompact ($3,500, 28 mpg)	42,100	÷	=	1,800 per mile	×	=	÷	=	+	÷	=
Bicycle	2,600	÷	=	(25 per mile personal energy cal.)	×	=	÷	=	+	÷	=

Bus ———
Railroad ———
Urban mass transit ———
Jet transport ———

400 per mile
750 per mile
950 per mile
2,100 per mile
1,250,000 per hour

Total Daily "Ownership" Calories for Transportation:

Transportation Totals:

HOUSING 7
Housing costing
$10,000 14,000
$20,000 28,000
$30,000 42,000
$40,000 56,000
$50,000 70,000

HEATING THE HOUSE 8
Equipment and operation
(Central heating)
(Insulated house) 1,200 52,000 per day
(Uninsulated house) 1,200 104,000 per day

Total Daily "Ownership" Calories for Housing and Heating:

Housing and Heating Totals:

Item HOUSEHOLD APPLIANCES AND ELECTRICAL CONVENIENCES:	"Ownership" Calories Per Day 9 (Owning or renting)	Sharing Factor	My "Ownership" Calories	"Use" Calories Per Hour or Day	Amount Factor	Total "Use" Calories Per Day	Sharing Factor	My Daily "Use" Calories	Total Daily Multiplier Calories (Ownership plus use)	Personal Energy Calories	Energy Slaves (Multiplier Calories Divided by Personal Energy Calories)
Water heater	400	÷	=	51,100 per day	X	=	÷	=	+	=	
Water heater (quick recovery)	610	÷	=	92,000 per day	X	=	÷	=	+	=	
Air conditioner (room)	1,200	÷	=	1,350 per hour	X	=	÷	=	+	=	
Attic fan	160	÷	=	320 per hour	X	=	÷	=	+	=	
Window fan	80	÷	=	170 per hour	X	=	÷	=	+	=	
Portable Heater	140	÷	=	1,100 per hour	X	=	÷	=	+	=	
Washing machine (automatic)	1,000	÷	=	450 per hour	X	=	÷	=	+	=	
Clothes dryer	810	÷	=	4,200 per hour	X	=	÷	=	+	=	
Steam iron	80	÷	=	870 per hour	X	=	÷	=	+	=	
Hair dryer	80	÷	=	6 per min.	X	=	÷	=	+	=	
Heat or sun lamp	200	÷	=	230 per hour	X	=	÷	=	+	=	
Electric Blanket king-size	140	÷	=	150 per hour	X	=	÷	=	+	=	
double	120	÷	=	120 per hour	X	=	÷	=	+	=	
twin	80	÷	=	80 per hour	X	=	÷	=	+	=	
Vacuum cleaner	400	÷	=	540 per hour	X	=	÷	=	+	=	
Oven cooking range	1,000	÷	=	5,300 per hour	X	=	÷	=	+	=	
Oven (self-cleaning)	1,000	÷	=	2,500 per hour	X	=	÷	=	+	=	
Oven (self-cleaning)	1,400	÷	=	4,100 per hour	X	=	÷	=	+	=	
Oven (microwave)	1,600	÷	=	1,300 per hour	X	=	÷	=	+	=	

Appliance	"Ownership"	Operating
Hot plate	100	1,080 per hour
Broiler	240	1,200 per hour
Frying pan	120	1,300 per hour
Roaster	100	1,200 per hour
Dishwasher	1,100	1,030 per hour
Coffee maker	240	770 per hour
Toaster	80	990 per hour
Waffle iron	100	960 per hour
Waste disposal	400	380 per hour
Radio	400	60 per hour
Hi-fi	810	100 per hour
Television (black and white)	1,000	200 per hour
Television (color)	1,600	290 per hour
Electric clock	20	2 per hour

Total "Ownership" Calories for Household Appliances and Electrical Conveniences:

Household Appliances and Electrical Conveniences Totals:

FOOD [10]

Cost of producing and distributing: a person eating an average U.S. diet purchased from the supermarket uses 22,500 Calories per day invested in the production and distribution of the food consumed. Adjust this figure up or down as you judge appropriate, depending upon whether you eat more or less than 2,500 Calories per day, whether or not your food comes from your garden or the supermarket, etc.

CLOTHING [11]

On the average, *each dollar* spent on clothes uses 11,600 Calories. To find your approximate energy investment in clothing, multiply 11,600 by the number of dollars you spend each month on clothes and divide by 30. Enter in the column headed "Total Multiplier Calories."

SERVICES [12]

Through our taxes, we buy and "own" many services. Each uses energy. The following figures are the per-capita energy costs for some of these "services."

Government:
                 Federal military
                 Federal nonmilitary
                 State services
                 Postal service
Hospitals, public & private
Schools, public & private
Telephone service
Other public utilities
Water systems
Sewer systems
Trash collection
Conservation & Development of Resources

TOTAL "OWNERSHIP" CALORIES _____
(PER DAY)

	My Daily "Use" Calories	Total Daily Multiplier Calories (Ownership Plus Use)	Personal Energy Calories	Energy Slaves (Multiplier Calories Divided by Personal Energy Calories)
		—— ÷ —— = ——		
$ Spent on Clothes × 11,600 =		—— ÷ —— = ——		
		14,280 ÷ —— = ——		
		2,500 ÷ —— = ——		
		3,000 ÷ —— = ——		
		730 ÷ —— = ——		
		5,000 ÷ —— = ——		
		1,890 ÷ —— = ——		
		497 ÷ —— = ——		
		1,090 ÷ —— = ——		
		1,110 ÷ —— = ——		
		400 ÷ —— = ——		
		280 ÷ —— = ——		
		260 ÷ —— = ——		
Totals for Services:		31,057 ÷ —— = ——		

Grand Totals	——	—— ÷ —— = ——		
	My Daily "Use" Calories	Total Daily Multiplier Calories	Personal Energy Calories	Energy Slaves

The Calorie Counter presently includes only selected items and by no means accounts for one's total energy expenditure. It includes few possessions that require no energy to use or operate. For example, while housing is included, furniture is not. Some leisure items, such as television or automobiles, are included, but no recreational equipment or activities are listed. Recreation can have high energy costs—activities such as motorboating or downhill skiing, or hobby equipment such as cameras or power tools.

For high-energy-use items such as cars, refrigerators, hot water heaters, etc., we have included more than one type to provide some basis for making choices, but much remains to be done to develop this aspect of the Calorie Counter as well.

You may wish to use the Calorie Counter to count your Calories each day for a period of time, or you may prefer to use it only occasionally to estimate average daily Calorie consumption. Either way, we hope it may be a useful tool.

The Calorie Counter itself is still very much a work in progress, and we'd welcome your comments, ideas, and suggestions about things you find helpful, confusing, or hindering. Write us, care of American Friends Service Committee, 2160 Lake Street, San Francisco CA 94121.

NOTES

1. The Energy Addict's Calorie Counter was first presented as part of a lecture titled "Counting Calories in the Energy Crisis," delivered in March 1973 by Douglas C. Strain, president of Electro-Scientific Industries. The authors are indebted to him for the idea and the title of this chapter; however, they alone bear responsibility for the Calorie Counter in its present form and for any errors that it may contain. They also take responsibility for the accuracy of all calculations and conversions of other energy units to Calories.

2. All calculations in this section are based on figures given in the U.N. Statistical Papers, Series J, No. 17, *World Energy Supplies, 1969–1972,* United Nations, N.Y., 1974. Calories are rounded to the nearest thousand, hundred, or ten, depending upon the order of magnitude. Energy slaves are rounded to the nearest half, except for Burundi, where the value would have been zero.

3. The terms "developed" and "developing" are used here as defined by the Statistical Office of the United Nations. Specifically, this U.N. agency defines the "developed" parts of the world as "the Developed Market Economies of Australia, Canada, Israel, Japan, New Zealand, South Africa, United States of America, and Western Europe (including Yugoslavia); and the "developing" world as "the Developing Market Economies of Africa, Caribbean America, North America. South America, Middle East (including Turkey), Far East, and Oceania."

4. Calories-per-hour figures taken from Glenn Swengros, *Fitness with Glenn Swengros* (New York: Hawthorne Books Inc., 1971).

5. "Ownership" Calories were calculated by dividing the energy required to manufacture each item by the estimated average life of that item and prorating energy costs on a daily basis. Automobiles were given a life of 5 years; household appliances, bicycles, etc., were assumed to have a life of 10 years; and houses 30 years. Beyond these "life spans," the repair costs were assumed to equal the amortization costs during the assumed life of the item.

6. Production and marketing (i.e., "ownership") figures for automobiles were taken from Eric Hirst, *Direct and Indirect Energy Requirements for Automobiles,* ORNL-NSF Environmental Program, Oak Ridge Laboratory, February 1974. "Use" figures for automobiles from Eric Hirst, *Energy Consumption for Transportation in the U.S.,* ORNL-NSF Environmental Program, Oak Ridge Laboratory, March 1972. Figures for other forms of tranportation from Hirst and Moyers, "Efficiency of Energy Use in the United States," *Science,* March 1973.

7. Housing figures were calculated from Lee Schipper, *Explaining Energy*, Energy and Environment Division, Lawrence Berkeley Laboratory, University of California, June 1975.

8. Calories required for heating calculated from Susan Knox, *The Energy Crisis Survival Kit*, (New York: Manor Books, 1974), p. 24 ff.

9. Ibid.

10. Ibid.

11. Energy costs of clothing calculated from Schipper (see note 7).

12. Energy values for services from Albert J. Fritsch, *The Contraconsumers, A Citizen's Guide to Resource Conservation* (New York: Praeger, 1974).

13

Food

BY ALICE NEWTON

Queries

1. Do I take food for granted? What are my major considerations in choosing and buying my food?
2. Do I know what my personal nutritional requirements are? Can I meet them simply without exploiting others or the environment? Am I afraid of what changing my diet would be like?
3. How do my eating habits relate to the increasing hunger and starvation in the world, to the exploitation of farm workers, to the food policies of the U.S. government, and to proposed international programs of food distribution?
4. Could I use the arable land around my house to grow fruits and vegetables, perhaps sharing the work and harvest, or just offering the land? Is there a community garden in my neighborhood, or could there be? (Some cities furnish land and water, even fertilizer or compost, to gardeners.)
5. Could I get along without those foods grown as cash crops (e.g., coffee, tea, bananas)?
6. Am I consuming more protein than my body needs? Am I making an effort to use protein foods other than meat? Do I feed pets high-protein foods that could be used to feed people? Are pets (especially big eaters) a luxury I should reconsider?
7. Where do I buy my food? Am I supporting the large supermarkets and agribusiness with my economic power? Is there a small independent grocer, a local farmer, a co-op market, or a food co-op that I could be supporting instead?
8. Can I get along without packaged, canned, or convenience foods—those "gross national products" of industry? Why do I buy these foods? To what extent are my eating habits influenced by the media?

9. Are there conferences, workshops, or speakers in my community that could inform me and others more about protein consumption, nutrition, food co-ops, community gardens, and the world's food needs? Is there a need for some of this educational work in my community? Could I move to fill that need? Could I join my efforts to those of neighboring communities in an educational project to reach a greater number of people?

10. How should food production and distribution be rightly managed to provide adequately for all the world's people? Who should make policy decisions and how should decisions be enforced? What changes should be made now to move toward long-range goals?

To us, living simply has many implications for the way we eat. One of them is that our food should be produced and consumed with as little harm to us, to others, and to the environment as possible. The present world food system does not minimize this harm; on the contrary, it is steadily increasing it. In affluent parts of the world like the United States, we are practically force-fed a diet full of ingredients that waste resources and damage our bodies. In the underdeveloped nations, hunger and famine stalk millions of people while vast areas of food farmland are used for non-nutritional cash crops like coffee and tea.

Thus, a second implication of simple living for us is that we should be informed about the present food system and concerned to change it so that adequate nutrition might become available to all people. We agree with those experts who feel that it *will* be possible to feed the growing world population adequately if profound changes in production, distribution, and consumption patterns are achieved. Change always produces some feelings of insecurity, and in the case of food, it strikes literally at the gut level. What would it *really* mean to "share the world's resources"?

In order to move towards change, we need to be informed about the world's food situation and to know how our own eating patterns relate to it, we need to be in touch with our personal feelings about food, and we need the help and support of our friends and community. In this chapter we will review the major factors contributing to the current world food situation and then see how some people who purposely changed their diets and shopping patterns feel this has affected their lives and families.

The Recent Famines

In 1972, nearly unprecedented adverse weather conditions occurred simultaneously in parts of the U.S.S.R., Asia, and Africa, causing grain production which had been rising annually to plummet. In the mid-1960s, when the Soviet Union had experienced massive crop failure, they had compensated by cutting back on the amount of grain fed to livestock. In 1972, they chose to cut exports to Eastern Europe and arranged to import grain from the United States. World reserve stocks (mainly held in the United States) fell to a 20-year low. Additional acreage was put into cultivation.

Then the energy crisis came, the United States suffered the worst growing season in 25 years, and famine was occurring in Africa and India. These events, plus the grim statistics (100,000 deaths by starvation in Africa's equatorial Sahel region and another 100,000 in Ethiopia) and the fact that it was not possible to mobilize enough food and resources to relieve the famines, shocked many people into examining the global food situation.

One of the first realizations this reexamination produced was that famines were likely to occur again. William and Paul Paddock, in *Famine 1975,* predicted that this decade would become known as the "Age of Famines." Norman Borlaug, Nobel Prize winner for high-yield wheat and an expert on the international food situation, estimated that 20 million people could starve in 1975. According to the United Nations Food and Agriculture Organization, nearly 500 million people are now suffering from some form of hunger, and in May 1974 the United Nations Children's Fund declared a state of emergency for the first time in its 27-year history. The problem is critical and the solution will not be easy. There are those who actually see starvation as nature's method of birth control. Some experts and political leaders are saying that with food production nearing its limit and population continuing to increase, food will replace nuclear weapons as the primary tool of political power. This process is already beginning. *Time* (November 11, 1974) quotes Secretary of Agriculture Earl Butz as stating, "Food is a weapon. It is now one of the principal tools in our negotiating kit."

Increasing world population is one factor affecting the hunger picture. At present growth rates, world population will increase by 75 percent, from 4 to 7 billion, by the year 2000, an increase of 200,000 people a day. Such growth would require increased food production of 30 million tons a year just to maintain present per-capita consumption levels. Moreover, it has become apparent that imported population control programs do not work among poverty-stricken people struggling for day-to-day survival. Birth rates reflect the social situation. Population growth in the United States, Western Europe, Cuba, and China began to stabilize only when physical needs were met and people felt more secure about the future.

Although world population will continue to increase, there are major areas in which profound change would significantly offset the food shortage: land use and agricultural systems; the present use of arable land for cash crops (such as coffee) instead of food crops; the world market system that forces Third World countries to export foodstuffs and raw materials for low prices and to import food commodities at high prices; and the overconsumption of beef by affluent countries, coupled with excessive use of grain as livestock feed.

Land Use

It is no longer possible to produce more food simply by plowing more land. There is essentially no unused land in the world that can be feasibly converted to large-scale agricultural use.

Recent studies indicate that there are, at most, about 3.2 billion hectares of land (7.86 billion acres) potentially suitable for agriculture on the earth. Approximately half of that land, the richest, most accessible half, is under cultivation today. The remaining land will require immense capital inputs to reach, clear, irrigate, or fertilize before it is ready to produce food. Recent costs of developing new land have ranged from $215 to $5,275 per hectare. Average cost for opening land in unsettled areas has been $1,150 per hectare. According to an FAO report, opening more land to cultivation is not economically feasible, even given the pressing need for food in the world today.[1]

The United States has now committed its last reserve, 50 million acres previously held in the "soil bank" since the mid-1950s, to all-out production.[2]

But if there is no more land, the best hope for growing more food would seem to be to produce more on the land now in use. The high-yield wheat and rice strains introduced as the "Green Revolution" in the early 1960s seemed promising. Wheat production in India expanded from 11 million tons to 27 million between 1965 and 1972.

However, the new grains require large amounts of water and nitrogen fertilizer (a petroleum by-product), as well as fuel to run irrigation pumps and machinery. During the "energy crises" of 1973, the cost of fuel skyrocketed and supplies of fertilizer became limited. The United States, the primary manufacturer of fertilizer, cut back exports, and countries that had become dependent upon the new agricultural methods were suddenly caught short.

The higher water requirements of the hybrid strains are cause for concern, too, because there is *not* an unlimited supply of water in the world, and many areas may have already reached maximum feasible water use. International food expert George Borgstrom argues that the most limiting and most ominous food-related crisis we face is that of providing sufficient water to meet increased demand.[3]

Other problems have been associated with introducing the high-yield seed. Only the rich farmers could afford to buy the required fertilizer and machinery or get bank credit for them. As a consequence, small farmers were put out of business. Again a few got richer while many were worse off.

In addition, there are other kinds of limits to the green revolution. First, there are questions as to whether higher yields can be sustained over long time periods, let alone increased, if the intensive use of fertilizers scorches the delicate soils. Second, the green revolution tends to develop monochrome strains of grain that are less resistant to disease, requiring the costly application of pesticides. Third, the use of chemicals has also led to chronic food poisoning via pesticides and fertilizers. Fourth, the environmental costs have been great, as reflected in depleted soils, water pollution, flood hazards, disruption of natural plant and animal populations, and depletion of natural resources.[4]

Since the green revolution is essentially the U.S. model of energy-intensive agribusiness exported abroad, we are also confronted with the above problems. Since 1943, more than three million farms have disappeared into large corporate land holdings.[5] It seems clear that large-scale mechanized agriculture is exploitative of human and natural resources and, therefore, self-limiting. Alternatives must be sought.

China shows one such alternative. The Chinese have greatly increased agricultural production by efficient use of labor without extensive use of machinery or artificial fertilizers. They have developed a system of "intercropping," where two or more crops grow simultaneously in one field, with staggered harvests allowing as much as 50-percent increase in total annual yield. Mechanical harvesters cannot be used. All land is utilized, even roadsides and dooryards. A high-yield rice strain is used, but field stubble and human and animal waste are composted and used for fertilizer, along with some artificial fertilizer. Even exhaust heat from kitchen stove pipes is directed through large blocks of subsoil, where the heat presumably hastens bacterial action in the soil, increasing fertility. Energy-wise,

> figures supplied by the Chinese show that for every BTU (British Thermal Unit) of human energy expended in their rice production, they reap a harvest of 53.5 BTUs in rice. In the United States, where human labor has been largely supplanted by gasoline-fired machines, recent studies have shown that one BTU of expended energy, on the average, yields only one-sixth BTU of food value.[6]

There are other examples, too. In Japan, families farming eight acres have been highly successful in food production. So have small farmers in Taiwan.

Food Crops Instead of Cash Crops

Another approach would be to convert cash-crop lands to food crops. Much of the agricultural land in Third World countries and most of the agricultural research (usually U.S.-financed and carried out by U.S. institutions) goes toward these crops, grown for profit, many of which are luxury items with little or no nutritional value. Coffee alone "is the lifeblood of forty developing countries." [7]

Why do countries that need food grow and export other crops? The production and exportation of cash crops dates back over 300 years to the establishment of the plantation system and is part of the general pattern of exportation of natural resources from Third World countries to affluent countries, as discussed in chapter 3.

By supporting military dictatorships and imposing import taxes on manufactured goods from these countries, the United States exercises much control over their economies and ensures continued export of their products at low prices. These hungry countries, then, are forced to import food. The U.S. Department of Agriculture favors the free market system of supply and demand, which results in higher and higher food prices as the demand goes up. When the world demand for pinto beans rose 601 percent between September 1972 and September 1973, for example, the price rose 602 percent.[8] For poor people who spend between 75 and 80 percent of their income on food, such price increases are disastrous.

The price for Third World exports does not necessarily go up even as the cost of food to them rises, so their debt to the United States increases and the economic noose becomes tighter.

What could happen if we did not have bananas and coffee for breakfast? Some people have abstained from consumption of cash crops as a personal testimony and consciousness-raising experience. Whether such abstinence by large numbers of consumers would help improve conditions in the Third World is not clear; the processes leading toward political, economic, and land reform in countries producing cash crops are complex.

Grain for People Instead of Beef

Most of us have read statistics showing that an average American uses five times as much of the world's resources as the average Indian. We use about a ton of grain per year per capita in contrast to the Indian's 400 pounds. Most of this grain goes to feed cattle. According to an article the *New York Times*, October 25, 1974, if Americans cut back their meat consumption 10 percent for one year, twelve million tons of grain could be freed for human consumption. The article also noted that by 1973 Americans consumed 116 pounds of meat per capita annually, but that 60 pounds, which is the amount we were eating in 1950, was all the protein our bodies could use. Excess protein is burned for energy rather than being used for tissue regeneration. Such gross overconsumption by Americans is directly related to hunger elsewhere in the world.

There are several reasons why consuming meat, particularly beef, is costly to world resources and the food supply. First, in order to fatten livestock to marketable size in about half the time that grazing takes, cattle raisers give their animals high-protein feed. In 1973, U.S. livestock were fed protein equivalent to six times that consumed by Americans, or as much grain as the 800 million people of China and the 600 million people of India together eat in a year.[9] Ironically, cattle do not require high-protein feed. They need only a nitrogen source (even urea) and a carbohydrate (even orange pulp or coffee grounds) to convert cellulose to protein.

Secondly, meat is costly in terms of water and energy use. Wheat requires about about 500 pounds of water for every pound of grain produced, and 21.4 pounds of grain are required to produce one pound of beef. That means it takes at least 10,000 pounds of water to produce one pound of grain-fed beef. By contrast, hogs require only 8.3 pounds of grain to produce one pound of meat; chickens, only 5.5 pounds.[10] In addition to water use, feeding puts demands on other resources such as fertilizer and fuel.

Finally, the impact of U.S. meat consumption does not stop at the border. The United States imports meat as well as livestock feed.

In 1968, we imported 332 million pounds of meat from Latin America—much of it coming from the poorest areas of Central America. At least 20 per cent of this meat is protein, enough to provide 60 grams (average daily requirement) of protein per day for an entire year to 1.4 million people, or most of the population of a country like Costa Rica.[11]

In that same year "we imported primarily from Chile and Peru 700,000 tons of fishmeal, enough to supply 15 million people—more than the whole population of Peru—with protein for a year."[12]

Cattle are fed grain for two reasons: first, it makes them mature faster, and secondly, it makes them fatter, which makes the meat more flavorful. All livestock spend their first months grazing. Then animals to be "fed" go to feedlots.

"Grass-fed" or "range-fed" beef (i.e., animals allowed to graze until maturity rather than being fattened in feedlots) is available in some stores. It is good meat, less expensive, with less fat content, and although it might have to be cooked a little longer to become tender, the problems relating to the feedlot method are avoided. Virtually all Latin American and Australian beef is grass-fed. In 1974 in the United States, 23.9 million head of fed cattle were slaughtered compared to 4.6 million head of nonfed cattle.[13] To supply the current demand for beef with grass-fed beef would require a total transformation of the beef industry. However, according to an article in the *Christian Science Monitor* (February 11, 1975), "a 20% shift away from grain-fed beef would free enough grain and concentrate to meet the entire nine-million-ton-famine relief need estimated at the recent World Food Conference." The article also states that experts agree that such a shift is readily possible and that "there is no reason why all U.S. table beef should not be grass fed within another five years."

Is Meat Necessary?

The argument that meat is the only, or even the best, source of protein is completely unfounded. The body needs 21 amino acids for maintenance. Eight of these 21 amino acids, the so-called "eight essential amino acids," cannot be produced by the human body itself and must be consumed through foodstuffs. Some foods have all eight of these amino acids, and they are referred to as "complete proteins." Soybeans and soy flour, wheat germ, and nutritional yeast are foods in addition to animal products (meat, fish, poultry, eggs, milk, and milk products) that contain complete proteins. However, the amino acid deficiencies found in grains and vegetables can be overcome by complementing proteins. This means combining, at the same meal, foods that are low in a given amino acid with others high in the same one, thus increasing the amount of usable protein (that is, the amount that has the eight essential amino acids). Generally speaking, the protein complementary groups are: grains and milk products, grains and legumes, and legumes and seeds. The National Academy of Sciences has determined that we can calculate our daily protein need by multiplying our ideal body weight by 0.42 grams. So, with educated care we can acquire our full protein needs on a meatless diet. In *Diet for a Small Planet,* Frances Moore Lappe thoroughly discusses the politics of protein in the world food shortage and shows how to combine nonmeat foods for adequate protein in delicious recipes. She points out that the amount of vegetable protein wasted in livestock feed equals 90 percent of the yearly world protein deficit—a clear mandate for working to change America's high fed-beef eating habits, starting with our own.[14]

Other Links in the Connection

U.S. Food Industry and Agribusiness

In the United States food is no longer thought of as a substance for survival; it has become primarily a profit-oriented industry. Family farms are being replaced by agribusiness holdings. Giant corporations control 80 percent of food production in this country. The top 50 of more than 32,000 food-producing firms in the United States had 61 percent of the industry's profits, according to a 1966 study by the Federal Trade Commission, the most comprehensive study to date.[15] The percentage of the total market controlled by the four leading firms is known as the "Four Firm Concentration Ratio" and is used as an indicator of economic concentration in industry. Dr. William Shepherd, an authority on economic concentration, reported an *average* ratio of 55 percent in the manufacturing of food and kindred products in 1966. The ratio for cereal preparations, for example, is 87 percent; for bread and prepared flour, 75 percent; and for fluid milk, 60 percent.[16] He also found that four farm machinery corporations hold 70 percent of the market.[17] Fifty-five percent is well into what experts call a "tight oligopoly," subject to "noncompetitive behavior practices." Incidentally, this is the same level of concentration enjoyed by the oil companies.[18]

With comparatively little competition left in the food industry, it's no wonder food prices have been going up. In an *Anti-Trust Law and Economics Review* article, Ralph Nader observed that "a secret staff report now at the FTC estimates that if highly concentrated industries were deconcentrated to the point where the four largest firms control 40% or less of an industry's sales prices would fall 25% or more." [19]

Concentration and vertical integration are the key terms. Large corporations control the food operation from "seedling to supermarket," as one author describes it. Such corporations hold almost monopolistic control, squeezing out or contracting the small independent farmers. Del Monte is a prime example of vertical integration.

[It] is the world's largest canner of fruits and vegetables. But it does more than processing and canning. It manufactures its own cans and prints its own labels; it conducts its own agricultural research; it grows produce on its own land, as well as putting 10,000 farmers under production contracts; it distributes its produce through its own banana transports, tuna seiners, air-freight forwarding stations, ocean terminal and trucking operations; it operates its own warehouses; it maintains 58 sales offices throughout the world; and it caters 28 restaurants and provides food services to United Air Lines.[20]

While small farms are going out of business, an increasing amount of Del Monte (and other) produce is grown and canned in Mexico. This system hurts American workers and exploits Mexican farmers for 23¢ an hour and cannery workers for 27¢ an hour. Del Monte saves 40 percent of its production costs by growing in Mexico, but charges the same high prices for the product.[21] This is one more example of food grown abroad and sent to the United States and Europe. Mexicans consume very few of these products because the retail price is often higher in Mexico than in the United States.

The same thing is occurring in the meat and other food industries. Nonfarm corporations such as ITT (Wonderbread), Boeing (potatoes), Greyhound (Armour), and Standard Oil (250,000 farm acres in California) are diversifying into the food industry.

Vertical integration and diversification are profitable. As prices to the consumer rose in 1970, Tenneco, a large multinational corporation, received $1.4 million in land subsidies for not growing food, paid no federal income taxes at all, and made out with $73.8 million in profits.[22] In 1973, Del Monte's profits were up 21 percent over 1972, Pillsbury was up 38 percent, United Brands was up 58 percent, and Iowa Beef 77 percent.[23] Profits and control are further assured by shared board members and stocks.

Rising food prices cause difficulties for middle-class Americans, but at least they can "spend down," i.e., buy less expensive types of food and cut into luxuries. The poor were already buying at the bottom of the scale; there was nothing cheaper for them to buy. However, as the demand for less expensive items increased, so did the price. For example, between December 1971 and March 1974 margarine increased 63 percent in price while butter increased only 8.9 percent. While hamburgers increased by 60.3 percent, porterhouse steaks increased by only 38.2 percent.

Dried beans increased by 256.3 percent.[24] Ironically, it has been found that identical items are generally higher in low-income neighborhoods than in well-to-do areas. Studies indicate that the lower one's income, the higher is the percentage paid for food.[25] Although federal funding for food programs such as the National School Lunch Program, the Elderly Feeding Program, and the Food Stamp Program tripled from $1.6 billion in fiscal 1970 to approximately $5.1 billion in 1974, these programs have not offset the effects of inflation. America's poor are worse off now than at any time in the last few years.

A further irony is that among those poor who frequently do not have enough food are the very workers whose stoop labor produces the fruits and vegetables in our markets. USDA figures published in 1972 indicate that 2.8 million farm workers average 88 days of work per year for an average annual wage of $1,160. Three separate studies (by the USDA, a research group at the University of Denver, and a subcommittee of the California Assembly) each show that 75 percent of all farm workers have annual incomes below federal poverty guidelines.[26] In Kings County, California, where individual corporate cotton and grain farmers receive up to $4 million each in federal subsidies, a study of 250 preschool-age children of farm workers revealed that 49 percent suffered from "functional anemia," an indication of possible malnutrition.[27] In Colorado, a pediatrician from the University of Colorado medical school studied 300 migrant children from 151 families. Clinical tests showed signs of serious malnutrition, including evidence of growth retardation and rickets; 50 percent of the children had serious vitamin deficiencies.[28] In 1960, the National Committee on Education of Migrant Children (NCEMC) reported that "while migrant children went hungry, almost a million dollars, or about 31% of the migrant education funds budgeted for food services were not spent." [29]

In addition to the economic exploitation just described, we are offered foods sprayed with poisonous insecticides; devitalized by processing; artificially textured, flavored, colored, and "enriched"; artificially preserved for long shelf life; and wastefully packaged to distract us from all of the above. It is the advent of these new technological processes that has made the "food" industry possible. Food research is primarily concerned with development of these processes, not with the nutritional value of foods. The hard tomatoes mechanically harvested while green and chemically ripened contain less vitamin A and vitamin C than those ripened on the vine. Yet, as inflation, property taxes, and agribusiness force increasing numbers of people to move from the country to urban centers, dependence on agribusiness and industry-produced food increases. To ensure this dependence, Del Monte's advertising budget is in excess of $15 million a year, and General Mills's advertising budget in 1972 was larger than the entire budget of the FDA's Bureau of Foods.[30, 31]

How long a food system as dependent upon enormous energy use as ours can last is questionable. The U.S. agribusiness and food industries use vast amounts of energy in the production, distribution, maintenance, and advertising of food. Lester Brown and Erik Eckholm in *By Bread Alone* assert that "if all the world were to eat as the U.S. does, and if their food were produced in the way we produce it, all known resources of oil would be totally exhausted in 29 years."[32] Almost 80 percent of the world's annual energy expenditure would be required just for the food system.[33] The most effective way to decrease energy use by the food industries is simply to eat less processed food, get locally grown food and buy directly from the farmer if possible (or grow your own), buy in bulk to avoid packaging, and recycle everything you can.

United States Food Aid

Just as domestic government food aid programs are inadequate due to design and funding limitations, the political priorities of our international aid program, Public Law 480, or "Food for Peace" are such that it has not necessarily provided the generous sharing of our bounty with the needy that many of us have assumed. Most of this food has not been given away according to need, but *sold* to "security-related" countries.

> In fiscal 1974, of the $152 million in food aid, 43% went to South Vietnam and Cambodia alone, while only 10% went to all of Africa. (Latin America received 6%, Asia 28%, other countries 13%.) It is quite clear that the "Food for Peace" funds were used in support of American interests in these countries. Any cover of humanitarian aid is quickly discounted in the realization that neither Vietnam nor Cambodia is on the United Nations' list of 32 countries most seriously affected by the global economic crisis.[34]

PL 480 was established during a farm crisis in 1954, primarily to provide price supports for farmers faced with huge surpluses due to technological advances. In the late 1940s these surpluses were primarily given or sold to U.S. allies in postwar Europe under the Marshall Plan, until Europe recovered economically. PL 480 served to protect farm prices by disposing of surpluses, supported agribusiness expansion, provided for disaster relief, and facilitated trade expansion and foreign policy designs. The law authorizes sales of surplus commodities to "friendly" food-deficient countries. Federal famine relief and other urgent assistance to any "friendly" nation or people in need of it (including some long-term feeding programs) is administered largely through CARE, Catholic Relief Services, and Church World Service, which account for over 90 percent of these programs. Government funding amounts to more than half the total budgets of the two religious groups.[35]

Analyses of food aid show that it has primarily been used "both as a tool for furthering the economic interests of those who control the American market systems, and as a weapon to enforce the international policies of the United States and its allies."[36] Nearly two-thirds of the food aid shipped between 1954 and

1969 was sold for foreign currency. PL 480 delineated uses of this foreign money. It could be used for grants for "common defense" of the recipient country. It could also be used for "economic assistance"; and since many recipient countries have large military budgets' this money often went for military expenditures. In their May–June 1971 newsletter, the North American Congress on Latin America (NACLA) reported that "the Food for Peace program has provided money for other governments to buy $693 million in military equipment over the past five years." [87] In 1973 Congress legislated against use of these funds directly for the military. However, receipt of large amounts of food aid frees other funds for military use.

Another major use of PL 480–generated funds has been for "agricultural export market development." That is, food aid has helped create a dependency situation necessitating continued importation of American grain, giving the United States strong political and economic control over recipient countries. Some countries now importing grain from the United States were previously grain exporters themselves, but have been transformed over the last two or three decades into exporters of cash crops such as coffee. Native growers unable to compete with free or cheap food turned to more lucrative crops with the encouragement and assistance of the U.S. Department of Agriculture. At home during these years, the feedlot method of raising beef cattle was replacing range feeding.

Pushing for modernization of agriculture by such means as the "Green Revolution" in developing countries also ensured dependency upon the U.S. corporations that produce the necessary seed, fertilizer, and machinery. Sometimes corporations benefit directly from PL 480 assistance.

Although PL 480 has throughout its history been most concerned with the expansion of exports, there is evidence that the program is increasingly being utilized by large agribusiness for their overseas subsidiaries. There are two fundamental ways in which this can be done. The first is to participate in specific PL 480 projects which ultimately benefit the corporations' activities in a given country. For example, Ralston Purina, which operates a feed mill in Colombia, "worked with the U.S. Agency for International Development (Food for Peace) Program and the Columbian government to improve local storage and transportation facilities." Since the profitability of an investment in one area of the agribusiness sector is very much dependent on the proper functioning of all the areas, it was important for Ralston Purina that the facilities be built. In effect, then, this multinational corporation was able to use public capital (both U.S. and Colombian) to enhance the profitability of its private investment. This "new partnership" in the world agribusiness market is the talk of the trade, and an important part of the "green revolution." [38]

From 1964 to 1974 there was a steady decrease in food aid donated and loaned in favor of sales by commercial companies. With foreign markets now assured, with hunger and demand increasing, with U.S. balance of payments deficits becoming more crucial as the cost of oil rises, the "Food for Peace Program" is being shunted aside in favor of sending exports to countries who can pay for them. In the late 1950s and early 1960s' when there were surpluses, PL 480 exports were 25–30 percent of total U.S. agricultural exports.

In 1972, when the huge commercial Russian grain deal helped to raise paid exports 25% over the preceding year, P.L. 480 was only 12% of total exports. In 1973, a year that world famine had drastically increased, P.L. 480 had dropped to a mere 4% of the total. In 1974 agricultural exports again rose sharply, for that was the first year that American farmers were not paid to let fields lie fallow. But although agricultural exports increased by nearly 20%, P.L. 480 exports remained at about the previous level, 5% of the total.[39]

It is apparent that the "Food for Peace Program"

has served the political and economic interests of corporate America. Rather than helping underdeveloped countries to be able to meet their food needs more adequately themselves, it has caused them to depend upon imports. Through its support of agribusiness it has contributed to domestic price increases. Now, in a time of increasing hunger, it is providing neither food nor peace. It was based upon getting rid of surplus instead of sharing. Now that countries must buy to survive, there is no more "surplus" and the program cannot continue. The little that is sent still goes mainly to politically important countries rather than to the hungriest ones.

Other Food Aid

As part of the reexamination of the world food situation produced by the famines and the energy crisis, the first World Food Conference was held in Rome. At the conference, representatives of 130 countries established the following bodies:

1. A *World Food Council* to serve as an umbrella organization to see that goods are directed toward needy countries.
2. A *Food Information or Early Warning System* operated by the U.N. Food and Agricultural Organization to send data around the world to inform countries of world production and shortages. (Agreeing to its establishment was a major shift in policy for both China and the Soviet Union.)
3. An *International Grain Reserve System* to help avert future shortage.
4. A *World Agriculture Development Fund* to provide needed funds for development in Third World countries.

These are notable steps. Participation by Russia and China and the commitment made by oil-producing countries to build new fertilizer plants lend hope that effective action may begin. It was discouraging, although not surprising, that the United States refused to increase its relatively small commitment to the grain reserve.

In their article entitled "How We Cause World Hunger" (WIN magazine, January 30, 1975), William Moyer and Pamela Haines stress that although it is important to support both short-term and long-term aid efforts such as those mentioned above we must remember that it is the exploitative political and economic policies of our government, military, and transnational corporations, as well as our consumption habits, that are the real causes of hunger and poverty in the Third World.[40] Poor and hungry people are the victims of the problem. Providing a little more food aid is like putting a Band-Aid on a systemic disease.

Summary

The world food situation is very complex. Yet it seems clear that if production, distribution, and consumption changes are achieved, it *will* be possible to feed a great many more people adequately than we now do. China and Cuba have managed to overcome hunger and solve other poverty-related social problems by being need-oriented instead of profit-oriented.

Moyer and Haines outline four steps the United States could take to begin to end world poverty and hunger:

1. Stop supporting military dictatorships.
2. The United States must undergo massive dedevelopment. We must greatly reduce our consumption of material resources, perhaps by as much as 80 to 90 percent, and do without many of our wasteful and environmentally destructive modern technologies. There just aren't enough resources for the world's poor and future generations unless we do, and we can never be safe in this world unless we do.
3. End the domination by our multinational corporations of the economic and political affairs of poor nations.
4. The United States must redevelop, basing our so-

ciety on *minimum* production, consumption, and waste.

Specific suggestions for U.S. food-related policies listed in the American Friends Service Committee's packet *Hunger on Spaceship Earth,* urge that:

a) The U.S. focus its development aid on agricultural and rural development with emphasis on involving the poor directly in the program's planning and implementation.

b) U.S. aid emphasize land reform and agricultural inputs and credit arrangements for small farmers, to help the developing nations become self-sufficient.

c) The U.S. increase its development aid at least to the U.N. standard of .7 of 1% GNP.

d) At least 10% of U.S. food exports be set aside for long-term sales or grants to poor countries. Currently only 2½% of our annual production is so used.

e) Food for Peace be brought back at least to its 1972 levels of 9 million tons, and that this be allocated solely to the most needy nations, rather than sales (Title I) which can be used for military purposes, and should be increasingly channeled through the U.N. World Food Program.

f) Proceeds from concessional food sales (Title I) be granted back to the most needy nations as agricultural help for small farmers.

g) The U.S. establish government held reserves under international control as the U.S.'s participation in the U.N. World Food Reserve System.

h) The U.S. participate in the International Fertilizer Supply Scheme to organize international credits for fertilizer purchase and shipment, and for plant production in developing countries. Fertilizer aid shipments are needed immediately.

i) The U.S. support research in agricultural production and distribution in developing nations by an amount equal to at least 1/5 of our arms spending.

j) Institute grading standards for *100% grass-fed beef,* and change current standards to clearly reflect to the consumer the degree of leanness.

k) Increase the budget of the Bureau of Land Management to upgrade and better manage the use of public range lands.[41]

What can you and I do about the way food and hunger are produced by American agribusiness here and abroad? Many responses are possible, and there is plenty of room for imaginative personal responses to the situation. At the same time, we can suggest three general categories of action which concerned people might explore. I call these speaking up, organizing, and contributing.

Speaking up is just that: letting manufacturers, regulators, and legislators know how we feel about the outlook and practices of the food industry and the changes we would like to see made. It also includes filing complaints when a product or official action seems particularly offensive or antihuman. There are now several books available which list names and addresses of consumer protection agencies, state and federal regulators, and private agencies and corporations, organized by industry and products. Among these are *The Angry Buyer's Complaint Dictionary* by White, Yanker and Steinberg (New York: Wyden, 1975); *A Guide to Sources of Consumer Information* by Thomas and Weddington (Washington, D.C.: Information Resources Press, 1973), and *Consumer Complaint Guide* 1975 by Rosenbloom (New York: Macmillan, 1975). One or more of these books should be on the reference shelf at your library. (If they aren't, perhaps the librarian ought to be asked to get them.) In some of these books, you can also find tips on how to make complaints most effective. By themselves, of course, letters and complaints won't change the system; but they can have an impact, especially in coordination with some of the projects described below. And the work of people like Ralph Nader, who started as an unknown private citizen without a personal fortune or a powerful institutional position' shows that individual efforts, however small they appear, need not be meaningless. The people who run the food industry know this, too.

Much organizing around food issues is still young in

this country. But there are groups that are actively at work trying to change the public and private policies that shape our food production and nonproduction. Food co-ops have been around in many parts of the country for a long time; they and similar alternative food distribution systems have been undergoing a renaissance of interest and activity in recent years. The Food Co-op Project, 64 E. Lake St., Chicago IL 60601, is a clearinghouse for information about them. (See also bibliography.)

Among the issue-oriented groups in the field, one of the most vigorous is the Center for Science in the Public Interest, 1757 S St. N.W., Washington DC 20009. CSPI pushes for better regulation of food additives and wider public awareness of food and nutrition issues. It was a founding sponsor of Food Day. The center publishes a newsletter, *Nutrition Action,* and an excellent series of pamphlets, reports, and books on both domestic and international food concerns. Bread for the World, 235 E. 49th St., New York NY 10017, is a Christian group which is attempting to mobilize grass-roots pressure on Congress to change American international food policies to make them more humane and just. The Friends Committee on National Legislation, 245 Second St. N.E., Washington DC 20002, also lobbies in Congress on food issues, especially their international dimensions, and works with people in local areas to help make maximum impact on legislators. Oxfam America, Box 288, Boston MA 02166, in addition to being an international relief organization' was cofounder of Food Day with the Center for Science in the Public Interest, and it is involved in many of the antifamine efforts that came out of the event. Incidentally, Food Day is held on April 17, and the activities have deliberately been decentralized in focus; the idea is for many groups in many places to raise the issues in the ways that best suit their situations. Write for more information.

The Churchmouse Collective of the Movement for a New Society, 4722 Baltimore Avenue, Philadelphia PA 19143, is reaching out to churches in various places, challenging them to increase their awareness of and response to the demands of their faith in a hungry world. This is part of the Collective's Simple Living Campaign, an effort with which we feel considerable sympathy.

In most major U.S. cities, and some smaller ones, there is a boycott support organization for the United Farm Workers. The boycott organization is seeking to apply consumer pressure in very specific strategies toward the end goals of dignity, self-determination and union contracts for farm workers. UFW contracts result in better wages, job security, hiring based on seniority rather than discrimination and favors to a labor contractor, controls on the use of pesticides, an end to child labor, and drinking water and toilets in the fields. In the UFW, farm workers from many ethnic groups—Chicano, black, Filipino, Arab—have the experience of negotiating and then enforcing their own contracts with their employers. They have built a strongly democratic union which provides such services as a credit union, day care, clinics, a medical plan, a retirement center, a pension plan, and legal help. By seeking out produce bearing the UFW black eagle label and refusing to buy or eat boycotted products, consumers lend strength to this nonviolent movement to create a better life for farm workers.

As we speak up and organize for structural changes that we hope will redistribute resources to feed everyone adequately at some point in the future, people are still starving to death today and tomorrow. There are many relief agencies which work to bring food to as many of these people as their resources can reach, and they deserve our support too. Among these we will mention only a few: The American Friends Service Committee, 160 North 15th St., Philadelphia PA 19102, operates relief, reconstruction, and development projects in many countries, as does Church World Service, Room 656, 475 Riverside Drive, New York NY 10027, and the Advance Program of the United Methodist Church, Room 1439, 475 Riverside Drive, New York NY 10027.

A long list of other international relief groups can be found in the Alternative Celebrations Catalogue (see bibliography). An extensive listing of food-related organizations is contained in *Food for People Not for Profit* (see bibliography). A recently established monthly newsletter *AgBiz Tiller*, PO Box 5646, San Francisco CA 94101, is attempting to monitor agribusiness and the public interest organizing involved in the field. Here is a brief additional list of related groups:

Community Nutrition Institute
1910 K St. N.W., Washington DC 20006

National Farmers Union
1012 14th St. N.W., Washington DC 20005

Consumer Federation of America
Suite 1105, 1012 14th St. N.W.
Washington DC 20005

Center for Consumer Affairs
University Extension, University of Wisconsin
600 West Kilbourn Ave., Milwaukee WI 53203

Food Resource and Action Center
25 West 43 St., New York NY 10036

American Freedom from Hunger Foundation
1028 Connecticut Ave., N.W., Suite 614
Washington DC 20036

National Farmers Organization
Corning IA 50841

Federation of Southern Cooperatives
Epps AL 35460

Center for Rural Affairs
PO Box 405, Walthill NB 68067

National Catholic Rural Life Conference
1312 Massachusetts Ave. N.W.
Washington DC 20005

Because the food industry affects all of us daily in many ways, taking charge of what and how we eat is a personal matter as well as a social or political one.

The personal stories that follow describe some experiences of people associated with the author as they have tried to apply a simple living perspective to their own living situations. Most of us in the United States have the luxury of choices. With each purchase of a food product, a political, social, and ecological, as well as a nutritional, choice is being made.

From Mom on Kids and Food

Changing diets with kids can be tricky. Most of all, they like to keep eating what they always used to eat. I was met with great resistance when I said, "No more sweets and junk foods. Now we're going to eat whole grains and things that are good for us." Each new food was met with "Yuk!" and each banned food was craved and enjoyed with self-pity at friends' houses.

I finally gave up. It was almost two years before I tried in earnest again—this time very slowly.

I attacked breakfasts with granola and eggs. I served cracked wheat and whole wheat bread, once a month at first "just for variety." After they stopped complaining and even admitted that it was good, I'd alternate it with white bread. We also bought French bread, potato bread, rye bread, soy bread, bagels, rye krisp, and any other breadstuff that they or I wanted to try. Slowly I cut out the white bread and continued to buy or make a variety of whole grain breadstuffs.

Even when we were eating a fair amount of whole grain bread, they still didn't like the whole wheat spaghetti. Whole wheat lasagna was okay. I stopped buying Kool-aid and soda pop and bought fruit juices instead. I stopped buying candy and bought granola cookies or made my own. The kids were allowed to buy candy and cookies and such with their allowances; however, I stopped providing it for them. It was very important for the kids to know that the new diet did not mean that they could never again have some favorite food. I bought peanuts, sunflower seeds, apples and oranges, raisins, prunes' and occasionally dates and dried apricots for them to snack on. I tried to make pies with whole wheat pie crust, but our tastes were slow to adjust to that. Apple tarts with nuts, honey, and whole wheat crust were good. About this time I'd joined a food co-op, which helped make nuts, dried fruit (and fresh fruit), whole grain pastas, etc. more available and affordable.

Next to be worked out of the diet was meat. I stopped buying luncheon meats, though I continued to buy salami occasionally. Sandwiches were made of peanut butter, cheese, egg, or leftovers (sometimes meat loaf, chicken, or beef roast). I began making more casserole meals, using a small amount of ground beef together with beans, chunks of chicken in rice (Chinese-style or with gravy), or turkey with bulgur wheat and black-eyed peas. About once a week, or less often, I'd try a vegetarian dish, using soybeans, whole wheat pasta, or complementary proteins from *Diet for a Small Planet*. Some of the things none of us liked. But the ones we liked I made again, slowly making them a normal part of our diet and phasing out meat. Our favorite vegetarian meals are lasagna made with whole wheat lasagna and mushrooms, pizza with a whole wheat crust, tacos with beans and cheese, omelettes, cottage cheese and yogurt with fruit and nuts, and baked beans.

Here are some tips I have found to be time-savers in cooking vegetarian foods:

Soybeans can be frozen in water in the ice cube tray, instead of being presoaked, and then used any time you need them. Also, beans can be covered with boiling water (if you have not presoaked them the night before) providing that you let them stand for one hour before cooking. If you have a pressure cooker, even beans that were not presoaked will cook in 30–40 minutes.

Cook enough rice or beans for more than one meal.

Make a big pot of vegetable bean soup and eat it for the rest of the week.

Always have nuts, eggs, cheese, cottage cheese, and yogurt available.

Don't think meat and potatoes.

From a Busy, Single, Male Graduate Student

Healthful eating habits based on foods that represent efficient use of agricultural resources can be *easy, tasty, and emotionally satisfying*. Drawing on my own experience, I want to illustrate all three of these nice features—convenience, appeal, and peace of mind.

There's no denying that a drastic departure from supermarket shopping can be intimidating. Fifteen minutes spent in a health store looking over the shelves, skimming through books, and eavesdropping on conversations among salespeople and veteran health food faddists may leave a newcomer feeling baffled and sadly inadequate. At first, eating simple, healthful foods may seem to demand expertise in biochemistry, crop geography, brand-name folklore, and home economics—plus determination to organize one's life around the purchase, storage, and preparation of food. Some people *do* become versatile food experts, but it isn't *mandatory* for those of us who just want to eat well on the cheap and keep our ecological consciences content.

I make it a practice to draw on my food-fascinated friends as free consultants. Being real enthusiasts who have a lot to offer, they get a kick out of pouring wisdom into my ears. I show plenty of lively interest (it's real, and it's cheap), and in return they do my homework for me. Just by asking a question such as, What are these little yellow beadlike things in the gallon jar? I learned about millet, an inexpensive grain high in food value and low in calories. By inviting a wise friend to dinner and exposing a cabinet to view, I've evoked a thoughtful cost-benefit analysis of my whole food supply. My guess is that just about anyone can learn enough to begin eating well and cheaply in ten hours or so of careful listening.

Like food selection, food preparation can be easy and quick. I'm too busy to lavish hours daily on my belly, but I do like variety, zippy flavors, and lots of vitamins. My day usually begins with a bowl of home-made yogurt (½ gallon takes 15 minutes to mix, plus six hours unattended culturing in a warm, dark place), crunchy granola, and one or more fresh fruits. The combination is packed with energy and can vary greatly in flavor and texture, depending on the fruit used. For lunch, I usually have a chunk of cheese and some whole grain bread, usually accompanied by mixed nuts and seeds and followed by fruit. Often I toss the cheese between pieces of bread, with a pile of alfalfa sprouts, some avocado, and mayonnaise. Such a sandwich would be cheap at $1 in a restaurant; I make it for 35¢ or so.

For supper, I invent variations on any of several basic recipes. For example:

All-Purpose Meatless Stew

Combine one or more varieties of dried beans with rice and/or millet. (One cup rice plus ¾ cup bulgur wheat, plus ⅔ cup soybeans will yield complete protein, as detailed in *Diet for a Small Planet,* by F. M. Lappe, p. 146.) For each cup of mix, add 2¼ cups of water. Chop in any veggies you like—zucchini, carrots, celery, onions, tomatoes. Add some spices (bay leaves, garlic, oregano, rosemary, etc.). Pressure-cook for about 30 minutes. If beans are too crunchy for you, heat some water to boiling while you brush your teeth in the morning and drop the beans in. In the evening, add the other stuff and cook.

Bean Sprouts Exotica

Add a little water to a can of tomato soup or sauce. Chop in almost anything (tuna, tofu, vegetables), and add spices. Heat, stirring occasionally. Put sprouts in a colander and run hot tap water over them. Immediately top sprouts with the sauce and sprinkle with chunks of cheese. Garnish generously with sunflower seeds, sesame seeds, or mixed nuts.

I think these recipes illustrate ease and at least hints of *tastiness*. What about emotional satisfaction? Won't it feel oppressive to abstain from junk food? Personally, I find now that a lot of the advertiser-inspired appeal has faded from buns made of nutrition-free white flour straddling a feeble slab of chemically

treated beef· to be washed down with a glass of fizzy
sugar water with artificial flavoring. A few days of
subsistence on restaurant food leaves me feeling dissatisfied and hungry for simple, nourishing foods.

I would like to comment that a little sinful eating
can be tolerated by all souls and most wallets. If you
get a serious "Big Mac fit," indulge. In a more serious
vein, the fact that food habits are *learned* deserves
repetition. Over time, healthy foods become satisfying
to eat. This happens earlier if you share food with
others who can be supportive and enjoy *eating well*
together as well as being together. For me, it took
just a few months.

(*Editor's Note:* I happen to know that this busy
person found a couple of hours a month to participate
in a food co-op, too, which helped him to make that
sandwich for 35¢.)

Our Cooking Co-op

Two evenings each week, a delicious and complete
dinner for my family of four comes through the front
door in the hands of a friend. On another evening of
the week, I prepare dinner for the families of my two
friends as well as my own. We live within a few blocks
of each other, so that delivery can be accomplished
within ten to fifteen minutes. We find it convenient to
eat in our own homes rather than together. Our families
each consist of two adults and two young children, so
the same amount of food is prepared for each family.
Variation in the size of the "family" (added guests,
absent family members) results in leftovers or requires
that the receiving family add bread, a salad, or another
dish.

The benefits of our "cooking co-op" are many. The
feeling of mutual supportiveness is at least as important
as the liberation from cooking every night. Preparing
food is a challenge and a pleasure for the cook, providing an opportunity to try unusual or more elegant
meals, and to give a much-appreciated "gift" to a

friend. Receiving dinner is wonderful! The recipients have the opportunity to spend a relaxed afternoon with their families and to enjoy a greater variety of food than one family is likely to prepare. A bonus for Mother Earth is greater efficiency in shopping and preparing meals.

We find it most pleasurable to provide and receive complete meals: main course (often including rice or "pasta" of some sort), cooked fresh vegetable, salad (optional), and bread (optional), including dressing, butter, and sauces if appropriate. Every so often a special drink or dessert is included as a surprise. We often cook vegetarian meals, taking care to provide complementary sources of protein, and we also attempt to prepare healthful, nutritious foods, avoiding non-food ingredients as much as possible.

Our co-op will soon begin its fifth year, with limited turnover in participants. The present members are good friends, who also share child-care and car-pool responsibilities. We are open to experimentation with our co-op, and are trying out an arrangement whereby we exchange food only two nights per week, with one member household preparing both meals. This adjustment is in response to the problem of too much leftover food and also is an attempt to increase the liberation from preparing food so frequently.

Other alternatives open to people interested in setting up a cooking co-op include sharing only main courses, exchanging with friends who live farther away by putting food in containers and delivering it at convenient meeting places, or eating together. The possibilities are vast, and a co-op can be developed to suit the personalities and needs of members with imagination and a willingness to be adaptable.

Neighborhood Food Co-ops

Belonging to a food co-op is one way to "take charge" of your life in a creative way. You will find yourself eating better, saving money, and making friends. All it takes is a few people who share the idea of working together for their own good.

Our co-op in Palo Alto, California, started in 1973 as a cheese-buying club with fifteen members. We found a wholesale cheese company and got a list of their cheese prices. Someone dittoed an order form with eight types of cheese and distributed it to friends and neighbors. People filled out the order form and paid in advance. The orders were totaled and we bought the bulk cheese. We cut it into pieces according to what was ordered and refigured the actual cost. Order forms for the next time were distributed and it happened again. We found an apple grower and a thrift bread store. Soon we began buying fruit and vegetables with another co-op one day a week. Most of the produce was bought at a farmers' market and a large commercial produce terminal. Some was picked up at a local farm and some came from a community garden. Gradually we added staples like grains and beans, dried fruit, and dairy products to our weekly list. The food was fresher and cheaper than what we were used to at the supermarket. Most members were surprised at how much good food they received in their first order. It was much more pleasant working with friends and involving the children than shopping in noisy sales-oriented supermarkets. People would comment on how the quality of their diets had improved. The co-op made fresh foods more affordable. Also, preordering meant that we planned our meals in advance instead of being tempted to buy expensive, unnecessary "convenience foods" at the store.

Members of the co-op do the work and decide how it will operate. The work is divided into work teams of ten people or less, who work together on a certain job in the co-op (e.g., cheese cutting, boxing orders, buying produce, etc.). The teams choose a team leader to communicate with the rest of the co-op. Small groups working together can get to know each other and decide how to do their work.

There are hundreds of food co-ops in the United States now, including cooperative supermarkets, a number of small co-op stores, and lots of groups of from

10 to 200 families like ours, who order and buy food regularly, then divide and distribute it from garages, churches, schools, etc. The only overhead costs involved for groups like ours are transportation costs, any packaging materials necessary (people can usually bring their own containers and bags), expenses of printing order forms, loss due to a few spoiled fruits per box, and initial expenses like simple scales. Some co-ops pay a few people for coordinating. From 5- to 10-percent mark-up over wholesale usually covers these expenses. Savings vary from 10 to 50 percent. In most places, and especially for small groups, permits, licenses, and health department inspection are not required. Business licenses, resale numbers, etc., if required, are usually fairly easy to obtain. Food stamp authorization to accept food stamp payment is easy to get. In the bibliography are three excellent references for further information on food co-ops: *The Food Co-op Handbook, Food Co-ops—An Alternative to Shopping in Supermarkets,* and the *Food Co-op Nooz.* All three contain a national listing of food co-ops complied by the Food Co-op Project, publishers of the *Nooz.*

Father and Son in the Food Co-op Store

what does the food co-op mean to me?
working with my son jacob four and a half years old
wheeling out the produce
jacob sorting out the bruised or overripe peaches
            and tomatoes
snitching some fresh peas
putting out all the different breads
small hands dipping into the grain bins to check
            if they need refilling
cutting weighing wrapping and pricing all the
            fine cheeses
snitching a nibble of each as we work together
jake and i
four hours
                    go by
        one saturday morning each month

jacob's attention
out and eager and full of useful things to do
interested in his store
and how it works
and what he can do to help

as for me
that feeling at first
when i came to the cash register without pricing
          my own items
the slowness at first of my friends adding up
            my purchases on the cash register
oops, i forgot to bring a jar to put oil in
consciousness of what people do in stores
and how much sense and easy it is to recycle
unthinkable now to waste as much glass and paper and
      gas (we plan our shopping better now so that
            our once-a-week binge cuts down on driving)
a store of organics and
it's incredible that you get everything you need
            in such small space
without rows and rows of softdrinks and potato chips
      and cookies and cat foods and plastic stuff and
      muzak and everything wrapped
and nothing touchable or out of color
it's so refreshing to own your own store
it feels different
it feels fine
and you never do a quick shopping there
your friends and you stop to chat
you count up how much you save this time and decide
            to buy another share in the store
you don't feel so rushed
when the vibes are home grown and cooperatively
                                    marketed

Projects

1. List everything you eat in one day and analyze it
   as to its nutritional value, additives, and social,
   political, and ecological considerations. At the end
   of the day, add them up and see if your nutritional

requirements were met. Would you want to make any changes? *Let's Get Well*, by Adele Davis, has good food-composition tables which include whole grains, seeds, sprouts, etc. The USDA *Food Composition Handbook* is also good. You can also find the daily minimum nutritional requirements for your height and weight in these books. For information on additives and other considerations, refer to *Diet for a Small Planet* by Frances Moore Lappe, *The Poisons in your Food* by William Longgood, and *Eater's Digest* by Michael Jacobson.

2. Make an inventory of your cupboards and refrigerator with nutritional, ecological, and social considerations in mind.

3. Go on your own supermarket awareness tour. Take some friends. Note advertising, packaging, placement of items to get attention, sales, ingredients, etc. Note what people are buying. Look for excessive use of plastic and paper bags. Do you see any smaller or irregular fruits and vegetables which are less expensive offered on sale? What happens to the produce that develops a bruise or bad spot, or the cheese with a mold spot?

4. Try meatless meals for a few days or a week. You may be in for a pleasant surprise. Refer to *Diet for a Small Planet* by Frances Moore Lappe or *Recipes for a Small Planet* by Ellen Buchwald for recipes emphasizing protein complementarity. If decreasing meat consumption is difficult for you, try eating meat progressively fewer times a week or using only very small amounts for flavor. *The Vegetarian Epicure* by Anna Thomas has delicious recipes. Have vegetarian potlucks focusing on protein complementarity. Go out to dinner at restaurants featuring vegetarian specialties.

5. Write letters or even brief postcards to congresspersons urging support of the food policies listed earlier.

6. Join or start a neighborhood food co-op. Write

Chicago Food Co-op Project, Loop College, C.C.E., 64 E. Lake St., Chicago, IL 60601, for a national directory of co-ops and information on starting them.

7. Start a cooking co-op with several families, where each family cooks once or twice for others and delivers the meals or invites the others over.

8. Find out what your local schools serve for lunches. What is served at school parties? At P.T.A. meetings? What changes could be made to reflect nutritional, ecological, and social concerns? Choices such as herb teas with honey, dried fruit, and nut snacks could be offered in addition, with a note explaining why.

9. Try to get your local market to stock grains in bulk and provide information on how to use them to combine proteins properly. If they sell books, do they have *Diet for a Small Planet* and *Recipes for a Small Planet* available? Does your library have these books? Would they do a display on protein complementarity? Such a display could be used at special events or group meetings, too.

10. Does your local market sell grass-fed beef? How many signatures on a petition would be required to persuade them to offer it as an option? What about your local school cafeteria, church dinners, restaurants?

11. Deliberately fix less than "enough" for a meal and experience what it is like to remain hungry. Try this as a surprise at a group dinner and discuss people's responses.

12. A group might sponsor a "sacrificial meal" with only rice and tea. You might do this as a benefit for UNICEF or another hunger-related project. The meal might be eaten in meditative silence with relevant informational material or poetry read at intervals and perhaps a film or speaker afterwards.

13. Simulation meal. Group people by continents for dinner. The number of people in each group might represent that continent's percentage of the

world population. The number of plates and utensils allotted each group might represent that continent's share of the world's GNP, and the amount of food served might represent that continent's daily per-capita consumption of animal protein. (See chart for actual percentages.) Instruct people to deal with the situation realistically, i.e., the United States may sell food to allies, barter leftovers, etc., but give away *very little*. Discuss feelings and reactions. The education and action packet· *Hunger on Spaceship Earth,* put out by the American Friends Service Committee (see bibliography) includes a similar game with detailed information and instructions.

PEOPLE

Continent	Percent
Africa	10
Asia	59
Europe	17
Latin America	8
North America	6

SHARE OF WORLD GNP (Plates and Silverware)

Continent	Percent
Africa	3
Asia	33
Europe	31
Latin America	5
North America	28

SHARE OF DAILY CONSUMPTION OF ANIMAL PROTEIN (Food)

Continent	Percent
Africa	8
Asia	23
Europe	36
Latin America	11
North America	22

14. Find out if there is a local UFW boycott organization (check United Farm Workers in your phone

listings or write UFW, P.O. Box 62, Keene CA 93531). Volunteer to hold a "house meeting" (a boycott organizer explains the movement to you and friends at a meeting in your home). Join in the current action program of the boycott, which may vary from letter writing and petition circulating to picketing a liquor store or produce market.

NOTES

1. Donella H. Meadows and Dennis L. Meadows, *The Limits to Growth* (New York: Signet, 1972), p. 58.
2. William Paddock and Paul Paddock, *Famine 1975. America's Decision: Who Will Survive?* (Boston: Little, Brown and Co., 1967), pp. 50–51.
3. *U.S. News* magazine, January 25, 1974, p. 50.
4. Adam Finnerty, "The World Food Conference— Hopes and Realities," *WIN* magazine, October 17, 1974, p. 8.
5. Mary Harvey, "Agribusiness and the Food Crisis," *The Corporate Examiner* (New York: Corporate Information Center, Room 846, 475 Riverside Drive NY 10027, 1974). Available for 60¢.
6. Ibid.
7. *Los Angeles Times,* December 19, 1974.
8. Geoffrey Barraclough, "The Great World Food Crisis," *The Catalyst,* The Publication of the Stanford Forum, Stanford University, Stanford, California, 1975, p. 17.
9. Ibid.
10. Frances Moore Lappe, *Diet for a Small Planet* (New York: Ballantine, 1971), p. 16.
11. *U.S. Bean Market Report,* U.S. Dept. of Agriculture, October 16, 1973.
12. Frances Moore Lappe, "Fantasies of Famine," *Harpers* magazine, February 1975, p. 52.
13. Frances Moore Lappe, *Diet for a Small Planet,* p. 7.
14. Ibid., p. 5.
15. Susan De Marco and Susan Sechler, *Corporate Giants in the Food Economy,* Appendix B: "Some Facts and Figures Supporting Action against Concentration in the Food Industry." Agribusiness Accountability Proj-

ect, 1000 Wisconsin Avenue, N.W., Washington DC 20007, p. 1.

16. Ibid., pp. 2–3.
17. Ibid.; Jim Hightower, "Statement of the Food Action Campaign before the Monopoly Subcommittee of the Senate Select Committee on Small Business," December 10, 1973, p. 7.
18. Ibid., p. 2.
19. Ralph Nader, *Anti-Trust Law and Economics Review*, vol. 5, no. 2.
20. Jim Hightower, op. cit., p. 9.
21. Kay Patchner and Nancy Mills, "Family Farmers and Concentration in the Food Industry," California Food Action Campaign, 370A Hayes Street, San Francisco CA 94102, p. 4.
22. *The Case of Food Price Blackmail* (San Francisco: United Front Press, 1973), p. 10.
23. Jim Hightower, op. cit., p. 32.
24. Michael Jacobson and Catherine Lerza, editors, *Food for People Not for Profit* (New York: Ballantine Books, 1975), p. 308.
25. Ibid., p. 307.
26. Gary Bellow and Jeanne C. Kettleson, "The Facts about Farmworkers," *The Harvard Crimson*, November 5, 1974.
27. Ronald B. Taylor, *Sweatshops in the Sun* (Boston: Beacon Press, 1973), p. 156.
28. Ibid., p. 157.
29. *Wednesday's Children*, National Committee on the Education of Migrant Children, New York, 1971, p. 77.
30. Jacobson and Lerza, op. cit., p. 305.
31. Polchnir and Mills, op. cit., "Consuming In a Concentrated Food Economy," p. 5.
32. Lester Brown and Eric Eckholm, *By Bread Alone* (New York: Praeger, 1974).
33. Ibid.
34. Mary Roodkowsky, "PL480: Aid for Arms and Agribusiness," written for *World Food Crisis—A Self-Education Packet*, April 1975 (available from Committee for Self-Education, 11 Garden St., Cambridge MA 02138, $2), p. 3.
35. Israel Yost, "The Food for Peace Arsenal," *North*

American Congress on Latin America (NACLA) News-letter. vol. 5, no. 3, May–June, 1971, p. 3.

36. Mary Roodkowsky, op. cit., p. 1.
37. Israel Yost, op. cit., p. 1.
38. Ibid., p. 4.
39. Mary Roodkowsky, op. cit., p. 3.
40. Pamela Haines and William Moyer, "How We Cause World Hunger," *WIN* magazine, January 30, 1975.
41. "Action Suggestions," *Hunger on Spaceship Earth,* an education and action packet available for $2.50 from AFSC, 15 Rutherford Place, New York NY 10003.

SOURCES OF FURTHER INFORMATION

The following is a limited list of materials available on this subject. Items listed with an asterisk (*) contain extensive listings of reading matter, organizations, and media materials.

Limited Resources and Hunger

*American Friends Service Committee. *Hunger on Space-ship Earth.* Available for $2.50 from AFSC, 15 Rutherford Place, New York NY 10003.

Contains some educational material, a "Simulation Game," alternative recipes, action suggestions, religious background. Intended for groups.

Barnes, Peter. *The People's Land.* Emmaus, Pa.: Rodale Press, 1975.

An anthology of readings on land reform with a major section on the implications of land reform for food production.

Brown, Lester, and Eckholm, Erik. *By Bread Alone.* New York: Praeger, 1974.

An overview of the problems the world will be facing —and the opportunities mankind has—in the next quarter-century.

*Committee for Self-Education. *World Food Crisis—A Self-Education Packet.* Available for $2 from the Committee for Self-Education, 11 Garden St., Cambridge MA 02138.

Contains 28 articles which deal with the various aspects of the world food situation and an excellent bibliography.

Finnerty, Adam. "Hunger Crisis: At Stake 400,000 Lives," *Fellowship* magazine, January-February 1975.

Lazar, Ed. "A Decentralist Approach to the World Food Crisis." January 1975. May be obtained from the American Friends Service Committee, 48 Inman St., Cambridge MA 02139.

Meadows, Donella H., et al. *The Limits to Growth*. New York: Ballantine, 1971.

A study of the future if present growth rates continue by a team of scientists from the Massachusetts Institute of Technology.

Moyer, William, and Haines, Pamela. "How We Cause World Hunger." *WIN* magazine, January 30, 1975. Available for 25¢ from the authors at 4713 Windsor St., Philadelphia PA 19143.

Paddock, William, and Paddock, Paul. *Famine—1975. America's Decision: Who Will Survive?* Boston: Little, Brown and Co., 1967.

A now-classic statement of the threat of world hunger.

Simon, Paul, and Simon, Arthur. *The Politics of World Hunger*. New York: Harpers Magazine Press, 1973.

A humanitarian look at the world food problem that points the finger of blame at the U.S. failure to place human needs before economic gain.

Transnational Institute. "The Transnational Institute Report." Available for $2.50 from the Institute for Policy Studies, 1901 W St., N.W., Washington DC 20009.

A radical view of the reasons for world food shortages. The report, prepared for the 1974 World Food Conference, advocates land reform and redistribution of world resources as the only long-term solutions to the food crisis.

Food Industry

Burbach, Roger, and Flynn, Patricia. "U.S. Grain Arsenal," *Latin America and Empire Report*, October 1975. Available for $1.25 from NACLA, Box 226, Berkeley CA 94701.

An in-depth study on how U.S. grain is being used as a diplomatic and economic weapon throughout the world.

Fenton, Thomas. "Coffee—The Rules of the Game and

You." Available from The Christophers, 12 E. 48th St., New York NY 10017.
Fenton focuses on coffee to illustrate a thorough discussion of exploitation of Third World workers through the system of cash cropping. Written in Christian context.

Hightower, Jim. "Corporate Giantism in the Food Economy." Available from the Agribusiness Accountability Project, 1000 Wisconsin Ave., Washington DC 20007. Statement of the Food Action Campaign before the Monopoly Subcommittee of the Senate Select Committee on Small Business. December 10, 1973.

Katz, Deborah, and Goodwin, Mary T. *Food: Where Nutrition, Politics and Culture Meet: An Activity Guide for Teachers*. Washington D.C.; Center for Science in the Public Interest, 1976.

Krebs, A. V. "The AgBiz Tiller." One-year subscription for $10 available from San Francisco Study Center, P.O. Box 5696, San Francisco CA 94101.
A monthly newsletter which monitors and reports on the activities of agribusiness from a public-interest perspective.

*Lerza, Catherine, and Jacobson, Michael. *Food for People Not for Profit*. New York: Ballantine, 1975.
A complete source book on the world food crisis prepared for National Food Day 1975. Contains a number of articles by authors already mentioned in the above list.

Lobenstein, Margaret, and Schommer, John. *Food Price Blackmail*. San Francisco: United Front Press, 1973.
Uses cartoons as well as script to expose some of the politics behind rising food prices in America.

McWilliams, Carey. *Factories in the Field*. Peregrine Publishers Inc., 1971.
The classic history of migrant farm workers and California agribusiness.

Robbins, William. *The American Food Scandal*. New York: William Morrow and Co., 1974.
An excellent description of the abuses of power by agribusiness corporations and food manufacturers.

Sechler, Susan, and De Marco, Susan. "Some Facts and Figures Supporting Action against Concentration in the Food Industry." Available from the Agribusiness

Accountability Project, 1000 Wisconsin Avenue, Washington DC 20007.

——. *The Fields Have Turned Brown.* Washington D.C.: Agribusiness Accountability Project, 1974.

A critical examination of the Food for Peace Program, the U.S. grain trade, the Green Revolution, and American agribusiness abroad.

Food and Nutrition

Ackerman, Caroline. *The No-Fad, Good Food, $5 a Day Cookbook.* Toronto: McClelland and Stewart, 1974.

Brown, Edward. *Tassajara Cooking.* Berkeley, Calif.: Shambala Publications, 1973.

Center for Science in the Public Interest. "Nutrition Action." Monthly newsletter. One year subscription available for $10 from the Center for Science in the Public Interest, 1757 S St. N.W., Washington DC 20009.

A publication aimed at nutrition and public health activists. Reports latest scientific information on food and health, as well as information on the activities of food action organizations and concerned individuals.

Consumers Co-op of Berkeley, Inc. *The Co-op Low-Cost Cookbook.* Richmond, Calif.: Co-op, 1965.

Davis, Jeanne M. *About Community Gardening.* Available for $3.25 from Alternatives, P.O. Box 20626, Greensboro NC 27420.

Ewald, Ellen B. *Recipes for a Small Planet.* New York: Ballantine Books, 1973.

Introduction by Frances Moore Lappe, author of *Diet for a Small Planet.* Description of "the art and science of high protein vegetarian cookery" and extensive recipes based on principles of protein complementarity.

Goodwin, Mary T., and Pollen, Gerry. *Creative Food Experiences for Children.* Available for $4 from the Center for Science in the Public Interest, 1779 Church St. N.W., Washington DC 20036.

A resource book for teachers and parents. Focusing on natural foods, it encourages children to use all five senses in exploring foods—not only with nutrition exercises and recipes, but also with activities applicable to science, art, and other subject areas.

Jacobson, Michael. *Eater's Digest—The Consumer's Fact-*

book of Food Additives. Garden City, N.Y.: Anchor Books, 1972.

————. *Nutrition Scoreboard*. Available from the Center for Science in the Public Interest, 1779 Church St. N.W., Washington DC 20036.
Rates and discusses the nutritional value of foods. Many foods are mentioned by brand name. Foods are rated by a single number reflecting the protein, vitamin, mineral, sugar, fat, and fiber content.

Lappe, Frances Moore. *Diet for a Small Planet*. New York: Ballantine Books, 1971.
A clear discussion of the ecological and political reasons for eating vegetable, rather than meat, protein. Also details how to combine vegetables properly to get maximum protein benefit.

Mittleider, J. R. *More Food from Your Garden*. Santa Barbara, Calif.: Woodbridge Press, 1975.

Olkowski, Helga, and Olkowski, William. *The City People's Book of Raising Food*. Emmaus, Pa.: Rodale Press, 1971.

Food Co-ops

Co-op Handbook Collective. *The Food Co-op Handbook*. Boston: Houghton Mifflin, 1975.

Food Co-op Project. "Food Co-op Nooz." A quarterly newspaper available for $2 per year from the Food Co-op Project, 64 E. Lake St., Chicago IL 60601.
Published largely by and for food co-ops and alternative warehouses, containing information about various co-ops, the food industry, nutrition, etc. A national directory is published semiannually.

Ronco, William. *Food Co-ops, An Alternative to Shopping in Supermarkets*. Boston: Beacon Press, 1974.
Describes history of the cooperative movement, gives contemporary food co-op forms, and contains the national directory of food co-ops compiled by the Food Co-op Project (above).

14
Another View of Economics
BY MARIE SIMIRENKO

Queries

1. What would an economic system be like that promoted harmony with the environment and the rest of the world family?
2. How can we create economic structures that would reflect our values? What could we do to stop or disengage ourselves from economic structures that go against our values?
3. How far are we willing to go to maintain our standard of living? How closely is the quality of life related to standard of living? What values would you like our economy to embody or protect?

In 1973 I joined a group of people associated with the Palo Alto Friends Meeting, to learn more about the problems facing the world today through a macroanalysis seminar, a study-action program developed by the Movement for a New Society. We met weekly to share the main ideas and significant details of the long list of books and articles we read. We discussed the readings and the interrelationships of the major study areas: Ecology, U.S. Relations to Third World Nations, U.S. Domestic Problems, Visions of a Better Society, How to Get from Here to There. Each of us took turns facilitating the meetings.

I became interested in the macroanalysis seminar and Movement for a New Society through actively involved friends I'd met while working with the AFSC in Reno, Nevada, and Palo Alto, California. I had also been active with the League of Women Voters in Reno and had taken part in getting a peace plank on the 1967 state Democratic platform. The work with the Democrats was frustrating, because although the plank was adopted, the candidates would not support it for fear of losing elections. I was interested in finding a new vision. The old one wasn't working for me and I didn't understand why.

My concerns were idealistic: how can we best live in harmony with nature and our fellow man without exploiting and being exploited? But they also came out of my own experience. For instance, for five years I had been the single parent of two small daughters working part-time for low wages. When the kids got sick, I hired older women to stay with them and paid them even lower wages. I identified with them—if I had been 30 years older I would probably have been doing the same thing—and I didn't like either their situation or mine. I felt both exploited and exploiting. How could we get out of this fix?

The rest of the seminar members were predominantly liberal students, professionals, and spouses. We were not surprised to learn that Americans use more food, energy, and resources per capita than people of any other nation. But it was a sobering shock to most of us to learn just how much more we used, and that there isn't enough for everyone in the world to do the same. Our sense of helplessness grew when it became clear that the economies of both this country and the world are dominated by large corporations whose concerns and priorities often run counter to our own.

Having studied the problems and their complexities, we became depressed. What could we do? We all tried to simplify our lives to consume less and be less dependent on the large corporate businesses. I cut down on my family's meat consumption, did more recycling, and got a bicycle.

These efforts didn't feel like enough, though. I wanted to join some model city in which solutions to these problems were already in existence. But I didn't know of any such model city, or what one would be like, or what I would do there if I found it. Instead I joined with some others from the seminar and a changing group of friends to help write this book as an attempt to develop for ourselves, and share with others, positive alternatives to the things we felt kept us from living our values.

There are two areas I want to reflect on here: first,

some of the broad questions of economics, seen from a different direction, and second, some alternatives that may help us gain control over our economic lives. I'm not an expert and don't pretend to exhaust either subject; but these descriptions can provide a basis for acceptance or rejection of these experiments, and a jumping-off place for further exploration.

Exploring Economics from Different Directions

The function of an economic system is to take care of our basic human needs (food, clothing, shelter, health). The system encompasses the ways in which these needs are met (jobs, building, manufacturing, transportation, energy use, buying, selling, bartering, sharing, etc.). Only to the extent that the economic system reflects and supports our values can it be a positive factor in our lives. It becomes a negative and destructive factor when it conflicts with our values or makes it impossible for us to live according to our values.

But our current economic system equates maximization of profits with good business and sees growth as a basic necessity to maintain healthy business. Human and ecological values suffer when business success is measured by high profits alone. Unlimited growth ignores the natural limits of resources and can threaten world peace. But changing to an economy of limited growth and limited profits will be hard, because our economy is dominated by large corporations which depend on growth to survive.

The economic terms we use today place greater importance on the quantities in life and money value than on the qualities of life and the well-being of people. The current dictionary definition of the word *wealth* stresses the possession of objects and property that have money value, and one's ability to acquire these. An earlier definition of wealth, which is now considered obsolete, stressed welfare, well-being, and happiness. It is interesting to contemplate how different our economic dealings would be if we returned to that earlier definition. Economics itself would have to become much broader and take into account the factors that contribute to human well-being and happiness as well as the management of affairs with reference to money. This could return the emphasis to the quality of life rather than the quantities in life.

Affluent, according to the dictionary, means "wealthy; abounding in goods or riches. Abundant; copious; plenteous." It would follow, then, that in an affluent society all the people's material needs are easily satisfied. Marshall Sahlins, in his book *Stone Age Economics,* claims that the unrestricted hunter and gatherer tribes of Paleolithic times constituted the most affluent society, because their needs were simple and easily met. In a society of infinite needs, people are poor, because their needs are never met. Such a society, based on scarcity and striving for the unattainable, is what we live in now. We want more; therefore we want growth.

When growth is used as an indication of economic health, high consumption is viewed as good. Luxuries become needs. Hot running water, which is a luxury to most people in the world, is considered a necessity in American homes. Some families also consider having three cars to be a necessity in their lives. More and more resources are used up increasing the demand and competition for resources and our dependency on them. The conflict that comes with increasing dependency on decreasing amounts of resources and its threat to world peace has been discussed earlier in this book.

We measure economic growth by quantifying the Gross National Product. GNP is based on the value of goods and services, or the quantity of possessions produced and sold in one year. By using growth in the GNP as the standard measure, the sheer mass of production replaces the meeting of human needs as an economic indicator. Whose well-being does GNP actually reflect? Brazil's GNP has risen greatly in recent years because of industrial development. But

Brazil's finance minister admits that only 5 percent of the people, the top income group, have benefited from this rise. Half of the people live as they did before, and 45 percent have had their standard of living eroded.[1] No one has attempted a comparable analysis of our own country. But of what importance is it to a country to have a high GNP if large numbers of its people are unemployed, unable to afford decent medical care, and desperately in need of adequate housing? Even during its most productive years, this country has never met its housing needs.

Unfortunately, growth and high consumption are necessary for the survival of the large corporations that dominate our national economic system. The size alone of these corporations gives them great power, and our dependency on them increases our vulnerability to that power. The role of large corporations in world economics with regard to the environment, resources, energy, and human labor has been discussed in various parts of this book.

Different Ways to Meet Our Economic Needs

By redefining wealth and affluence, I found it easier to focus on meeting human needs, rather than growth and money for money's sake, as the goal of economics. But definitions were not enough. How was I to move from concepts to actually changing the forces that affected my life. How could I free myself from the system? Or, better yet, how could I help create a system that would more nearly meet my needs and values? As I became more involved in alternatives, my attitude towards these questions changed, until it has taken on the aspect of playing a game, like attempting a crossword puzzle or tackling a brain twister. It has become a lot more enjoyable than watching TV.

To begin with, I believe that things don't have to be the way they are. We can develop alternatives and create new structures. Each new way has its own weaknesses and strengths, which we should be aware of, but at least there are other ways to meet our needs. What are some of them?

To find out, I started reading the underground literature and talking to people who were experimenting with new life-styles. The alternatives listed here are intended to help people meet their own needs while supporting various people-oriented values.

In Madison, Wisconsin, it is possible for a person to earn money, buy food and clothing, purchase a bicycle, service a car, and even find housing without having to pay for anyone's profit. Through cooperatives and an association of service organizations, many citizens of that city are attempting to

> seize control of their lives and the resources needed to live their lives to the fullest potential. We [the co-op members] see ourselves as providing badly needed services to the people of Madison and in doing so creating an atmosphere of cooperation and trust in which people may begin to liberate themselves from existing social and economic roles which place people in positions of dominating and being dominated.[2]

The Earthworm Community in Champaign, Illinois, consists of about fifty groups, both cooperative businesses and community services, representing about two hundred people. To be eligible for inclusion in Earthworm, groups must have a collective decision-making structure and run on a nonprofit or low-profit basis.[3]

Collective decision making implies the absence of managers, bosses, or any kind of hierarchy. Tasks and decision making are equally shared so that people can control their own work lives and have power over the decisions that affect their work. Some businesses rotate managerial responsibilities, while in others all responsibility is shared all the time.

Running a nonprofit or low-profit business does not mean that people cannot make a living from it. It means that the business is not run to make profits.

It meets its costs and provides for overhead, maintenance, salaries, and projected needs.

Cooperative Business

Over fifty million people in the United States belong to some cooperative business: food retailing, repair services, housing, credit unions, farm equipment, and rural electricity, among many others.[4] Cooperatively owned businesses can respond more directly to people's needs than businesses oriented towards profits for the few. There are three types of co-ops: producer cooperatives, worker cooperatives, and consumer cooperatives.

In a producer cooperative, people producing similar things band together to market them. The size of producer co-ops can vary from the immensity of agribusiness to small groups of farmers. Small food-growing cooperatives, for example are now their own wholesalers. They have also begun contracting to supply urban food-buying cooperatives. Such guaranteed markets take much of the risk out of farming.

In worker-owner-and-operated cooperatives, workers provide the money to start and run the business and elect the board of directors. Any surplus earnings are distributed as bonuses. Worker-owner cooperatives can take other forms, for example, living communities. In such groups, each person has an equal say in the decision-making process and receives enough money to cover his or her low consumption needs.

Consumer cooperatives are owned and controlled by their customers, usually through an elected board. Some consumer cooperatives are run as nonprofit businesses that provide workers with an adequate income and consumers with low prices. These can be operated on a direct-charge basis; the Briarpatch Cooperative Market, mentioned elsewhere in this book, is an example. It meets its operating expenses through a monthly charge of fifty cents per member. The initial capital to start the store came from selling membership shares. Co-ops may also return profits to members in the form of patronage refunds, whereby profits are divided and returned to member patrons in proportion to their sales receipts. Some consumer co-ops have workers on their board of directors as well as members. Each member shareholder has one vote, so those with more shares do not have more power.

Cooperatively Owned Housing

In cooperative housing, all units are financed with a single mortgage, which is held by a nonprofit corporation. These units may be houses or apartments or both. The corporation, in turn, is owned by the residents of the housing cooperative through membership shares —one share per residential unit, one vote per share.

Cooperative housing can sometimes be 100-percent financed through federal or local government loans. In this way the corporation can purchase the housing without having to raise much capital from its members. The only down payment needed to live in the cooperative is the cost of a share, which can be as low as the total of the two months' rent deposit often required on similar housing, with monthly payments equal to, or smaller than, rent on comparable housing. Members can deduct property tax and mortgage interest payments from their state and federal income tax, and they are eligible for the homeowner's property tax exemption in California. When someone moves out, the cooperative buys back the share and resells it to a new resident at no profit. Because the mortgage is held by the cooperative corporation, there is no refinancing cost or 6-percent real estate commission in the transaction.[5] In this way, housing that could normally be afforded only by families with incomes of $14,000 or more a year could be made available to families with incomes as low as $7,500, assuming one-fourth goes to housing.

New York State loaned $234 million to one of the largest cooperatively owned housing complexes in the world, Co-op City in the East Bronx. The monthly payments Co-op City members make are well below prevailing rates in New York City.

Cooperatively owned housing is a good example of how basic needs can be met through cooperation with others. At the present time, most people cannot afford to own their own home, so they rent. The landlord pays property taxes and his mortgage, for which he gets federal income tax deductions, and he can claim depreciation on the building structure while the value of the land rises. The renter pays all the expenses related to the property through his rent, plus a profit to the landlord for his investment, and his full income taxes. The renter pays more to rent than he would pay if he owned the property he rents. But, separately, most people are unable to qualify for a home loan.

Land Trusts

Land trusts present a completely different way of relating to land and to ownership. In a land trust, the land belongs to those who use it. It is not theirs to abuse or sell, but theirs to care for, nurture, and live on as trustees. The trustees use and hold the land for future generations. One group, Landlords End in East Palo Alto, California, did not want to own any land, but did want to settle on some without the expense of renting. Landlords End is an example of land trusting as an alternative to renting. The residents, or trustees, of the land gain no equity in the property and improvements they make. These are retained in the trust. More frequently, in land trust arrangements, only the land is put in trust, with arrangements for residents to recover equity from improvements to buildings or property. One of the Landlords End group put it this way:

> The idea seemed simple. A land trust; the idea of mutuality between people and the land they use; the idea that between people and land there is a

caretakership; that land is to be used, but not used up. We would buy the houses we were already living in and put them together into a trust. Making payments would be no more than what we were already paying in rent, and when the last payment was made we would make no more. If any of us left, others would move in and make the payments. Perhaps as we paid off some of the houses we should lower the rents of all, or help others pay off houses. Slowly a rent-free housing zone would emerge. No landlords; people directly responsible for the houses they lived in; buying or taking over empty lots for playgrounds and gardens; perhaps one or two houses for meetings and small stores.

And so we did it. We bought a few houses; scraped up the money from friends—loans of $2,000 here, $5,000 there—friends who knew that the banks invested their savings into war industries but who didn't know what else to do with them; friends who wanted to help an idea get started with little or no interest. And the experiment began. Three years later there are seven houses in close proximity to each other, and between fifteen and twenty people. We didn't wait for a legal formula to do it, we just did it. And now that there is a legal form,[6] it seems important to say, both to ourselves and to others:

The Trust begins in our hearts. It worked out in our lives. The legal form can be used to give clarity. Writing it down seems to lend stability. But don't build trust on a legal system that is guaranteed to set us at each other's throats. The first requisite of Land Trust is a sense of the importance of community and the courage and willingness to struggle.[7]

Voluntary Community Tax

Often when people work together to meet a common need, a community is formed. These people will have other needs for which they may seek a common solution. One means of supporting groups or funding projects that meet community needs is through a voluntary community tax. Such a tax can give people a choice of whom and what they support. It can be used to make a community more self-sufficient and less dependent on the larger society to meet its needs.

Both the Earthworm Community in Champaign, Illinois, and the cooperative community in Madison, Wisconsin, have experimented with a voluntary community tax. Such a tax is often called a self-tax, because it is self-imposed. In the Earthworm Community, the funds generated from a voluntary 2-percent tax are allocated to various groups and individuals for the purpose of enchancing the quality of community life, promoting community-centered services, or satisfying community needs. Some allocations are made to new and existing member groups as requested, provided they have met the agreed-on criteria. Others are given monthly to service groups such as the Health Center and the Consumer's Union, or to needy workers as income supplements.[8]

The Madison Sustaining Fund collects and allocates that cooperative community's self-taxes to promote and support "a counter-economy which provides goods, services, employment, and a sense of community sharing without profits."[9] Its members include a free medical clinic, a consumer's co-op garage, a theater, a co-op food market, a free high school, a printer, a tenants' union, a restaurant, a bicycle co-op, and legal defense aid, among others. They have initiated a variety of taxes for their purpose and have acted as a planning group for the community.

Voluntary community tax funds are placed in the care of a committee of trustees, or council, who represent everyone and meet regularly to oversee the collection and distribution of the funds. The structure of the committee reflects the political principles of its members; decisions are made by consensus and the chairmanship rotates. Some self-taxes used by these and other communities are:

1. Businesses pledge 2 percent of their profit or 4 percent of their gross sales to the community fund.

2. Retail businesses ask customers to volunteer a percentage (1 to 3 percent) of their sales price, to be placed in a collection box near the cash register.
3. A five-cent mark-up at movie clubs or similar groups is levied.
4. Individuals pledge a regular part of their income to the fund.

Your Own Bank

If you want complete control of your money, including your savings, you will have to start your own credit union or even your own bank. I don't believe in wars and I don't want my money to contribute to them. But what bank can I put my money into and be sure it will not turn around and lend my money to some war industry? None that I know of. And there isn't any way I can check on what a bank does with my money. The small amount of savings I have is in a credit union; that's better than a bank in that I can help set its policies. But I can't write checks on my credit union account. A group associated with the Institute for the Study of Nonviolence tried to go further; they became their own bank for a while. One participant explained it to me.

We formed our own "peoples bank." We started off with a little box and we wound up with about ninety of us banking in it. The idea was that money should be used and that life should be based around the community. We tried to define community as using one another as resources. Human resources were the wealth and the joy that we had, and we were going to try and take the material parts of that to manifest a sense of small community. We began the bank wanting it to be a no-interest bank, but given an inflationary society where inflation is always eating out from under us, we felt an alternative structure was needed.

We had three different accounts, Fund A, Fund

B, and Fund C. Fund A was for saving money; a person could sign in an amount of money and know the money would be kept there and not used by others. Fund B was called the Sharing Fund. This was money that we felt we had in surplus, extra money within our wealth; it could be used back and forth by people. After toning down and refining, we come up with the idea that anybody in the group could take up to ten percent of the total money in Fund B without asking anybody else. They were to pay it back when they had the money to do so; it was floating money. Fund C was for those of us who were resisting war taxes. We set aside money that would be used for tax resistance projects. One year we bought a lot of medical supplies and tried to exchange them for bombs at a Navy base in Alameda. We systematically did something similar each year.

Overall though, the operation of the bank was very loose. The bank was totally voluntary, people's roles changed every month, people were busy with other projects. The bank ran for a couple of years, and we were able to loan funds to other land trusts and use the money in ways we wanted. In the end we had a problem with a friend who got heavy off into dope and ripped off the money; we lost a thousand and two hundred dollars. Even so, when we assessed ourselves for that loss, it turned out that the amount was basically what it would have cost to have had a bank account; at least the money was not used by the Bank of America.[10]

I came to Palo Alto after the close of the Peoples Bank, but I hope they will try something like it again. One of their key principles in setting up the bank was complete trust. There was no bookkeeper or audit of funds. Everyone was responsible for their own entries. I believe in trusting people, but I also know that I have trouble balancing my own checkbook. I would want at least a monthly, if not weekly, audit of the bank just to catch honest errors. This practice would also have caught any missing funds.

Sharing

Mutual sharing is a satisfying way of meeting our needs and building community. Car pools, potluck dinners, and baby-sitting exchanges are common ways of sharing. Tool sharing, communal kitchens, and many other forms are also becoming more common.

Lee Swenson belongs to one of four households that decided to buy and maintain tools together for everyone's use. Each household contributed five dollars a month toward the purchase of tools. The money accumulated quickly, but they waited for good buys on quality tools before purchasing. Together they bought a power drill, a power sander, a router, a power saw, and a chain saw. Each family paid a minimal amount of money in relation to the number of tools they have access to. The tools are kept at one house, where each family has easy access to them. Each time a tool is used, a quarter is put in an envelope to pay in advance for future repairs. In this way there is no wait for money for repairs, and the problem of deciding who pays to repair something everyone uses is eliminated. When they allow outsiders to use the tools, two or three dollars are collected to help offset purchase cost and repairs. Occasionally they have more money than needed for repairs, so they temporarily stop paying the quarter for each use. This system works very well. The only problem was with the chain saw. It was too hard to maintain. People just seemed to run it into the ground. So there are limits.

In setting up sharing arrangements, Lee cautions that it is very important to clarify things in advance. Trust breaks down when people expect something of each other, but the expectation is never stated or agreed on. "If I borrow your truck for a hundred-mile trip, and it breaks down, do you expect me to pay for the repairs or can I expect you to pay? If I don't do what you except me to do, you get mad at me. And then I start avoiding you, and the whole thing falls apart. It's usually lack of clarity where trust breaks down, so it is important to set up procedures and work for clarity of assumptions beforehand," Lee emphasizes.

Skill Pool

We can also share our skills. In an effort to meet economic needs without the use of money and to build the feeling of community, a group in Monterey, California, has been developing a skill pool. Each member makes his special skills, tools, services, or instructions available to the others. No money changes hands, but a community of concern and sharing has developed. This skill pool includes nurses, electricians, auto mechanics, typists, gardeners, sewers, and many others.

Barter

Barter is a form of exchange in trade without the use of money. We can barter skills and services as well as goods. Our own capabilities can be put to greater and more varied use when we step outside the limits of monetary exchange and meet our needs more directly. My friends and I barter handmade shirts for handmade toys, haircuts for bicycle repairs, artwork for baked goods, garden produce for an auto tune-up, or window repairs for mending. Barter can also be a way of giving different types of work value according to a more human scale. One man bartered with a lawyer to obtain his divorce. He did three hours of construction work for the lawyer to each hour the lawyer worked for him. Normally the lawyer would have received $50 an hour as his fee, but they were able to get much closer to a human relationship by exchanging their services.

Barter parties can be given where people get together to meet others with whom they can exchange goods and services. Bartering can be facilitated by keeping an open file of people, skills, and goods they wish to barter and the needs or goods they wish to obtain. Bartering can include a chain of people, where three or more people are involved in an exchange. If you can do something for me but I am unable to do what you need, I can still barter with you if I can find someone who can use my services in return for fulfilling your need. This sounds complicated, but it is possible to string out such a trade through five people before everyone's mind gets too boggled.

Conclusion

So where do I fit into all this experimentation? At the same time that I was part of the macroanalysis seminar, I joined an art and craft cooperative in downtown Palo Alto. The building was divided into individual booths in which we each produced and sold our own craft items. The rent and upkeep expenses were shared, and we each agreed to be in the store 20 hours a week to sell our and other members' crafts.

This was my attempt to live out the artist's fantasy of being able to make a living from my art. In Nevada I had been selling woodcut prints, collages, and constructions through galleries, but sales were slow there and I had not put much effort into it. I hoped sales would be higher here and thought I could supplement my income by teaching printmaking at the numerous recreation centers in the area.

I did woodcut prints at the co-op, but the teaching never worked out. At the end of a year I was still not making enough money to support myself and my two young daughters. The decline in the economy in 1974 cut back new sales, even though I was gaining return customers. I took a part-time job and half a year later, due to lack of energy, quit the co-op and temporarily quit making woodcuts.

The potters and jewelry makers are still there, along

with some others. But otherwise the co-op has a large turnover in membership. Working there was one of the nicest experiences I have had. I'd like to try again, but next time I'll work my art into something people can use rather than just hang on the wall.

Now I work a 40-hour week doing what the man says. The bills get paid, some money gets saved, and I keep looking for an opportunity to try to make it on my own again or get a job in a cooperative business.

I also keep joining cooperatives and doing my share of the work, but I fall down on attending all the meetings. I belong to the Briarpatch Cooperative Auto Shop and was part of a food conspiracy before joining the Briarpatch Cooperative Market. Bit by bit my model city is growing up around me. Or at least that is the way it seems to me.

A city needs houses, and I've been looking into buying a house in Palo Alto. But there is almost no low-income or moderate-income housing here. I have enough money to make a modest down payment on the very cheapest house on the market, but I don't earn enough to make mortgage payments with today's 9-percent interest rate. And house prices are going up faster than I can save.

Recently, however, a group of Briarpatch Market people have begun meeting to create a land trust and a network of cooperatively owned houses. I want to be part of that group. With a lot of time and work, we may be able to do it and start building our model city in earnest. I hope I can get a house with them. Otherwise I have no choice but to continue to pay rent increases, which keep better pace with the cost of living increase than my salary does.

Although I am sick of meetings and enjoy my independence, I can't find a way to do what I want to do alone. But then again, it's nice to work with people who share the same goals.

Writing this chapter has been a discovery and learning experience for me. And I have also made some very good friends in the process.

Suggested Projects

1. Find out what economic alternatives are available in your area, such as sharing, consumer co-ops, and cooperative businesses. Are they caring and consumer- and worker-oriented, or are they maximum-profit oriented?
2. Brainstorm governmental or legal changes that would make the economic system more responsive to human and ecological needs.
3. Discuss in what ways we as individuals or in groups could make our economic dealings more illustrative of our values and more responsive to our needs.
4. Brainstorm changes that would occur if a steady-state economy were achieved instead of a growing economy. What would be needed to bring this about?

Trust Agreements of Landlords End

"I conceive that land belongs for us to a vast family of which many are dead, few are living, and countless numbers are still unborn."—A Nigerian tribesman.

"Sell the land? Why not sell the air, the clouds and the great sea?"—Tecumseh.

WHEREAS the use of land for speculation and profit has often been at the expense of that land and of resources that could be more humanely used to benefit other peoples and other generations

NOW THEREFORE the undersigned parties agree to and do hereby enter into the following agreement:

This trust agreement is made this 24 day of January 1973 by and between [names of parties in agreement]. This agreement is the written statement of a verbal agreement made by and between the aforementioned persons on or about the tenth day of October, 1970.

For good and valuable consideration the persons named in deeds annexed to this form hereby convey real estate (herein after referred to as "land") described in those deeds annexed hereto and by this reference made a part hereof [names of trustees] as Trustees. Said Trustees agree to hold said land in trust upon the following terms and conditions:

1. The name of the trust shall be Landlords End.

2. The trust shall be a charitable trust in perpetuity.

3. The purpose of the trust shall be to return land to its place as a natural resource to be used with care by all peoples for sustaining life, to eventually dissolve the borders between nation-states and to seek an end to war and exploitation of humankind.

4. The trustees of Landlords End agree that any person living on trustheld land shall become a Trustee after one year's residence thereon, and upon common agreement of the Trustees. Upon agreement of the Trustees, persons conveying land to Landlords End will automatically become Trustees if they continue to live on that land after it is held by Landlords End. All Trustees must be residents of Landlords End. In case of incapacity, resignation or death of all of the Trustees without appointment of any successor, the Institute for the Study of Nonviolence, Palo Alto, California, shall be the Trustee of this trust, Landlords End.

5. The powers of the Trustees shall be exercised by consensus decision reached in general meetings with every Trustee, (even those absent from the meeting), offering opinion and discussion before a decision is finalized. The relationship between Trustees and other people living on trustheld land, besides being one of friendship, is based on the principle that people have the right to direct input to the decisionmaking process wherever their lives are affected. Therefore any two people living on trustheld land can call a general meeting and such meetings are open to all residents of trustheld land.

6. The trustees shall hold and manage the said land and any other property real or personal which may

be given or acquired by Landlords End, and apply the income or principal in whole or in part as deemed by them in their full discretion to fulfill the purposes of Landlords End. A lease arrangement shall be made with all persons, including Trustees, living on trustheld land. A lease form to be used by Landlords End is annexed to this form.

7. In addition to all of the powers conferred by law and the powers expressly conferred by this agreement, and the implied powers essential or proper to effectuate the purposes hereof, the Trustees shall have full powers to purchase, acquire, take, hold, own, improve, lease, convey, exchange, (but not sell) and otherwise handle real or personal property, make contracts, borrow money, construct buildings, and do any or all things which they may in good faith deem expedient and proper to effectuate the purposes of Landlords End.

8. The Trustees shall receive no compensation for their services as Trustees.

9. This trust, Landlords End, shall terminate at any time all of the property of the trust, Landlords End, shall have been expended or distributed in accordance with its purpose.

In witness thereof, we have hereunto set our hands and seals on the day and year first above stated.

[Signatures]

NOTES

1. See also A. Fishlow, "Some Reflections on Post-1964 Brazilian Economic Policy," Working Paper No. 19, Department of Economics, University of California, 1971. Also, "Brazilian Size Distribution of Income," *American Economic Review* 62 (May 1972), pp. 391–402.
2. *Community Market Catalog* (New York: Knopf, 1973), p. 92.
3. Ibid., p. 49.
4. Richard Taylor, *Economics and the Gospel* (Philadelphia: United Church Press, 1973), p. 37.
5. "Co-op Housing: How It Works," *The Public Works*, no. 1, Spring 1975. Available from 349 62nd St., Oakland CA 94618.

6. A copy of the form is included at the end of this chapter.
7. Will Kirkland, "Land Trusts," *Institute for the Study of Nonviolence,* vol. 1, no. 3, April-May 1973, pp. 17–22.
8. *Community Market Catalog,* p. 50.
9. Ibid., p. 94.
10. "New Persons, New Society," *In the Tracks of the Dinosaur,* June 1975, p. 8.

SOURCES OF FURTHER INFORMATION

(See also: Consuming Ourselves, Consuming the World, Food, Work)

Brigham, Nancy, and Bagson, Steve. *Why Do We Spend So Much Money?* Somerville, Mass.: Popular Economics Press (5A Putnam St.), 1973.

Cockcroft, James D., Frank, André G. and Johnson, Dale L. *Dependence and Underdevelopment.* New York: Doubleday/Anchor, 1972.

The Community Market Cooperative Catalog. New York: Alfred Knopf, 1973.

Daly, Herman. *Toward a Steady State Economy.* San Francisco: Freeman, 1973.

Ehrlich, Paul. *The End of Affluence: A Blueprint for Your Future.* New York: Ballantine, 1974.

Gandhi, M. K. *Sarvodaya (The Welfare of All).* Malaga, N.J.: Ahimsa, no date.

Illich, Ivan. *Tools for Conviviality.* New York: Harper and Row, 1973.

Philadelphia Macroanalysis Collective. *On Organizing Macroanalysis Seminars: A Manual.* Available for 75¢ from 4722 Baltimore Ave., Philadelphia PA 19143.

Sahlins, Marshall. *Stone Age Economics.* Chicago: Aldine-Atherton, 1972.

Taylor, Richard K. *Economics and the Gospel.* Philadelphia: United Church Press, 1973.

15
The Shakertown Pledge

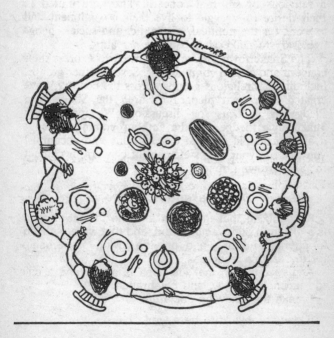

Many people throughout the country have come to believe that if the world family is to be cared for and fed, the United States must begin wide-scale dedevelopment. In order for this to happen, they feel American citizens need to adopt new ways of life in which they consume closer to their fair share of the earth's resources. The network of people moving thus to simplify their lives includes individuals and groups from many backgrounds and interests who are committed to bringing about a just world standard of living. One such group is the Shakertown Pledge Group, who act out of a religious or spiritual concern. They are united in their desire to struggle to live their commitment and to work for the political, economic, and social change necessary to make global justice a reality.

The Shakertown Pledge was written to express their concern and shared commitment. Several other groups, including nonreligious groups across the country, have created their own pledges or used the Shakertown Pledge as a focus for discussion. We include the Shakertown Pledge and the authors' comments about it as an example of what can be done and encourage you to write your own statement of concern or contact the Shakertown Group.

The Shakertown Pledge

Recognizing that the earth and the fulness thereof is a gift from our gracious God, and that we are called to cherish, nurture, and provide loving stewardship for the earth's resources.

And recognizing that life itself is a gift, and a call to responsibility, joy, and celebration.

I make the following declarations

1. I declare myself to be a world citizen.

2. I commit myself to lead an ecologically sound life.
3. I commit myself to lead a life of creative simplicity and to share my personal wealth with the world's poor.
4. I commit myself to join with others in reshaping institutions in order to bring about a more just global society in which each person has full access to the needed resources for their physical, emotional, intellectual, and spiritual growth.
5. I commit myself to occupational accountability, and in so doing I will seek to avoid the creation of products which cause harm to others.
6. I affirm the gift of my body, and commit myself to its proper nourishment and physical well-being.
7. I commit myself to examine continually my relations with others, and to attempt to relate honestly, morally, and lovingly to those around me.
8. I commit myself to personal renewal through prayer, meditation, and study.
9. I commit myself to responsible participation in a community of faith.

About the Shakertown Pledge

The Shakertown Pledge originated when a group of religious retreat center directors gathered at the site of a restored Shaker village near Harrodsburg, Kentucky. A number of us were personally moved by the global poverty-ecology crisis we saw all around us, and we covenanted together to reduce our levels of consumption, to share our personal wealth with the world's poor, and to work for a new social order in which all people have equal access to the resources they need. We have since been joined by others.

We believe that all people of faith should take this Pledge. We know from the Scriptures that God commands his people to make the cause of the poor and the oppressed their own. If we are truly to practice our faith then we cannot sit idly by while others starve. It's as simple as that.

What Would It Mean to Take the Shakertown Pledge?

Many people are attracted to the sentiments expressed in the Shakertown Pledge, but are not sure just what the Pledge might mean in their own lives. Here is a brief discussion of each item in the Pledge.

#1 I declare myself to be a world citizen.

Recognizing that we are citizens of one world can have a profound impact on our daily lives. Those who make this declaration should begin to think of the needs of all the people of the earth, and adjust their lifestyle, their social vision, and their political commitments accordingly. We must go beyond our familial, village, regional, and national loyalties and extend our caring to all humankind.

#2. I commit myself to lead an ecologically sound life.

Through this we pledge that we will use the earth's natural resources sparingly and with gratitude. This includes the use of the land, water, air, coal, timber, oil, minerals, and other important resources. We will try to keep our pollution of the environment to a minimum and will seek wherever possible to preserve the natural beauty of the earth.

Concretely, this should mean that we will participate in local recycling efforts. It means that we will try to conserve energy and water in our own homes. It means that we will try to correct wasteful practices in our communities, schools, jobs, and in our nation.

#3. I commit myself to lead a life of creative simplicity and to share my personal wealth with the world's poor.

This means that we intend to reduce the frills and luxuries in our present lifestyle but at the same time emphasize the beauty and joy of living. We do this for three reasons: First, so that our own lives can be more simple and gracious, freed from excessive attachment to material goods; Second, so that we are able to release more of our wealth to share with those who need the basic necessities of life; Third, so that we can move toward a Just World Standard of Living in which each person shares equally in the earth's resources.

Concretely, anyone who takes the Pledge should sit down with their family and review their present financial situation. Each item of expenditure should be looked at carefully, and unnecessary or luxury items should be reduced or eliminated. The surplus that is freed by this process should be given to some national or international group that is working for a better standard of living for the deprived. This surplus should be a regular budgeted item from then on, and each member of the household should endeavor to see how this surplus can be increased. In the future, families and individuals who have taken the Pledge might consider meeting together in "sharing groups" to discover new ways in which community and co-operation can free more resources for the poor.

#4. I commit myself to join with others in reshaping institutions in order to bring about a more just global society in which each person has full access to the needed resources for their physical, emotional, intellectual, and spiritual growth.

This complements and enhances our commitment to share our personal wealth with those who need it. Wealthy nations such as the United States need to "de-develop" those parts of their economies that are wasteful and harmful in ecological and human terms. Wealthy nations must reduce their overconsumption of scarce resources while supporting the ecologically wise development of the poor nations to the point where the basic needs of all "spaceship earth" passengers are met equally.

We commit ourselves to use our political and institutional influence toward these goals. This means that we will support those candidates who will do the most for the poor both here and abroad. It may mean that we will engage in lobbying, peaceful demonstrations, or other forms of "direct action" in support of the transfer of more of our resources and skills to the developing lands. It means that we will oppose and attempt to change those aspects of our economic system which create an unjust distribution of wealth and power here and abroad. This also means that we will support efforts to bring religious, intellectual, and vocational freedom to peoples who are being denied these basic human rights.

#5. I commit myself to occupational accountability, and in so doing I will seek to avoid the creation of products which cause harm to others.

This most certainly means that we will not allow our labor to go into making products which kill others. It should also mean that we will take a close look at what we are producing to determine if it is safe, and is ecologically sound. We should also consider our choice of a career, and whether it contributes concretely to a better world for all humankind. If our present occupation does not do so, or is only marginally helpful to others, we may decide to change it, even if we earn less money as a result.

#6. I affirm the gift of my body, and commit myself to its proper nourishment and physical well-being.

Many of us in the developed (or "over-developed") countries desecrate the "temple" of our own bodies through overeating or through consuming physically harmful and nutritionally "empty" foods. Also, through our meat-centered diets we consume protein in its most wasteful form, depriving people in other lands of desperately needed protein.

Serious attention to this point would mean: 1. A commitment to maintain our weight at the normal healthy level; 2. A reduction in the consumption of animal protein in our diets; 3. Regular attention to healthy physical exercise; 4. A reduction in consumption of empty calories, especially in desserts, candy, pastries, alcohol, and other food products which contain great amounts of refined sugar.

#7. I commit myself to examine continually my relations with others, and to attempt to relate honestly, morally, and lovingly to those around me.

We will seek to understand and improve our relationships with others, and to treat each person as our neighbor. We will try to affirm and nurture the gifts and talents of others. We support the development of the small group and face-to-face community in religious life—since here many people are learning new ways to communicate their love, their needs, their hopes and dreams, and their anguish. Small groups and communities have also been helpful in enabling people to see more clearly how they affect others.

#8. I commit myself to personal renewal through prayer, meditation, and study.

For many people, "prayer" and "meditation" are alternate terms for the same process of turning one's thoughts toward God. We believe that deep and continuing personal renewal can result from a discipline of prayer or meditation, and from reading and reflection. We encourage each person to find their own individual spiritual discipline and practice it regularly. For a start, we would suggest setting aside time twice a day for prayer or meditation.

#9. I commit myself to responsible participation in a community of faith.

We believe that God not only has a relationship with each of us individually, but also collectively—as a people. One of the obligations—and joys—of living our faith is that we are called to worship together with others. We recognize that common worship and the support of a community of common beliefs are essential to an active, creative, joyous life. Concretely, this means participation in a church or synagogue, or "house church," or other worship group.

Signing the Pledge

You are invited to sign the Pledge and let us know that you are making this commitment. Taking the Pledge simply means that you agree with the substance of the nine points that have been proposed, and that you want to join with others in a common community of support. The "Shakertown Pledge Group" is a loosely-knit association of people who hold the principles of the Pledge in common, and who are attempting to re-direct their lives toward creative simplicity and working for a more just global society.

The Shakertown Pledge was written to appeal to a broad audience composed of all people of faith. We encourage people from specific religious traditions to consider "writing your own pledge," in language that may be more uniquely suited to the language and practices of your community.

Resource

The Co-ordinating office of the Shakertown Pledge Group is a collectively operated information and communication center for people who are interested in radical simplicity. In addition to correspondence and information sharing, they are at present able to provide the following:

Training Workshops for Simple Living Organizers; plus ongoing support for their work.

Creative Simplicity, a monthly newsletter which keeps people posted on how the Pledge and the Simple Living Movement is progressing, what others are doing, notes and articles on simple living that are of interest to all, and reviews of books and magazines.

Literature on many topics for those who want to deepen their understanding of the times in which we live.

Speakers, workshops, and seminars for those who want to learn more about simple living and what it means.

Contact Persons for the Shakertown Pledge:

Churchmouse Collective, 4709 Windsor, Philadelphia PA 19143.

David Hartsough, c/o AFSC, 2160 Lake St., San Francisco CA 94121.

Dwight Sarson, c/o Mid Atlantic CROP, 30 West Side Ave., Hagerstown MD 21740.

Sr. Maureen Mange, John XXIII Center, Rt. 2, Box 303, Hartford City, IN 47348.

Charlie Springer, 217 N. 14th St., Richmond IN 47374.

Reg. McQuaid, 63 Beaty Avenue, Toronto, Canada, M6K3B3.

Susan and Michael McConnell, 4527 N. Malden, Chicago IL 60640.
Freddy Willoughby, 906 South 49th, Philadelphia PA 19143.
Co-ordinating Office: The Shakertown Pledge Group
West 44th Street & York Avenue
South
Minneapolis MN 55410

If you would like to be on the mailing list, send the group a check for $5 for one year. People on the mailing list receive the Newsletter, *Creative Simplicity,* and one copy of *Toward a Just World Economy: A Critical Introduction to Voluntary International Aid Agencies in the United States.*

If the world were a global village of 100 people, one-third of them would be rich or of moderate income, two-thirds would be poor. Of the 100 residents, 47 would be unable to read, and only one would have a college education. About 35 would be suffering from hunger and malnutrition, at least half would be homeless or living in substandard housing. If the world were a global village of 100 people, 6 of them would be Americans. These 6 would have over a third of the village's entire income, and the other 94 would subsist on the other two-thirds. How could the wealthy 6 live "in peace" with their neighbors? Surely they would be driven to arm themselves against the other 94—perhaps even to spend, as Americans do, about twice as much per person on military defense as the total income of two-thirds of the villagers.

Bantam Book Catalog

Here's your up-to-the-minute listing of every book currently available from Bantam.

This easy-to-use catalog is divided into categories and contains over 1400 titles by your favorite authors.

So don't delay—take advantage of this special opportunity to increase your reading pleasure.

Just send us your name and address and 25¢ (to help defray postage and handling costs).

BANTAM BOOKS, INC.
Dept. FC, 414 East Golf Road, Des Plaines, Ill. 60016

Mr./Mrs./Miss_____
(please print)

Address_____

City_____State_____Zip_____

Do you know someone who enjoys books? Just give us their names and addresses and we'll send them a catalog too!

_____

Mr./Mrs./Miss_____

Address_____

City_____State_____Zip_____

Mr./Mrs./Miss_____

Address_____

City_____State_____Zip_____

FC—6/77